Confederate Citadel

*Richmond and
Its People at War*

Mary A. DeCredico

UNIVERSITY PRESS OF KENTUCKY

Copyright © 2020 by The University Press of Kentucky

Scholarly publisher for the Commonwealth,
serving Bellarmine University, Berea College, Centre
College of Kentucky, Eastern Kentucky University,
The Filson Historical Society, Georgetown College,
Kentucky Historical Society, Kentucky State University,
Morehead State University, Murray State University,
Northern Kentucky University, Transylvania University,
University of Kentucky, University of Louisville,
and Western Kentucky University.
All rights reserved.

Editorial and Sales Offices: The University Press of Kentucky
663 South Limestone Street, Lexington, Kentucky 40508-4008
www.kentuckypress.com

Unless otherwise noted, photographs are courtesy of the Virginia Museum of History
and Culture, Richmond, Virginia, and the Valentine Museum, Richmond. Maps by Dick
Gilbreath, independent cartographer.

Cataloging-in-Publication data is available from the Library of Congress.

ISBN 978-0-8131-7925-4 (hardcover : alk. paper)
ISBN 978-0-8131-7928-5 (epub)
ISBN 978-0-8131-7927-8 (pdf)

This book is printed on acid-free paper meeting
the requirements of the American National Standard
for Permanence in Paper for Printed Library Materials.

Manufactured in the United States of America.

 Member of the Association
of University Presses

To the memory of Joseph and Alexandra DeCredico
and Martha Reynolds Belk

Contents

Prologue

Death of a Nation

Died: Confederacy, Southern.—at the late residence of his father,
J. Davis, Richmond, Virginia, Southern Confederacy, aged 4 years.
Death caused by strangulation. No funeral.
—*Richmond Whig,* evening ed., April 7, 1865

The Confederate death certificate given as this chapter's epigraph was published shortly after General Robert E. Lee surrendered the Army of Northern Virginia to General Ulysses S. Grant at Appomattox Court House. Confederate president Jefferson Davis and members of his cabinet were on the run, attempting to make their way to the Trans-Mississippi theater.

Davis and his cabinet left behind a capital city that was a shadow of its former self. As the Confederates evacuated Richmond, they put tobacco to the torch. A south wind whipped the flames out of control, and as the Federal army marched in, the business district was ablaze. Working to put out the fire, many of those in Union blue must have wondered if the loss of more than 300,000 Federal troops over the past four years was worth the cost of this victory; others probably questioned how such an upstart, largely overgrown town could have assumed such importance.

But it was in the rubble that locals and other curious onlookers could perceive Richmond's legacy. The burned-out business district bespoke of a diversified, developed commercial entrepôt. The hulking silhouette of the Tredegar Iron Works, saved by its workforce from an angry mob, testified to Richmond's singular importance as an industrial powerhouse within the Confederate nation. Indeed, the city's detritus spoke in mute testimony to the reality that it had transcended its symbolism as the Confederate capital.

From the time Virginia seceded from the Union and the Confederacy made the fateful decision to relocate the capital from Montgomery, Alabama,

Women and ruins, 1865. Stereocard.

to the City on the James, politicians, the Northern public, and the Federal high command clamored, "On to Richmond." The *New York Times* captured the prevalent spirit in the spring of 1861: "Let us make quick work. The 'rebellion,' as some people designate it, is an unborn tadpole. . . . We have only to send a column of twenty-five thousand men across the Potomac to Richmond, and burn out the rats there."[1] Sadly for those in both the North and the South expecting a quick and glorious victory, the rebellion would become a long, drawn-out, very bloody affair. It is not off the mark to argue that the war lasted four years because of the contributions the city and the people of Richmond made to the Confederate cause.

Previous studies of Richmond during the war have focused primarily on the city and have argued it was a place enamored of its past. A venerable city, it was laid out in the eighteenth century and over the years became intimately associated with the revolutionary legacy. One only had to wander to Capitol Square to see the imprimatur of the author of the Declaration of Independence: the imposing capitol building patterned after the Maison Carrée in the south of France. Richmonders were proud of the role they played in America's fight for independence and were quick to associate the First Families of Virginia with major milestones in the early republic's history.

But declining economic fortunes and a rising tide of sectional politics jolted Richmonders and other Virginians out of their lethargy and spurred them to diversify the economy and to develop railroads. The result was a vibrant commercial, urban, and industrial complex by 1860. That renaissance laid the foundation for the city's remarkable wartime contributions. As locals

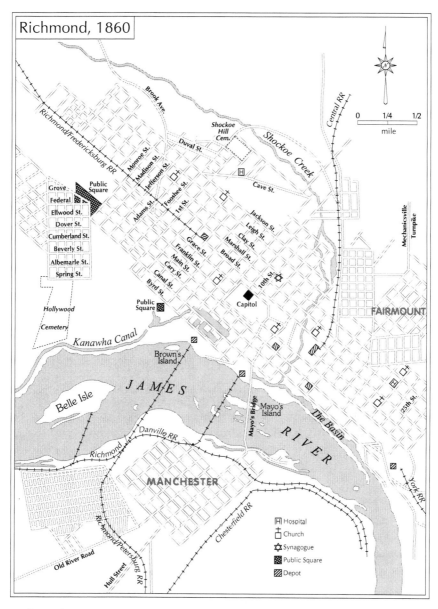

Richmond, Virginia, 1860.

mobilized and fought, they created a capital that transcended its symbolism as the center of the rebellion. Richmond and its people became the keystone of the Confederacy, the Southern nation's impenetrable citadel. Once that keystone cracked under the pressure of war in April 1865, the Confederate citadel collapsed, and Robert E. Lee would surrender the Army of Northern Virginia one week later.

In many ways, Richmond was an anomaly in the antebellum South. It stood as the future Confederacy's second-largest city, and it had developed a very diversified economy by the 1850s. Indeed, in 1860 Richmond ranked thirteenth in the United States in manufacturing.[2] The city enjoyed extensive trade relationships with the border South and with the Mid-Atlantic region. Richmond was heavily dominated by the Whig Party, although the national Whigs had died slowly during the increasing sectional conflict of the 1850s. The capital of Virginia also had a diverse population of Irish and German immigrants, Jews, free people of color, and slaves. As the war approached, Richmond's bondsmen played a critical role in the city's tobacco and iron industries.

Abraham Lincoln's election to the presidency in 1860 produced great consternation in the Deep South and led to the almost immediate secession of South Carolina. But Virginia would not join the Deep South's exodus. Because the two-party system stayed viable on the state level, Virginians in general and Richmonders in particular did not see an apocalypse on the horizon. They adhered to the Cooperationist "wait and see" stance—wait for the new president to make a hostile act. That act came in the aftermath of Fort Sumter, when Lincoln issued a call for 75,000 ninety-day volunteers, with a quota of that number to come from the Old Dominion. That, to the people of Virginia, was the hostile act they had waited for, and on April 17, 1861, Virginia voted to secede.[3]

In some respects, Richmond's tortured road to secession mirrored that of one of its favorite sons: Robert E. Lee. Both city and citizen decried secession and war, but when it proved impossible to avoid, both cast their lot with the nascent Confederate States of America. Over time, the fate of the capital and its chief defender would become inextricably tied together.

In mid-1864, with the Federal Army of the Potomac again on Richmond's doorstep, the *Richmond Daily Dispatch* printed an editorial that summed up the city's sacrifices on behalf of the Confederacy. Entitled "What Richmond Has Given Up," it cataloged the tremendous contributions the city had made to the Confederate cause:

WHAT RICHMOND HAS GIVEN UP to aid the Confederate Government in the prosecution of this war, has never been rightly estimated nor appreciated outside of Virginia. Her public buildings and institutions have been mainly monopolized by the general Government, of course with the consent of the authorities, for what would not the citizens of Richmond give if it were asked of them? This commenced with the transfer of the seat of government from Montgomery to Richmond. First, the State Capitol was occupied by the Confederate Congress; the Mechanics Institute by the War Department; the City Postoffice [*sic*] by the Treasury Department. . . . Since the army of occupation came our hotels have been pressed to supply other government accommodations; court martials sit in our churches; committees in our school houses; Yankee prisoners cram our warehouses; the wounded fill our dwellings; the refugees are quartered upon us by the thousands, and the original citizens are pushed into the smallest possible corner. We do not make these assertions in a spirit of fault finding; far from it. Richmond does not murmur, while the grand old mother of States and statesmen utters not a groan, no matter how much friend and foe trample upon her and tear her fair bosom. She battles and suffers in hope, and looks for the day of her deliverance.[4]

Sadly for Richmond, its "day of deliverance" would be a calamitous one, and as the evacuation fires burned, Richmond's hopes of being the capital of a newly independent nation would be consumed in the fires that extinguished all hopes of independence. It remained to be seen, as the evacuation fires continued to burn days after the city fell, whether Richmond would regain its wartime prominence in the Reconstruction era that followed.

1

From the City on the James to Confederate Capital

In early March 1861, Richmonder Alfred Paul wrote to a friend that "the city of Richmond is extremely excited. Anarchy openly reins here. It is noisy . . . and sometimes menacing." This local went on to note, "The [Virginia] convention does not wish to be under the influence of the North nor of the South to which, nevertheless, its members make speeches on every corner." Paul then mentioned that the Stars and Stripes, the state flag of South Carolina, and the flag of the "Confederation of the South" flew in the capital. But as to the business of the convention, Paul told his friend it could "be summed up in three words . . . nothing, nothing, nothing." Another Richmond resident, Sallie Brock Putnam, believed, "To the anxious and restless inhabitants of Richmond, the proceedings of the Virginia Convention during the winter of 1861 seemed slow, undecided and uncertain. Separated, by the action of the other Southern states . . . they chafed under the apprehension that they would be compelled to remain in the Union."[1]

In late March, ardent secessionists, who were definitely in the minority in the capital city, were led by former governor Henry Wise. He planned to convene a "Spontaneous Southern Rights " convention in the city on April 16. Throngs gathered at Metropolitan Hall on that day in the hopes they could add pressure to the convention during its deliberations. Although Governor John Letcher and others continued to counsel moderation, public demonstrations in favor of secession continued.

En route to Richmond on April 10 and 11, J. B. Jones noticed that "as we approached Richmond . . . the people were more and more excited, and seemed to be nearly unanimous for the secession of the State. Everywhere the Convention then in session was denounced with bitterness, for its adherence to the Union." Jones went on, "Gov Letcher was almost universally execrated for the chocks he had thrown under the car of secession and Southern independence."[2]

Richmond-Howe's, Virginia, 1850.

Undaunted by Governor Letcher's open declaration of Unionism, prominent local citizens staged "spontaneous" torchlight processions. J. B. Jones arrived in the city just in time to witness the aftermath of the fall of Fort Sumter. "To-day the secession fires assumed a whiter heat," recorded Jones. "In the Convention the Union men no longer utter denunciations against the disunionists. They merely resort to pretexts and quibbles to stave off the inevitable ordinance."[3] The *Richmond Enquirer* reported, "A procession of citizens was formed which marched up Main Street . . . bearing the flag of the Southern Confederacy." That group quickly "swelled to about three thousand persons, by the time the column halted at the Tredegar Iron Works to witness the raising of a large Southern Confederacy flag over the main building." Joseph R. Anderson, Tredegar's owner, addressed the crowd, as did several prominent Richmond secessionists. While a band played the "Marseillaise," people cheered lustily.[4]

Those in Richmond who favored secession fervently hoped the fall of Fort Sumter would precipitate action in the convention. Sentiment toward secession had increased markedly in the aftermath of Sumter, but it was President Abraham Lincoln's call for 75,000 ninety-day militia on April 15—including a quota from Virginia—that pushed all Richmonders and Virginians over the brink. As one local noted, "There has certainly been a great change in the opinions of the people in the last few days."[5]

According to one participant, during the April 16 gathering, former Governor Henry Wise told the assembly the Virginia militia was in the process of seizing the Federal garrison at Harpers Ferry and would move to procure the Gosport Naval Yard in Norfolk. Shortly thereafter, it was announced that the convention had chosen secession by a vote of 88 to 55; all three delegates from Richmond cast their ballots in favor of secession. "This announcement was followed by a thrilling moment of silence succeeded by tears of gladness and deafening shouts of applause."[6]

Pandemonium quickly spread through the city as word of Virginia's secession spread. Sallie Putnam observed after the vote for secession, "Suddenly—almost as if by magic—the Confederate flag was hoisted on the Capitol, and from every hill-top, and from nearly every house-top in the city, it was soon waving." Robert Graniss, a young Northerner who journeyed to Richmond in 1858 to work as a clerk, remarked that the excitement in the city was "intense. The wildest joy seems to prevail. All is war." Tucker Randolph could barely contain his glee when he wrote in his journal, "We had a grand torch light procession this evening. The houses all over the city were light [sic] up, rockets were fired, &c." He also noted local militia companies "have been drilling every night at 8 o'clock." J. B. Jones, who would soon become a clerk in the Confederate War Department, celebrated the decision and mused in his diary over whether Virginia's act could be considered revolutionary. "But what is in a name? Secession by any other name would smell as sweet. For my part, I like the name of Revolution or even Rebellion . . . for they are sanctified by Washington and his compeers." Sallie Putnam was equally ecstatic with word that Virginia had finally seceded. The celebration the night of April 19 included "the most extensive torchlight procession ever known here." Jubilant Richmonders thronged down Marshall Street to Broad Street and then to the Ballard House and Exchange Hotel. Speaker after speaker predicted a quick and glorious Southern victory, which roused the crowd even more. "As far as the eye could reach down the line of Franklin Street, and over the hill, more than a mile distant, gleamed the torches." According to Putnam, "long before the ordinance of secession was passed by the Convention, almost every woman in Richmond had in her possession a Confederate flag— ready at any moment, to run it out from her window." Those banners, she commented, were now unfurled amid the general revelry.[7]

Not everyone in Richmond greeted news of Virginia's secession with jubilation. The staunch Unionists in the city were heartbroken at the turn of events. John Minor Botts protested he would never "live under the rattlesnake authority of the cotton republic" and swore allegiance to no "other flag than the stars and stripes [*sic*]." Elizabeth Van Lew stood at her home on Church Hill in the city and was crushed to witness the torchlight processions that illuminated the night sky. "Such a sight! . . . the multitudes, the mob, the whooping, the tin-pan music, and the fierceness of a surging swelling revolution." Many Unionists in the city feared for their personal safety because the pro-secession mobs had gotten so large and aggressive.[8]

With the secession of Virginia, the nascent Confederacy would gain the largest, most populous state in the South and its major manufacturing center. In time, Richmond would also become the capital of the Confederacy, the symbol of the rebellion, and thus a major target of the Union high command in the East.

Yet how did a city laid out in 1733 attain such status? Perhaps, as one historian has noted, Richmond was tailored to be the capital of the Southern drive for independence because of its revolutionary legacy. Locals noted that Patrick Henry immortalized liberty at St. John's Episcopal Church; they pointed with pride to the Houdon statue of George Washington in the capital building and to the magnificent equestrian statue on its grounds, and they were immensely pleased when one of the Virginia dynasty, James Monroe, was reburied in Hollywood Cemetery in 1858. As this same scholar has argued, Richmonders carefully crafted a "civic religion" that centered on the "veneration of Revolutionary heroes." This sense of history—and of Virginia's destiny—was palpable.[9]

Some scholars have argued that Richmond tenaciously held on to its past because of its political and economic decline from 1820 to 1850. As Southerners migrated to the rich lands of Mississippi and Alabama and as years of tobacco cultivation exhausted its soils, the Old Dominion stagnated. The depression of the late 1830s and 1840s merely exacerbated conditions throughout the state. Richmond in particular and Virginia in general seemed more than happy to relive its bygone glory rather than adapt to the changing economic and political situation during the Age of Jackson.

But migration west fueled expansionism and conflict. The resulting Mexican War and the onset of sectional tensions jolted the Old Dominion out of its lethargy. Seemingly overnight, the state's urban press began to trumpet growth and development as a way to counter the growing economic might of the Northern states. The *Richmond Daily Dispatch* led the chorus of boosterism when it proclaimed, "Ought Richmond not to be one of the greatest manufacturing cities in the Union?"[10]

In some respects, Governor Henry Wise's speech on the occasion of the reinterment of James Monroe's remains in Hollywood Cemetery epitomized the city's embrace of progress: "Before you leave here, my friends from New York, look at the iron factories that are growing up around this noble scenery." Wise must have surprised some locals when he proclaimed, "I thank God that the old colonial aristocracy of Virginia, which despised mechanical and manual labor, is nearly run out. I thank God that we are beginning to see miners, mechanics, and manufacturers who will help to raise what is left of that aristocracy to the middlegrade [*sic*] of respectability."[11] It was Richmond's businessmen—its merchants, bankers, and manufacturers, the men Wise referred to in his speech—who would lead the city's economic renaissance.

Interestingly, the urbanization of Virginia's cities occurred during a period of growing sectionalism. According to one historian, "The rhetoric of the urban leadership, and their economic policies embodied a greater goal than local aggrandizement."[12] Richmond's business leaders were not oblivious to the reality that trade routes to the west had not been developed as well as they might. Nor could they ignore the rise of the port of New York and its monopoly on trade from the Midwest and Great Lakes. Too many were aware that the influx of immigrants to the urban-industrial Northeast was tilting the country's population—and hence U.S. House of Representative seats—to the free (nonslave) states. Finally, virtually every urban booster saw transportation links as a way to create prosperity, to counter the city's lagging position, and to take steps toward reestablishing its dominance nationally.

The James River–Kanawha Canal project was reflective of this drive. Local investors began the canal shortly after the American Revolution, but not until 1840 did it reach Lynchburg. In 1851, the canal was extended to the Shenandoah Valley town of Buchanan, and there were hopes it would eventually reach the Ohio River and tap the trade of the Midwest.[13] As Richmond chronicler Samuel Mordecai observed, "The progress of Richmond and of the James River Canal are so intimately connected that it is due to the one to notice the other."[14] Sadly for Mordecai and his fellow Richmond boosters, the dreams of extending the canal and thus enhancing Richmond's trade routes were not realized before the onset of sectional strife.

Hand in hand with the James River–Kanawha project went the development of railroads. Richmond's tobacco manufacturing and trade burgeoned during the 1840s and 1850s, which necessitated better and more extensive rail connections. Five railroads eventually terminated in Richmond: the

Richmond, Fredericksburg & Potomac Railroad linked the city to Aquia Creek, which in turn allowed Richmond's products to be loaded on Potomac River vessels for shipment elsewhere; the Virginia Central Railroad linked Richmond to Washington via the Orange & Alexandria Railroad; the Richmond & Danville Railroad ran to the North Carolina border; the Richmond & Petersburg Railroad ran to the Appomattox River; and the Richmond & York River Railroad linked the city to West Point on the York River. Yet, despite these trappings of modernity, not one of these lines ran through the city. Freight that arrived at one station instead had to be hauled by wagon to another depot. As with the failure to extend the Kanawha Canal, the lack of through rail lines would come to haunt Richmond in the not too distant future.

Nevertheless, the advent of railroads encouraged the development of other industries and commercial enterprises. Tobacco manufacturing had long dominated the local economy, but beginning in the 1840s flour milling also became more prominent. Several large mills, in particular the Gallego Mills and the Haxall Mills, gained national and international prominence for the quality of their product. In fact, the Gallego Mill's extensive trade with Latin America allowed the firm to become the largest mill of its kind in the country. By 1860, tobacco and flour manufacturing accounted for 60 percent of the city's industry.[15] Visitors to Richmond could not help but notice the high level of industrial activity—and its unsavory by-product. One individual, although proclaiming Richmond could well be considered the "Lowell of the South," was overwhelmed by the pungent and pervasive smell of tobacco: "One seems to breathe tobacco, to see tobacco and smell tobacco at every turn. The town is filthy with it."[16]

The brown cloud of tobacco was soon rivaled by the black cloud of coal that accompanied iron production. Richmond had manufactured iron products since the 1830s, but it was the establishment of the Tredegar Iron Works in 1837 that put the city on the map as a major producer of iron goods. The halcyon years of the Tredegar began with the arrival of Joseph Reid Anderson. A West Point–trained engineer, Anderson took the Tredegar to new levels of production and prominence: by 1860, the Tredegar Iron Works was the largest enterprise of its kind in the South. It counted among its clients the U.S. War Department and various Southern state governments and railroad companies.

But the production of iron at Tredegar—and in the South as a whole—faced significant obstacles that placed it at a disadvantage vis-à-vis Northern and European firms. The South's iron market was smaller. Only Virginia and Georgia enjoyed fairly extensive rail systems. Raw material was also limited, though Anderson availed himself of the rich coal pits in the Shenandoah Valley. Finally, labor was expensive, and many of the skilled immigrants who flooded the United States in the mid–nineteenth century chose to settle in the North rather than in the South. Anderson moved aggressively to meet these challenges. In an effort to cut costs and compete with his Northern rivals, he began to expand the employment of slave labor.[17]

Scholars have found that slavery thrived in the urban environment. Many studies of urban history in the United States testify to the significant impact that urban slavery had on the growth of the antebellum South's industries and the development of its internal improvement networks. Indeed, Richmond's success in using slave labor made it an urban celebrity of sorts among European and Northern visitors. Census statistics highlight that Richmond was a key beneficiary of urban slavery. In 1840, its slave population stood at 7,509. Twenty years later, that number had increased 56 percent to 11,700. In tobacco manufacturing alone, slaves made up almost 90 percent of the labor force.[18] The growth of urban industrial slavery in Richmond "is even more surprising given that the slave population in the city was shrinking in proportion to the white population."[19]

Richmond was also one of the few Southern cities that witnessed a large influx of immigrants during the 1840s. Both Irish and German immigrants found their way to the city by the James to take advantage of the opportunities in the capital's mills, foundries, and railroads. By the early 1850s, immigrant laborers accounted for almost 17 percent of the city's population.[20] But that increase also portended the potential for labor unrest. As a result, Richmond entrepreneurs, like their planter counterparts, found slaves a welcome alternative to white and immigrant labor that could paralyze production with an unwanted strike. Indeed, one could argue they preferred slave labor over free white labor.

Perhaps predictably, the growth of Richmond's industries and the use of immigrant and slave labor created deep divisions within the city's white working class. Unskilled Irish workers and skilled white Virginians worried that the increased use of slave labor would supplant them and thus jeopardize their livelihood. Although they grudgingly accepted slaves as unskilled laborers, they vigorously opposed putting slaves in more skilled positions. This situation faced Joseph Anderson and the Tredegar Iron Works in the spring of 1847 as the firm prepared to expand the slave workforce into skilled-labor areas, which precipitated a strike by the white workers. Undaunted by the threats coming from the white puddlers (the workers who stirred the molten iron), Anderson moved swiftly: he proceeded to hire slave puddlers and alerted the striking white workers they were no longer needed. The Richmond press and Anderson's fellow industrialists applauded his forceful actions. Nonetheless, the artisanal classes in Richmond lobbied the city council for tighter controls and restrictions on industrial slave labor and even on the labor of free people of color.[21]

The expansion of urban industrial slavery was not without conse-quences. Urban slave owners were increasingly aware that their bondsmen were becoming alarmingly independent, if not downright insubordinate. As more slaves were hired, a slave community developed in pockets of the city between Fourth and Belvidere and Broad and Leigh Streets as well as along Shockoe Creek. The living conditions in these areas were abysmal, but the slaves who inhabited these sections of Richmond were able "to create a com-munity that offered comfort, solidarity, protection and entertainment." The urban alleyways also encouraged autonomy, which further fueled white fears of slave resistance and rebellion. Not surprisingly, when those fears were borne out in 1852, Richmonders were stunned. In that year, the city was rocked by the news that local slaves had murdered three of their white owners. Those crimes precipitated the passage of a flurry of municipal ordi-nances that cracked down on slave activities. For example, new laws prohib-ited blacks from smoking in public, closed alleys in black neighborhoods, and decreed that slaves who worked in the city's industries could no longer take lodgings without being supervised by their owners. But local officials were stymied continually because white owners refused to enforce the regulations. As a result, Richmond's urban slaves became more resistant to restrictions and more independent as the antebellum era ended.[22]

By far the most lucrative business in antebellum Richmond was the slave trade. While tobacco sales and processing boomed, farmers and plant-ers throughout the Old Dominion exhausted their soil, rendering their field hands useless. The expansion of cotton farming to the Deep South in Ala-bama and Mississippi provided a great demand for slaves to work on farms and plantations in the Mississippi Delta. In 1860, only New Orleans sur-passed Richmond as a slave-trading hub.[23]

The slave traders could be found in some of Richmond's most promi-nent hotels. Here, the traders kept their offices, often near the capitol build-ing. Nearby would be slave jails, or "pens," where the slaves would be housed while awaiting sale. One historian estimates that around 1860 there were sixty-nine slave-trading establishments in the city that sold thousands of slaves to the Deep South. The period between Christmas and New Year's marked the height of the annual slave-trading period. According to the *Richmond Daily Dispatch,* "Streets were thronged with negroes[,] their owners[,] and buyers as was the annual custom. Thousands of dollars exchanged hands and thousands of negroes changed homes." The city was a "frenzied marketplace for human labor."[24]

Residents and visitors noted that "the selling and hiring of slaves was [*sic*] so fully recognized as a business of general public interest that the city directories usually indicated resident traders." Another observer opined, "The slave market was a flourishing institution . . . fully countenanced if not approved and defended."[25]

However, not all residents and visitors to Richmond looked favorably upon the trade of humans to plantations and farms in the Deep South. One gentleman described his journey to see a slave auction. "Out of the beautiful grounds and past the handsome residences we went, turning down Franklin Street towards the great Exchange Hotel." This man noted that as he and a companion walked, "the street became more and more squalid and repulsive, until at last we reached a low brick warehouse." A red flag hung from the door, and inside were a number "of negroes . . . to be disposed of." When a family was separated by sale, "my companion and I looked at each other in disgust." Tellingly, "neither [of us] spoke a word."[26]

The growth of tobacco and flour milling, the expansion of the Tredegar Iron Works, the development of railroads and their linkage industries, and the robust internal slave trade all accomplished what urban boosters hoped: Richmond flourished during the 1850s. The population grew almost 40 percent, which necessitated the physical expansion of the city. After years of discussion, city leaders finally allocated the necessary funds to complete the Richmond Gas Works. Gas streetlights flooded the city with illumination after dark and led one local newspaper to proclaim, "Richmond is making herself a worthy metropolis." But these vestiges of cityhood also underscored the class divisions within the city. Lawyers, doctors, manufacturers, and businessmen settled in fashionable residences on Franklin Street and Grace Street; free blacks and bondsmen congregated along Shockoe Creek; Irish workers could be found on Oregon Hill and Fulton; and the Germans congregated on Union Hill and Navy Hill. The diversity of the population led to the creation of tight-knit social, ethnic, and racial communities, which reinforced camaraderie, if not solidarity. By the end of the decade, Richmond's per capita wealth exceeded that of both Boston and New York.[27]

Scholars of Southern history have long argued that urbanization in the region was sui generis—that is, uniquely Southern and hence decidedly different from its Northern counterpart. Because agriculture dominated the Southern economy, these historians argue, the South's cities followed agrarian rhythms, with busy planting in the spring followed by slow summers, fall and the harvest season creating a lively urban scene followed by somnolent winters. The South, argues one scholar, witnessed "urbanization without cities." Similarly, many other historians contend that urban Southerners participated in but were not part of a capitalist economy. Although an urban middle class may have existed in the South, planters dominated that class socially, economically, and politically. The dependence on an enslaved labor force kept local markets small and hence militated against the true development of an urban industrial order. Thus, Southern cities never approximated their counterparts north of the Potomac.[28]

Such arguments, however, ignore the reality that the vast majority of *American* cities in the mid–nineteenth century revolved around agricultural growing seasons. Moreover, 90 percent of the population in the United States lived in rural areas. According to the 1860 census, the top industries in the country were agricultural processing industries. To be sure, the urban population was growing at a faster clip than the rural population. But with the exception of the Northeast, the United States was a nation dominated by farmers and small towns. The transportation revolution was in full swing, commerce and manufacturing were thriving, but in most instances growing cities in both the North and the South contained railroads that did not run through the towns and that often operated on different gauges. In short, few cities and towns in either region could approach the standard of New York, Boston, or Philadelphia. Nonetheless, people in Richmond and elsewhere in the urban South remained undaunted: they worked energetically to push their cities forward within the national urban hierarchy.[29]

Richmond and the Rising Tide of Sectionalism

Richmond's growth paralleled the country's increasingly tense political situation. The acquisition of new territories in 1848 and the Gold Rush in California precipitated a crisis that culminated with the Compromise of

1850. For Richmonders, as for their brothers and sisters in the other Southern states, the key element of that agreement was Northern enforcement of the Fugitive Slave Law. The death of the Whig Party on the national level led to the emergence of the nativist Know-Nothing Party. Though Whigs remained strong in Richmond, the Old Dominion did witness the rise of the Know-Nothings. To be sure, Richmond's Know-Nothings were alarmed at the large population of Irish and Germans in their midst, but they were even more concerned about "the danger that an immigrant and antislavery North posed."[30]

Equally troubling was the emergence of the Republican Party, with its mantra "free soil, free labor, and free men." Virginians in general and Richmonders in particular saw in the "Black Republicans," coupled with the fallout from civil war in Kansas, a serious threat to Southern liberty. The Richmond press warned its readers that the Republicans sought nothing less than "the 'subjugation' of the South and the destruction of its slave-based society."[31]

Perceived and actual Northern threats led Richmond's business leaders to again support the Southern Rights Association and the Southern Commercial Convention movement. These ostensibly nonpolitical groups followed a very political course: the championing of direct trade with Europe and a boycott of Northern goods. Richmond hosted the Southern Commercial Convention in January 1856, but a winter storm discouraged many from outside of Virginia from attending. At this meeting, politics played a larger role than in the past, despite the efforts of Marylander Tench Tilghman, who presided over the convention. Tilghman opened the gathering by stressing the value of the Union. Fiery Southern booster J. D. B. De Bow countered Tilghman and argued that the convention movement was designed to "secure southern prosperity either within the Union or outside of the Union." Before the convention adjourned, it adopted a number of pro-Southern resolutions, including the call to patronize only Southern commercial and manufacturing firms. Ominously, also for the first time, it passed resolutions praising the benefits of slavery.[32]

Richmond boosters who attended this Southern Commercial Convention and other Southern Rights Association meetings harped upon the need to unshackle Richmond's economic dependence on the North. Typical of the bromides uttered at these gatherings and in some of the Richmond press was the argument that Richmonders were mere "hewers of wood and drawers of water" to the Northeast.[33] Editorials in the Richmond press repeatedly called upon locals to be less dependent on Northern goods and services. But the economic reality was that Richmond was inextricably bound to Northern commerce. The example of the tobacco trade underscores this reality. During the 1850s, Richmond came to dominate tobacco inspections: on the eve of secession, 61 percent of all tobacco inspections took place in the city. Yet although the city may have monopolized inspections, it did not dominate final sales. All tobacco was instead shipped to the Northeast and thence to foreign ports. To be sure, Richmond developed other markets in the Deep South and in South America, but the Northern markets remained unchallenged. Those contacts were beneficial and allowed the city to prosper. Nevertheless, locals were painfully aware that despite prodigious growth, they still lagged behind their rivals above the Mason–Dixon line, especially New York.[34] In a sense, Richmond was entering its urban adolescence at a time when the cities of the Northeast were entering maturity.

Proponents of the Southern Rights Association and the Southern Commercial Convention saw their efforts to achieve economic independence from the North stall during the mid-1850s, but they were reinvigorated in the aftermath of John Brown's raid on Harpers Ferry in mid-October 1859. Brown's actions "struck at the heart of the slave republic." His subsequent trial and execution created panic and paranoia throughout the Old Dominion. But it was the North's reaction—the tolling of church bells and other public expressions of mourning—that shocked Richmonders and Southerners alike. Brown had attempted a slave rebellion, every Southerner's worse nightmare, yet Northerners treated him as a martyr to the cause of abolitionism. Renewed cries for separation and economic independence were raised while militia companies witnessed a surge in membership. But even those events were short-lived. Once again, moderates, led by the Whiggish element in Richmond, "crafted a political message committed to the protection of slavery but wedded to constitutionalism and Union." That temperate stance derailed the state's extremists and set the stage for the election of 1860.[35]

The Election of 1860

The Democratic Party that met in Charleston in 1860 was a deeply divided party. Southern Democrats were determined that front runner Stephen Douglas not get the nomination for president of the United States. They went to Charleston dedicated to adopting a platform that guaranteed constitutional protections for slavery. Unsuccessful, delegates from the Deep South walked out, in this way depriving Douglas of the two-thirds majority he needed to get the nomination.

Dejected, the delegates resolved to meet again in Baltimore, a city they hoped would be more congenial. Douglas supporters succeeded in getting pro-Douglas delegates from the Deep South seated at Baltimore, which led to another walkout. Those Democratic bolters traveled to Richmond. Meeting in Metropolitan Hall, they successfully nominated John C. Breckinridge on a state's rights ticket.[36]

That the Old Dominion was deeply divided in 1860 was apparent in the election returns. Both John C. Breckinridge, the Southern Rights candidate, and John Bell, the Constitutional Union candidate, did well in the commonwealth, but it was Bell who carried the city of Richmond and who squeaked out a victory in the state by a little more than 150 votes.[37] Given Richmond's Whiggish history, that result was not surprising. What was surprising, as the dust settled and fire-eaters surged to the forefront in the Deep South, was talk concerning secession. One local wrote to a friend that many in the city were discussing a secession convention and worried that "conservative Virginians . . . no longer count on the possibility of assuming the role of arbiters between North and South." Another Richmonder noted in his diary that although he had voted for Breckinridge, he would not support a secession convention until "an overt act has been committed by the Black Republican Government."[38] In general, the press in the state maintained a moderate stance. The *Richmond Daily Dispatch* wrote on November 8, 1860: "The returns received and published yesterday left little or no doubt of the election of Abraham Lincoln to the presidency. Today we publish enough to make it certain. The event is the most deplorable in the history of the country. The Union may be preserved. . . . We think it will, but are prepared to expect trouble." Only the *Richmond Enquirer,* in an editorial on November 10, 1860, thundered that "the idea of submission to Black Republican rule, under any pretext, is as dangerous as it is degrading." The editor pointed to the purely sectional nature of the vote—Lincoln was on the ballot only in the western part of Virginia and not at all in any other Southern state—and then charged: "This is a *declaration of war.*"[39]

Such conversations continued to roil Richmond, but it was the secession of South Carolina on December 20, 1860, that changed the parameters of the debate for many. Robert Graniss, now fearful of his Northern roots, observed how the Palmetto State's secession precipitated a "terribly distracted state" in Richmond. Many locals were calling for a state convention to discuss Virginia's course of action. Others in Richmond saw how the unsettled condition of political affairs was wreaking havoc on local business. A number of Richmond merchants received desperate entreaties from Northern colleagues, begging them to exercise their political influence and quell talk of disunion. Still more bemoaned sluggish trade and the element of uncertainty that pervaded all commercial transactions. As Richard Eppes of neighboring Petersburg observed, "Business is completely depressed [and] nothing doing but discussing politics. I believe it is agreed by all parties that a Convention should be called at an early date but whether any good can be accomplished to keep the Union together is a dubious question."[40] Many hoped that secession could be accomplished peacefully, but many more voiced the belief that "the South must defend her rights."[41]

The dawn of a new year did not bring any appreciable change to the atmosphere in Richmond. Moreover, the harsh winter did little to lighten spirits or to reverse the continued decline in business. Governor John Letcher sent a much anticipated message to the Virginia Legislature urging caution and suggesting that Virginia delay in calling a secession convention. Nonetheless, on January 19, 1861, the legislature announced that elections would be held on February 4, 1861.

The delegates who convened in Richmond reflected the commonwealth's conservative and moderate tone. The vast majority of the delegates opposed secession. Indeed, of the 152 delegates elected, barely a third could be considered secessionists. Richmonders elected one secessionist, George Wythe Randolph, whose views may have reflected those of his grandfather, Thomas Jefferson, and Jefferson's support of the right to secede in the Kentucky Resolution of 1799. Randolph's fellow delegates differed markedly from him. Marmaduke Johnson was a prominent Whig lawyer in Richmond and an avowed opponent of secession. Similarly, William MacFarland was an attorney and president of the Richmond Farmer's Bank. Like other moderates, MacFarland adopted the cooperationist "wait and see" attitude prevalent in the Upper South. Because Richmond in particular and Virginia in general had enjoyed a vibrant political culture throughout the 1850s—even after the death of the Whig Party nationally—most did not see the election of Lincoln alone as necessitating secession. Continued confidence in the political system and in the South's ability to thwart any hostile moves Lincoln might make caused these Virginians to delay hasty action.[42]

Others in Richmond contended that secession threatened the growth and diversification of the Old Dominion's economy during the 1850s and argued that the state was tied economically to the Upper South and Mid-Atlantic states rather than to the cotton South. Finally, virtually every delegate, especially those representing the city of Richmond, hoped for some resolution to the crisis because business remained terribly depressed.[43]

The situation in Richmond, the "Gibraltar of Whiggery," was more "complex" than in other cities in the Old Dominion. To be sure, there were outspoken radicals who clamored for immediate secession in the aftermath of Lincoln's election. But the legacy of the Whigs and their support of the city's urban working class, who were solidly Unionist, led to a more restrained reaction. City-wide meetings held in late December 1860 and again between the call for elections and Election Day calmed the electric atmosphere; in fact, these gatherings promulgated resolutions concerning the political crisis that were quite moderate in tone. Those meetings and the subsequent actions of both Cooperationists and Unionists succeeded in silencing the fire-eaters.[44] That remained the situation into the new year.

While Richmonders waited for the legislature to make up its mind, six other states in the Deep South joined South Carolina in the Southern Confederacy and met in Montgomery, Alabama, in February 1861 to frame a provisional government. After drafting a constitution modeled on the document of 1787, they chose the moderate Democrat Jefferson Davis of Mississippi as president and former Whig Alexander Stephens of Georgia as vice president. The selection of those two politicians was symptomatic of a major shift in Southern thinking. The men in Montgomery were only too aware that the secession tide had stalled in places such as Virginia. Fire-eaters precipitated a revolutionary act with secession. Now it was time to create a government that promised to protect Southern rights—this promise, they believed, would be attractive to the Upper South, the border states, and especially the Old Dominion.[45]

While the Confederates were putting the finishing touches on their government, the North was preparing for the advent of a new administration. On March 4, 1861, Abraham Lincoln became the sixteenth president of a deeply divided Union. His Inaugural Address exquisitely combined the olive branch with the sword in its promise to uphold federal law but not interfere with slavery where it existed. Nonetheless, Richmond residents and other Virginians could consider the penultimate paragraph in Lincoln's speech as throwing down the gauntlet: "In *your* hands, my dissatisfied fellow countrymen, and not in *mine,* is the momentous issue of civil war. The government will not assail *you.* You can have no conflict, without yourselves being the aggressors." New Yorker Robert Graniss noted as much when he wrote that Lincoln's words "foreshadowed coercion of the seceding states." Just two weeks later Graniss observed, "Politically matters remain much the same. The Southern Confederacy is in full blast and Va [*sic*] remains in the Union." But as Graniss—and others—noted in the aftermath of Lincoln's inauguration, "The secessionists are gaining ground here and it is impossible to tell the ultimate result."[46]

Sentiment in the city and the state was changing. As winter turned to early spring, Richmond's newspapers began to openly reject moderation in favor of secession. John Moncure Daniel and his paper the *Richmond Examiner* led the way. Daily, he lambasted the proceedings of the Secession Convention and likened it to "a vast manufactory of froth, soap, bubbles, treason and submission." The failure of the much anticipated February 1861 peace conference and Lincoln's unwillingness to endorse the Crittenden Compromise further eroded moderate support. Nevertheless, the convention authorized an eleventh-hour effort to resolve the crisis. George Wythe Randolph, Alexander H. H. Stuart, and William Ballard Preston (each of whom, interestingly, represented the respective sentiments in the divided state) were sent to Washington to meet with Lincoln about his intentions regarding Fort Sumter, off the coast of Charleston, South Carolina. That meeting was also fruitless: the Union's president informed the three Virginians he had every intention of protecting federal forts. It was increasingly clear to most in Richmond that constitutional measures had been exhausted; secession was now the only remedy.[47]

The Richmond convention continued to be dominated by Unionists. Yet many in the capital city were aware that the situation in Charleston Harbor was becoming more volatile by the day, and they worried whether the unionists could continue to hold sway if anything happened in Charleston. Several weeks after the inaugural, Lincoln determined to reprovision the garrison at Fort Sumter and alerted Confederate authorities that a relief expedition would sail on April 6. Tucker Randolph noted in his journal on April 9, 1861, that in Richmond "rumors afloat are pregnant with War [and] the dispatches say that a Fleet of seven or more vessels are lying of[f] the harbor of Charleston with the intention . . . of reinforcing the Fort."[48] Predictably, Jefferson Davis and his cabinet could not allow Sumter to be reprovisioned, so they directed the Confederate commander in Charleston,

General P. G. T. Beauregard, to demand the surrender of the fort before the arrival of the relief expedition. At 11:00 p.m. on April 11, 1861, three Confederate officers rowed out to Sumter to meet Major Robert Anderson and demand he surrender the fort. Should Anderson not turn over the garrison, South Carolina batteries would begin shelling at 4:30 a.m. Undaunted, Anderson refused to capitulate.[49]

At the appointed hour, Confederate batteries opened fire, and a fierce bombardment ensued. By April 14, telegraphs in Richmond were spreading the news that Fort Sumter had fallen to South Carolina forces. Bedlam followed. Samuella Curd wrote that in the "greatest excitement," a crowd "amounting almost to a mob" had gathered in the streets and proceeded to Capitol Square, where it "pulled down the Stars & Stripes off the Capitol & raised a Secession flag." Richmond native Sallie Brock Putnam declared the news of Anderson's surrender "was received with the wildest demonstrations of delight. . . . All night the bells of Richmond rang, cannons boomed, shouts of joy arose, and the strains of 'Dixie's Land,' already adopted as the national tune of the Confederates, were wafted over the seven hills of the city." Another resident noted the Virginia Armory fired off salutes in honor of the surrender, while people thronged the streets carrying torches and generally celebrating the Southern victory.[50] Many in Richmond must have wondered how a staunchly Unionist city had seemingly overnight embraced secession.

Night after night of "grand illuminations" in Richmond underscored the short-war mentality that gripped both North and South in the aftermath of Lincoln's call for militia and the secession of Virginia, North Carolina, Arkansas, and Tennessee. It was not uncommon to hear boasts that one Southerner could whip seven Yankees. Even some of the South's leading political figures bragged they would drink whatever blood was spilled in the conflict.[51] Parades and military musters, heartfelt farewells at the train stations as husbands and sons went off to enlist, and promises to wait for a suitor to return from the front covered in military glory—all were predicated on the notion the war would be over in a month or two. Those who counseled it would be a protracted affair were rejected as Cassandras or reacted as diarist Mary Boykin Chesnut did. When told by none other than the president of the Confederacy that the war would be a long one, Chesnut admitted, "That floored me at once. It had been too long for me already. . . . He said only fools doubted the courage of the Yankees or their willingness to fight when they saw fit."[52]

Richmonders received an early jolt of the reality of war just four days after the Old Dominion's secession. On Sunday, April 21, word spread quickly that the U.S.S. *Pawnee* was headed up the James River "to retake the steamers that had been seized by the Governor of Virginia." Church services hastily concluded as parishioners flooded the streets to gather the latest news. Officers quickly mustered local militia units, and hundreds flocked to Rocketts Wharf to observe the action. Local officials deployed artillery at the entrance to the city, but no Federal warship appeared. But the idea that a Yankee vessel could mount a challenge to the city caused more than a few to realize how woefully unprotected Richmond was.[53]

No one in Richmond could know that as they were panicking over the possibility of a Federal gunboat shelling the city, messengers were en route to northern Virginia. Their destination was Arlington Mansion, and they bore a communiqué from Governor Letcher offering Colonel Robert E. Lee command of Virginia forces. Although Lee opposed secession and war, once Virginia cut its ties to the Union, he tendered his resignation to the U.S. Army. Lee journeyed to Richmond on April 22, and the next day he was officially appointed major general in charge of the commonwealth's forces. This was a fortuitous selection, for the West Point–trained engineer became Richmond's and the state's chief advocate for building fortifications to stave off any Northern military advances. As one historian has written, "The safety of that city was to be the supreme care of the military life of Robert E. Lee."[54]

Perhaps not surprisingly, one of the first groups to approach Lee regarding the need for local defense was the Richmond City Council. The *Pawnee* threat doubtless added to the council's desire to protect the capital from assault. On May 9, 1861, the council resolved "to ask [Lee] his advice in regard to taking steps to put this City in a state of defence [*sic*] by erecting batteries around or near it." The councilmen also informed Lee they would direct Mayor Joseph Mayo "to furnish, so far as possible, the necessary labor from among the unemployed Negroes now in the City."[55] This instruction would mark the beginning of the extensive use of free black and slave labor in the Virginia war effort.

Lee had a daunting task. Not only was he responsible for creating Richmond's defenses, but he also had to ensure that all areas of the Old Dominion—from Norfolk on the coast to Harpers Ferry in the west—were similarly protected. Less than a week after taking command, he directed his former army superior, Colonel Andrew Talcott, to erect fortifications along all riverine approaches to the city. He also dispatched commanders to vulnerable spots at Norfolk and Harpers Ferry. Finally, Lee authorized newly appointed Virginia commanding officers to begin enlisting companies from the various locales. These troops would journey to Richmond and add to the martial atmosphere there.[56]

Lee was forced to move quickly, for once the Confederate capital relocated to Richmond, its defense had to be secured; moreover, all Virginia forces would then be tendered to the Confederate government.[57] The general informed Governor Letcher in early June that the dearth of laborers was delaying severely the creation of an adequate defensive perimeter around the city. Neither for the first nor for the last time, Lee recommended "that all available persons in and around Richmond be organized for the defence of the city, and that they provide themselves with such arms as each can procure." Lee admitted these were "precautionary measures" only but concluded his missive by noting they were "better made now, than upon the eve of the emergency, should it arrive."[58]

Once again, the Richmond City Council answered Lee's request. On July 8, 1861, the council "*resolved,* That the Mayor of the City be requested to impress the services of such free Negroes as he may think proper, to work on the fortifications around the City." The council also directed those impressed free people of color to be assigned to the "Superintendent of the Defences." Finally, the council promised to confer with the Confederate government about the need for additional redoubts to protect the city.[59]

Confederate Capital

Virginia's secession set off renewed debate concerning the location of the Confederate capital. Perhaps sensing the import of Virginia's action, the Confederate government sent Vice President Alexander Stephens to Richmond just four days after Virginia's vote in favor of secession. Stephens and other government officials in Montgomery were not oblivious to Richmond's advantages. They knew Richmond was the nascent Confederacy's most industrial city and the Old Dominion was the largest Confederate state. Stephens urged Virginians to join the Confederacy because "the enemy is now at your border." He also held out the talisman of Richmond becoming the capital: "There is no permanent location in Montgomery— and should Virginia become . . . the theatre of the war, the whole may be transferred here." The Secession Convention thereupon voted to form a temporary alliance with the Confederacy. Although the delegates had every intention of formally joining the new nation, they were cognizant of the promise to hold a popular referendum on secession. That election was scheduled for May 23, 1861.

Anticipating the benefits of hosting the Confederate government and swayed by Stephens's forceful appeal, the Virginia Convention next extended an invitation to President Davis and the Confederate government "to make the city of Richmond, or some other place in the State, the Seat of the Government of the Confederacy." Shortly thereafter, the Confederate government passed a resolution "to hold their session in July in this City, and to make it the seat of government." The government acknowledged Richmond's offer and "accepted [it] by the authorities and the citizens with the liveliest satisfaction." With the passage of the popular vote on secession in Virginia, the door was open for the Confederate government to change residence to the city on the James. By the end of May, Davis and the government had physically relocated to Richmond. The *Daily Dispatch* reported that when Davis arrived, he spoke to the crowd that assembled to welcome him, and "his remarks, though brief, were to the point, and convinced every one [*sic*] who heard them that Jefferson Davis was the man for the occasion."[60]

Despite discussion and debate by contemporaries then and historians since, the decision to remove the Confederate capital to Richmond was not only a logical one but also a necessary one. There was really no other city in the Confederacy that had the industrial infrastructure that Richmond did. Moreover, it was the capital of the richest, most distinguished Southern state. The city carried the mantle of the country's Founding Fathers. Making Richmond the capital created even more symbolic importance to its role and hence added to the absolutely crucial need to defend it. As government bureaus opened, people flocked to Richmond seeking security, sinecures, and status.

The thousands of first-time visitors to the city were amused, amazed, and stunned at what they saw. Thomas Cooper DeLeon, who lived in both Montgomery and Richmond, wrote: "Passing out of the cut, through the high bluff, just across the 'Jeems' river bridge, Richmond burst beautifully into view, spreading panorama-like over her swelling hills, with the evening sun gilding simple houses and towering spires alike into glory. The city follows the curve of the river, seated on amphitheatric hills, retreating from its banks; fringes of dense woods shading their slopes, or making blue background against the sky. No city of the South has a grander or more picturesque approach." DeLeon also spied the hulking silhouette of the Tredegar Iron Works, a firm that was destined to play a critical role in the city's military mobilization. "Rising above [Gamble's Hill] . . . are the slate-roofed Tredegar Works; their tall chimneys puffing endless black smoke against the sunshine." Fiery secessionist and staunch Virginian Edmund Ruffin was similarly impressed by Anderson's firm: "All of us, as must all who see this great workshop, come away with a greatly enlarged appreciation of the military resources of these southern states, in having this establishment to call upon."[61]

First Lady Varina Davis was rather surprised to realize the city "was one great camp—men hurried to and fro with and without uniforms and arms, with that fixed look upon their faces they acquire when confronted with danger." Confederate officer E. P. Alexander echoed her observations: "Richmond was very far from dull, for troops from all over the South were arriving every day & resigned Southern officers out of the old army were coming in from every territory & camps of instruction were formed near the city where raw troops were drilled." Another Virginian, forced out of her home in Alexandria, noted that "letters from Richmond are very cheering. It is a great barracks. Troops are assembling there . . . [and] Ladies assemble daily, by the hundreds, at various churches, for the purpose of sewing for the soldiers."[62]

Longtime residents of Richmond could not ignore the transformation. Sallie Putnam noted, "In a very short time the population of Richmond increased in a wonderful ratio. Strange faces greeted citizens at every turn; and the city, even at that early period, began to wear the stern and remarkable characteristics she has ever since retained." German-born resident John Gottfried Lange remarked that after the arrival of the Confederate government and the beginnings of military mobilization, "Richmond was not the same quiet city anymore." Lange went on to comment: "Nobody could remember that there had ever been such a reversal in the machine works and iron works [industries after the election of Lincoln]. Factories were converted to cast all kinds of canons [*sic*][,] of which the large Anderson Foundry supplied the best models."[63]

Not all locals reacted favorably to the influx of newcomers. The peripatetic Thomas Cooper DeLeon averred that news that the Confederate government would relocate to the city caused many old Richmonders to feel "as much as the Roman patricians might have felt at the impending advent of the leading families of the Goths." Because of the crush of outsiders, Richmond "was thoroughly jammed." "Richmond hotels," he continued, "always mediocre, were now wretched." No one could remain oblivious to the consequences: "The *flotsam* and *jetsam* that had washed from Washington to Montgomery followed the hegira to Richmond. Echo from the 'Cradle of the Confederacy' had penetrated to the banks of the James and . . . sent cold chills down the sensitive Virginia spine. These soon wore away, but they early differentiated the personality of the leaders of the 'official set."[64]

Varina Davis also noticed not all Richmonders were enamored of the influx of government bureaucrats. She thought Richmond women seemed sincere enough, but "I was impressed by a certain offishness in their manner towards strangers; they seemed to feel an inundation of people of perhaps doubtful standards, and at best, different methods, had power over their city, and they reserved their judgment and confidence while they proffered a large hospitality." Davis and her husband endeavored to break the proverbial ice of Richmond society by hosting levees and receptions, as had been the custom when Jefferson was a U.S. senator in Washington. They met with mixed success. Although they continued this tradition throughout the war and although these gatherings were well attended, Richmond society never really accepted the Davises.[65]

One thing that surprised newcomers to the city was the number of unmarried and unchaperoned women. Longtime residents took that reality as a given; visitors from the Deep South were amazed if not shocked. One visitor boldly inquired as to the habit and was told, "Visitors always remark that. . . . But it is not the result of the war or the influx of strangers. Since I can remember, only unmarried people have been allowed to go to parties. . . . As soon as a girl marries . . . she must fold up her party dresses. . . . The pleasant Indian idea of taking old people to the riverbank and leaving them for the crocodiles . . . is overstrictly carried out by our celibate Brahmins. Marriage is our Ganges."[66] For obvious reasons, soldiers and other single men found that custom extraordinarily attractive. Throughout the war, Richmond would enjoy a very active social whirl—dominated by single women—which often appeared at odds with the ongoing arrival of the dead and wounded.

Mobilization in Earnest

Spirits in Richmond were high after the arrival of the Confederate government. Business rebounded quickly, and the depressed markets of just a few months earlier became faded memories. The fairgrounds were converted into a military camp—Camp Lee—and people routinely gathered there to observe as Virginia Military Institute cadets taught basic drill to the assorted units in an effort to transform local citizens into Confederate soldiers.[67] Everywhere one looked, one witnessed activity and optimism. The *Richmond Daily Dispatch* spoke for many when it wrote on June 26, 1861: "When the war is ended and the Capital of the Confederacy is established permanently here, Richmond will have the brightest future before her of any inland city on the continent. . . . Our city has already assumed an appearance of business activity quite cheering to see, while every day from morn to sundown the pavements resound with the tread of gathered thousands of all shades of complexion and degree in life, and of both sexes. We never saw people look more contented than those now."[68] As spring turned to summer, the stream of newcomers continued, and the city's economy strained to meet the demand for lodging, food, and the other necessities of life. Lincoln's naval blockade of Southern ports and the Davis government's self-imposed embargo of Southern cotton caused prices to rise, and some in Richmond began to notice shortages of certain goods. Beneath the prosperity that the city press trumpeted was a dark underside of vice and crime.

Sallie Putnam was one of those who observed these changes. She had no problem in accepting the reality that Richmond was "a city of refuge." What did bother her was the appearance of "the vilest extortioners," who preyed on locals and refugees alike by charging high prices for goods such as cotton, wool, and coffee. She was equally shocked to see that "in the course of time prosy Richmond was acknowledged 'fast' enough for the fastest." For Putnam, the rapid decay of decorum and civility was deeply disturbing. Another local, Kate Pleasants Minor, was disturbed by "the numbers of reckless criminal characters who flocked to the center of excitement for what they might find to profit themselves." Like Minor, T. C. DeLeon noticed newcomers taking advantage of the diversions the wartime capital offered. Gambling was especially prevalent, and many soldiers and fellow travelers frequented the city's saloons and gambling dens: "So the faro-banks flourished and the gamblers waxed fat like Jeshurun, the ass, and kicked never so boldly at the conscript man."[69]

That locals and visitors would comment on such changes to the social order is significant. They witnessed the mobilization effort transforming the social order and its conventions. As the war progressed, these changes became even more prominent and reflected the decay of what had been a bastion of First Families of Virginia.

Local authorities eventually clamped down on these "dens" in a series of raids. "The community will be greatly rejoiced to learn that steps have at last been made to cleanse Richmond of these vile habitations, and to relieve the community of one of its worst moral pests," wrote the *Richmond Examiner*. But the editor was dismayed that the mayor and police had been so tardy in addressing the problem. Locals soon discovered those "vile habitations" were in the city to stay.[70]

Equally troublesome to Richmond residents was the brazen appearance of ladies of ill repute. As one historian has noted, Richmond became a veritable "mecca of prostitutes." And these women were far from discreet in peddling their sexual charms. One madam had the audacity to set up shop across the street from the Young Men's Christian Association (YMCA). The YMCA's manager was irked enough to register a complaint with the city's provost marshal, arguing that the men under his care were not recovering from their maladies sufficiently because of the prostitutes, "'who appeared at windows in semi-undress and made gestures calculated to lure convalescents to chambers of vice, and whose efforts were not devoid of success.'" The *Daily Dispatch* recorded that complaints had been made about "a row of houses in the rear of the Exchange Hotel." Those dwellings apparently were "occupied by parties of a dubious and uncertain character." The various bivouacs in the city and its environs predictably saw a spike in the number of cases of venereal disease. The world's oldest profession never disappeared from the city, and the problem waxed and waned depending on the proximity of the Confederate army.[71]

Drinking, gambling, and prostitution had always existed in Richmond, but those pursuits exploded in popularity as soldiers continued to pour into the camps and as refugees flooded into the Confederate citadel. Gangs of young boys also became popular. Throughout the war, the local press castigated the "evil disposed boys, who seem to delight in throwing stones, using indecent language, and in other ways, annoying the neighborhood."[72] Juvenile delinquency seemed on the rise. Many began to worry about the state of the city's morals. These concerns did not go away, but they were relegated to lesser importance as word reached the Confederate capital that Union forces were determined to keep the Confederate Congress from meeting in July 1861.

"The Rebel Congress Must Not Be Allowed to Meet"

When the Civil War began, there were only 16,000 soldiers in the U.S. Army. The secession of the South saw large numbers of officers in the U.S. Army resign their commissions and offer their services to their Southern states. Because the Deep South seceded before Lincoln's call for troops, it managed to muster 60,000 men into service before the first Federal soldier donned the Union blue. Those 60,000 soldiers, combined with the units Lee raised in Virginia between late April and late May, proved critical to the Confederacy's early victories. Unlike the North, all Southern soldiers were required to serve for one year.

Richmond celebrated the first land victory, after Sumter, on June 10, 1861. Federal major general Benjamin Butler had advanced up the peninsula between the James and York Rivers from Fort Monroe. Any hopes he had of assaulting the capital from the east came to naught at the Battle of Big Bethel, where he was repulsed by a Confederate contingent under the command of the dashing Colonel John Bankhead Magruder. This action would approximate a mere skirmish in comparison to the bloodletting of 1862, but it was an intoxicating victory for the Confederate capital and was savored as such.[73]

A more ominous situation loomed in northern Virginia. There, pressure mounted on the Federal commander, General Irvin McDowell, to engage the Confederate forces positioned at Manassas Junction, near Bull Run Creek, just thirty miles from the Federal capital in northern Virginia. McDowell had 35,000 soldiers, whose ninety-day enlistment was due to expire; he faced the hero of Fort Sumter, General P. G. T. Beauregard, and his 20,000 Confederates. McDowell hoped General Robert Patterson, a veteran of the War of 1812, could keep General Joseph E. Johnston and his 15,000 Confederates in the Shenandoah Valley from reinforcing Beauregard, so he could bring his superior numbers to bear against Beauregard's left flank. Johnston's covert move to Winchester and hence to the railroad that took him to Manassas dashed this plan. So, too, did the greenness of McDowell's troops. It took twice as long to get his army into position because the soldiers were unaccustomed to marching in the hot, humid weather of July in Virginia.[74]

The Battle of First Manassas on July 21, 1861, was really more a slugfest between two armed mobs than a battle between two disciplined armies. Considering that this encounter was the first combat experience for most of the soldiers there, they fought well under fire. The battle surged back and forth across Bull Run and Henry House Hill. Confederate general and native Virginian Thomas J. Jackson finally stemmed the Federal tide on that slope at about 1:00 p.m. In the process, he earned the nickname "Stonewall" and became one of the Confederacy's first bona fide heroes. By late afternoon, the Confederates were advancing all along the Federal front. Union soldiers suddenly heard a terrifying sound—the high, eerie pitch of what became known as the rebel yell. The Union lines wavered and broke, and the men in blue stumbled in retreat toward the fords that would take them back to Washington. What began as a fairly orderly retreat quickly became a full-blown rout. In their haste to return to safety, the Union soldiers became entangled in the large number of civilians who had journeyed to Manassas, picnic hampers in hand, to see the great spectacle. As one eyewitness told a fellow Virginian, these civilians "came not as Florence Nightingales to alleviate human suffering, but to witness and exult over it." Happily for the Confederates, the rebel army sent the spectators "flying back to Washington, in confusion and terror, pell-mell, in the wildest excitement. And where were their brave and honorable escorts? Flying too . . . with self-preservation alone in view."[75] Nothing epitomized the short-war mentality more than the presence of these civilian noncombatants picnicking as men from North and South fought to exhaustion.

In Richmond, President Davis was anxious about the action unfolding in northern Virginia. Some in Richmond believed Davis entertained thoughts of assuming overall command of Confederate forces. A West Point graduate who had served with distinction in the Mexican War, Davis chafed at being in the Confederate capital while a battle that might seal the South's independence raged less than one hundred miles to the north. Delayed by an address to Congress and by other business, Davis was kept from leaving for Manassas until late afternoon. Finally, he and an aide boarded a train for Manassas Junction. What should have been a short journey took most of the day because of bad tracks and insufficient cars. When Davis did finally arrive, he could hear artillery and could see Confederate stragglers. His presence, according to one of his biographers, seemed to bolster the men's courage. Hoping for a complete rout, Davis was disappointed. When he finally found his commanders, Johnston wisely cautioned restraint. As Johnston noted after the battle, "Our army was more disorganized by victory than that of the United States by defeat."[76]

According to T. C. DeLeon, people in Richmond had "every eye . . . strained to the Manassas plains." The battle fell on a Sunday, and Sallie Putnam believed all seemed normal in the capital as people wended their way to church services. "But the interior of the churches presented an aspect until late foreign to them. As the eye glanced over the concourse assembled within," Putnam noticed, "one was struck at once with the great majority of females." The husbands and fathers who frequented the churches were for the most part serving in the army. Locals would continue to reflect upon the men who were missing from the pews. That situation remained unchanged throughout the war.[77]

According to most in Richmond, the city remained calm even as word spread of the Southern victory. As Sallie Putnam observed, "The news of the great victory was received by the Southern people with no violent manifestations of joy. . . . There were no bonfires kindled, no bells rung, no cannon fired, none of the parade which the event might have expected to call forth." DeLeon recorded, "There was no sleep in Richmond that night. Men and women gathered together in knots and huddled into groups on the corners and doorsteps, and the black shadow of some dreadful calamity seemed brooding over every tree top."[78]

That sense of a "dreadful calamity" became all too apparent later, on July 22, when the first of the Confederate wounded began to arrive in the city. "Day after day the ambulance trains came in bearing their sad burdens, and the same scene was ever enacted," wrote one local. "Strangers, miles from home met the same care as the brothers and husbands of Richmond; and the meanest private was as much a hero as the tinseled officer." Sallie Putnam realized, as did most residents, that the city did not have sufficient hospital space to take care of the constant stream of wounded soldiers: "Our hospital accommodations at that time are scarcely worthy to be mentioned." Indeed, the city's hospitals were quickly overwhelmed by the more than 1,600 wounded Confederates as well as 1,400 Union prisoners, many of whom were also wounded, coming into the city.[79]

Nonetheless, Richmond citizens sprang into action. One Richmond woman stated, "Our citizens are doing everything they can, bringing the wounded that can be moved to the city, and placing them in private families." Another noted, "Every delicacy of the soil and season, and the treasures of the pantry and cellar . . . were cheerfully brought forth to regale the wounded soldier." The crush of the wounded forced Richmonders to come to terms with the consequences of battle. The Confederate government moved quickly to establish a system of hospitals and worked to have them staffed with a sufficient number of doctors and nurses. Richmond women played a pivotal role in the establishment and evolution of the city's hospitals.[80]

As Richmonders tended to the arrival of the first wave of wounded, President Davis returned to the capital. Crowds followed him to his lodgings at the Spotswood Hotel, where he was entreated to tell them what he had seen on the battlefield. Davis did not disappoint his listeners. According to war clerk J. B. Jones, "Never heard I more hearty cheering. Every one believed our banners would wave in the streets of Washington in a few days; that the enemy would be expelled from the District and from Maryland, and that a peace would be consummated on the banks of the Susquehanna or the Schuylkill." The Richmond press was similarly effusive in its praise. Even the usually reticent *Richmond Whig* proclaimed, "The breakdown of the Yankee race, their unfitness for empire, forces dominion on the South. We are compelled to take the sceptre of power. We must adapt ourselves to our new destiny."[81]

Not everyone in Richmond was as sanguine as the Richmond press and other boastful residents. Mary Chesnut fumed, "Here we dillydally and Congress orate and generals parade, until they [the Union] get up an army three times as large as McDowell's that we have just defeated." Chesnut also recorded in her diary a conversation she had with a prominent South Carolinian: "[He] says this victory will be our ruin. It lulls us into a fool's paradise of conceit at our superior valor." T. C. DeLeon echoed these sentiments when he noted everyone in the capital was parsing the victory and declaring "one Southron was equal to a dozen Yanks. Instead of using the time, so strangely given by the Government, in making earnest and steady strides toward increasing the army, improving its *morale* and adding to its supplies, the masses . . . were upon a rampage of boastfulness." This attitude, concluded DeLeon, "was most injurious."[82] Neither Chesnut nor DeLeon could know just how prescient they were.

Summer turned to fall and early winter. Setbacks in western Virginia and continued fears of Federal raids depressed many, but on the whole the Virginia front was quiet. The citizens of Richmond, however, remained quite busy. Concern for the families of soldiers dominated discussion within the city council. On September 9, 1861, the city council resolved to appropriate and distribute $5,000 "for the benefit of the families of the volunteers from the City of Richmond now in the public service, by the committee of the Richmond Soldier's Aid Fund." The fund grew to more than $16,000 and allowed local families to receive, according to need, between $7 and $14 a month. The council repeated these actions in November and December, when it appropriated additional money for soldier's families. It also labored to procure additional funds for the defense of the city to augment what General Lee had accomplished. Cognizant of the continued need to tend to wounded and ill soldiers, the council resolved to convert the city almshouse into a hospital.[83]

Richmond's churches also became actively involved in assisting those who were at the front. Many were deeply concerned about the material condition of the Confederate armies. Although the conflict was barely six months old, people in Richmond were shocked to learn many of the soldiers were ill clad and ill shod. The approaching winter precipitated a renewed effort to supply the troops. St. Paul's Episcopal Church was one of many churches that heeded the call: "Let us look over our stores, and see whether in the present emergency some articles might not be spared for the soldiers who are fighting for our dearest rights."[84]

As 1861 drew to a close, people in Richmond were aware that much in their world had changed. The city now included three separate governments—city, state, and Confederate. Its population was steadily increasing as Southerners arrived to work for the war effort and to escape Yankee incursions elsewhere. The Confederate government had established a number of hospitals clustered at the corner of Twenty-fifth Street and Main. Luther Libby's warehouse was converted into a Union prison, and as the number of Union prisoners increased, they would be placed on Belle Isle in the river. Tredegar Iron Works and Gallego and Haxall Mills were working around the clock to supply the Confederate war machine's increasingly insatiable needs. Smaller firms were also garnering government contracts and producing for the war effort. Finally, the city bore a decidedly martial aspect as trains continued to ferry soldiers to the front.

Christmas in Richmond dawned cold and wet. Sallie Putnam spoke for many in Richmond when she observed: "Never before had so sad a Christmas dawned upon us. Our religious services were not remitted, and the Christmas dinner was plenteous as of old; but in nothing further did it remind us of days gone by. We had neither the heart nor inclination to make the week merry with joyousness when such a sad calamity hovered over us. Nowhere else could the heart have been so constantly oppressed by the heavy load of trouble as in Richmond, and friendly congratulations of the season were followed by anxious inquiries for dear boys in the field."[85] Others in the city found cause for celebration. With the exception of reverses in western Virginia, 1861 had been very good to the Confederacy. The holidays were a time to rejoice in Southern arms and to celebrate the birth of a new nation. As a consequence, locals and visitors engaged in what one observer deemed "a long season of more regular parties and unprecedented gaiety." "[T]he first winter of the war was one to be written in red letters, for old Richmond rang with a chime of merry laughter that for the time drowned the echo of the summer's fights and the groans of wayside hospitals."[86]

As December ended and the snows fell heavily upon the city, many wondered what the New Year—and the renewal of the military campaigning season—would bring. Few could have imagined that the horrors of Manassas would return some tenfold in yet another "On to Richmond" campaign.

2

The Campaigns of 1862

"On to Richmond"

The new year in Richmond dawned cold and dreary, and the news from the various fronts did little to lift people's spirits. For Richmonders, the gods of war proved very fickle indeed. The war had begun gloriously with victories at Fort Sumter, Big Bethel, and Manassas, but the casualties, especially from the latter battle, sobered many who believed the rebellion would be a short, relatively bloodless affair. Then came a wave of bad news in the early months of 1862, and many in the Confederate capital quickly began to despair for their cause.

February 1862 was an especially bitter month. An obscure Union officer named Ulysses S. Grant stunned the Confederacy by seizing Fort Henry on the Tennessee River and Fort Donelson on the Cumberland River. Those reverses led to the fall of Nashville, a key manufacturing and supply hub, on February 23, 1862.

Southerners had barely digested word of the reverses in Tennessee when they were rocked with the news that Union infantry and gunboats had seized Roanoke Island and Cape Hatteras off the North Carolina coast. The battle at Roanoke Island was especially a blow that hit locals hard: O. Jennings Wise, the son of former governor Henry A. Wise, was killed in action while leading the popular Richmond Light Infantry Blues. On the heels of that news came tidings that Confederate outposts on the Mississippi were threatened. These defeats shocked a people convinced of the worthiness of their revolution, especially after its early successes. Richmond native Maria Clopton wrote to a relative, "The times are very gloomy, [and] we hear nothing but disaster on all sides, but my trust is still in Him who rules the universe." Another Richmond lady recorded in her diary, "The state of public feeling at this time is very distressing, because we have met with some reverses." She went on to note that many were predicting "the

Yankees will get to Richmond." Thomas Rutherfoord also cataloged the string of setbacks and observed that locals were despondent and believed "we are on the eve of greater reverses [and] that we are no where [*sic*] in a state of preparation to meet the overwhelming forces that surround and press upon us by sea and land on all our borders." The *Richmond Daily Dispatch* editorialized, "These are the times that try men's souls," and exhorted its readers not to "sink into the dust of despondency." It concluded, "Subjugation! Perish the thought! Let it not be dreamt of for a day, an hour, nay a single minute." The acerbic editor Edward Pollard summed up the sentiments of many when he wrote after the war, "No one who lived in Richmond during the war can ever forget these gloomy miserable days."[1]

This was the backdrop to Jefferson Davis's swearing in as permanent president of the Confederate States of America. To prove yet again that Southerners were the true heirs of the revolutionary tradition, the date chosen for the inauguration was purposeful and symbolic: February 22, the 130th anniversary of the birth of George Washington. Because of the disastrous reverses out west, the local press remained mute on those events so as not to add more dark clouds to the day's proceedings. Indeed, the weather on that day reflected the mood of most. According to Thomas Cooper DeLeon, it was "dark and dismal enough to depress still more the morbid sensibilities of the people." Refugee socialite Constance Cary wrote that the weather disheartened "even the stoutest spirits." Capitol Square was "one mass of open umbrellas." Edmund Ruffin saw in the deluge an "inauspicious day for the President's inauguration." The rain never let up and succeeded in soaking everyone who stayed to listen to President Davis's address. Not surprisingly, Davis referred to the revolutionary legacy and the Founders' resolve in the midst of despair: "To show ourselves worthy of the inheritance bequeathed to us by the patriots of the Revolution," Davis intoned, "we must emulate that heroic devotion which made reverse[s] to them but the crucible in which their patriotism was refined." One onlooker noted that after raising the cry "God Bless Our President," "men and women left the Square with solemn brows and serious voices."[2]

Perhaps predictably, people in Richmond who believed their cause was just and their armies without peer sought reasons, if not scapegoats, for the wave of defeats. Many very quickly came to believe it was the government's doing and more specifically the Confederate commander in chief's doing. George Bagby reflected upon the string of reverses and averred that the people could bear the sad tidings if they "retained confidence in the President." Mincing few words, he went on to write: "Cold, haughty, peevish, narrow-minded, pig-headed, *malignant,* he is the cause of our undoing. While he lives there is no hope for us. . . . Alas for the Southern Confederacy." Maria Clopton confided to a friend that people in Richmond were losing faith in the president, the cabinet, and the Confederate Congress. She went so far as to state that favoritism among those in the highest echelons of government was causing the country ill. Some, such as Catherine Cochran, were cognizant of the government's failings. She recognized the "spirit of disaffection and the faulty-finding" but observed, "The President is held responsible for every calamity from the loss of a battle to the washing away of a bridge." Nevertheless, thought Cochran, "[Davis] is not the man to be swayed by popular clamor." Even Davis's staunch friend Mary Chesnut despaired. "The Confederacy done to death by the politicians. What wonder we are lost. Those wretched creatures of the Congress and legislature could never rise to the greatness of the occasion. . . . The soldiers have done their duty. All honor to the army."[3]

The *Richmond Daily Dispatch* tried to find a silver lining in the clouds, both literal and figurative, that cast a pall on the capital. In an editorial titled "Fresh Courage—Vigorous Action," it opined, "It is difficult to decide whether an excess of confidence or a deficiency of it is the greater coil to a nation at war." It went on to discuss the great odds against the Confederacy but urged that reality and the recent setbacks should "awaken our energies and intensify our determination to retrieve our fortune." The *Dispatch* concluded with an admonition: "Let the Government be as sagacious . . . and energetic as the people; let the military leaders be not only cautious, but aggressive, and give full scope to the genius and spirit of our volunteers, and the clouds now overhanging us will be swept from the sky, and a radiant firmament once more gladden our eyes."[4]

Davis was not blind to the dismal situation, and he acted quickly to address some of the most pressing issues, both in the capital of Richmond and in the Confederacy at large. The resignation of Secretary of State Robert M. T. Hunter offered Davis the opportunity to reorganize his cabinet. He shifted Judah P. Benjamin from the position of secretary of war to secretary of state. Benjamin, like Davis, had borne a disproportionate share of the blame for the defeats in 1862. Davis pleased locals immensely when he named Richmond resident and prominent citizen George Wythe Randolph as secretary of war.[5]

A rising crime wave, rumors of slave insurrections, and concerns that Union spies were actively undermining the Confederacy wracked Richmond during the winter of 1862. Thefts, burglaries, and general lawlessness seemed the rule. Samuel Mordecai wrote to his brother that he feared excessive drinking was the cause: "The streets of Richmond exhibit the most disgusting scenes—hundreds of drinking shops are open and all filled." He added, "It is rumored that Richmond will be under martial law . . . it is the safest way to repress crime, detect spies and arrest impious characters."[6]

Rumor became reality on March 1, 1862, when Davis declared martial law to combat those deleterious developments. That proclamation followed on the heels of the suspension of what the president considered the "privilege" of habeas corpus, but most locals welcomed these decisions. Adelaide Clopton wrote to a friend that at least 1,500 individuals had been arrested. She reported that locally "there is no doubt but the Germans & the Italians here were in a plot headed by some Yankees . . . to put the city in the hands of the Federals." Clopton also noted that "*among* the most prominent of those arrested" was Richmond Unionist John Minor Botts: "How the mighty are fallen! . . . I am afraid he really is a traitor of the vilest." Clopton noted approvingly that the proclamation of martial law closed all liquor stores and watering holes in the city: "This alone will have a most excellent effect." Another Richmond woman recorded in her diary, "Things seem to be getting on very well now. . . . Every citizen has had to give up whatever private arms he possessed to the government." Even Edmund Ruffin, that staunch states' rights defender of individual liberties, thought the proclamation of martial law "salutary" and was especially pleased that it also forbade the distilling and selling of alcohol. "For some time," Ruffin noted, "the great assemblage of soldiers . . . & their drinking have made Richmond a sink-hole of drunkenness, rowdyism, & crime." Not all greeted the advent of martial law with enthusiasm, however. John Gottfried Lange, a German immigrant who owned a beer hall in the city saw his livelihood affected. "Whoever has lived in a city under martial law," Lange wrote, "will remember the depressed mood and the repugnancy of the population."[7]

Martial law did not totally curb excesses. The *Richmond Daily Dispatch* railed against the "Cyprians . . . as well as loose males . . . [who] have been disporting themselves . . . on the sidewalks and in hacks, open-carriages, &c., in the streets of Richmond, to the amazement of sober-minded citizens." The *Dispatch* urged Mayor Mayo to enforce the city's vagrant law to put a stop to such "vulgarity."[8]

Equally serious was the reality that the enlistments in the Confederate army were due to expire. Davis went to the Confederate Congress and told this body that manpower was needed for the renewal of military campaigns—and for a conflict he anticipated would be a long, drawn-out affair. The solution was a conscription law. The Congress approved Davis's request, and on April 16, 1862, the first conscription act in American history was implemented. Scholars still debate how effective the conscription legislation of 1862 and its subsequent iterations were, but it did succeed in keeping a Southern army in the field as the campaigning season opened that year. As one resident noted, "Companies are forming and recruiting quite rapidly it seems; a great many join now from fear of being drafted, who would not do so otherwise."[9]

With conscription, Richmonders and others in the Confederacy were learning the hard lessons of war. Ever mindful of their individual liberties, Southern white men were now finding the government taking those liberties away from them. Some in Congress urged Davis to assume even more power in executing the war. But he refused. Nonetheless, as the war went on, more and more individual liberties would be challenged.[10]

One of Davis's closest advisers, William Preston Johnston, "marveled at . . . his unwillingness to be a dictator, even when some of his friends in Congress urged that measures be passed vesting him with supreme civil and military power." To Davis, such an investment of power smacked of destroying the ideology of state's rights and individual freedoms upon which the Confederacy was based. Nevertheless, as one of Davis's biographers notes, the legislation Davis pursued in mid-1862 was remarkable.[11]

The pall that hung over Richmond did not lift with the advent of spring. If anything, locals grew more disheartened as bad news continued to filter into the capital. In early April, the Confederacy's attempt to regain Tennessee in an offensive launched from Corinth came to naught at the Battle of Shiloh. Sallie Putnam voiced what many felt when she observed: "In mute despair we listened [to word of defeat] until the heart grew sick, and grim war seemed unendurable. . . . [And] again arose the question: Who is at fault in this defeat?"[12]

Perhaps the crowning blow of that dismal early spring was the fall of New Orleans to Admiral David Farragut's fleet on April 25, 1862. Disbelief, shock, and grief overwhelmed the capital. "This disaster is to us most momentous," Edmund Ruffin confided to his diary. T. C. DeLeon averred that the "loss was the most stunning blow that had yet been dealt the cause of the South." Constance Cary recorded that the string of defeats, especially the loss of New Orleans, made people in Richmond "feel like the prisoner of the Inquisition in Poe's story, cast into a dungeon of slowly contracting walls." Sallie Putnam noted the economic impact "was felt immediately in Richmond in the increased prices charged for such articles of food as were brought from that section of the country."[13]

Shortages of food and inflated prices actually predated the fall of New Orleans. One resident informed a relative, "It is a bad time for strangers to come to Richmond, for we are really in such a state of I may say almost starvation, that it is utterly impossible to do more than get a scanty supply of provisions for the use of our immediate families." Phillip Whitlock observed that the continued depreciation of Confederate money caused the cost of "every thing [to get] very high." Both Sallie Putnam and J. B. Jones decried the "extortion" that seemed to pervade the city. Jones in particular noted that beef prices had more than doubled and that butter was fifty cents per pound. Putnam added, "The complaints of the people grew loud and terrible" and forced General John Winder, the provost marshal, to intercede: he "laid a tariff of prices on articles of domestic produce." Sadly for the residents of the city, the schedule of fixed prices provided little relief. As the *Richmond Enquirer* observed, "quite a contrary effect" resulted: "The supply of provisions is curtailed. The great scarcity . . . is acknowledged by everyone." The editor hastened to add, however, that "it is not to be wondered at when we consider the great increase of our floating population, together with the fact the hucksters refuse to furnish the markets at the established prices." The *Daily Dispatch* added to the chorus of complaints over high prices and shortages. "We have never heard of anything in the history of man like the high prices which prevail for every article of use and necessity." The *Dispatch* went on, "Whilst the mass of Southern people have given up everything to the war[,] . . . Congress has squabbled over the amount of its pay, the Legislature exempted itself from military duty, the speculators and land sharks drained the soldiers who were fighting for them of their life-blood. . . . It may be said to the extortioners and speculators . . . as was said to their predecessors in the Jewish temple, 'You have made it a den of thieves.'" All agreed, "Some other remedy should be sought for this evil." It would not come before the next "On to Richmond" campaign.[14]

"If the Yankees Can Get *Here*, They Can Get Anywhere"

The people in Richmond did not have the luxury to lament the military reverses for long because the Federal juggernaut was poised to launch another strike at the Confederate capital. After weeks of trying to get the new Federal commander, Major General George B. McClellan, to commit to a strategy of action, President Lincoln was finally persuaded that "Little Mac" had an offensive plan that also had the support of most of his subordinate officers. McClellan proposed nothing less than to move the Army of the Potomac to Urbanna, Virginia, on the Rappahannock River via the Chesapeake Bay. Once there, he would utilize the Richmond & York River Railroad to gather his forces at West Point, Virginia, and march north toward the Confederate capital. McClellan assured Lincoln he could fight the "Waterloo" of the rebellion and capture Richmond under this plan.[15]

Unfortunately for McClellan, the Confederates were unwilling to allow the Union army to operate at will. On March 8, 1862, the C.S.S. *Virginia*—the Confederates had salvaged the former Federal ship *Merrimack* and encased it in armor plates—steamed out of Norfolk and attacked the Union's blockading squadron off Hampton Roads. The Federal capital was thrown into a panic as Lincoln and Secretary of War Edwin Stanton feared nothing could keep the Confederate behemoth from steaming up the Chesapeake Bay and shelling Washington. Those fears were allayed on March 9 when the U.S.S. *Monitor,* the Federal ironclad, engaged the *Virginia* in a dramatic battle that ended in a draw. As Edmund Ruffin correctly observed, "This is one of the most decisive & remarkable naval combats in the annals of warfare. . . . Like all other true southerners, I have been greatly delighted & excited by this great naval success."[16] Word of the *Virginia's* exploits boosted, albeit briefly, Richmond's sagging spirits.

McClellan began his movements in mid-March, proudly proclaiming to one of his subordinates, "I shall soon leave here on the wing for Richmond—which you may be sure I will take." This massive undertaking—ferrying the Army of the Potomac, its artillery, horses, and supplies, from the Potomac River and Chesapeake Bay down to Fort Monroe—took less than three weeks. By the beginning of April, McClellan had assembled a massive force of 121,500 men, forty-four artillery batteries, and all the other accouterments of war. It was a staggering accomplishment.[17]

Meanwhile, in Richmond President Davis and his generals were deciding how to meet the threat just sixty miles to the east. The meeting in Richmond began at 11:00 a.m. on April 14, 1862, and included Davis, chief military aide General Robert E. Lee, and Secretary of War Randolph; commanding officer General Joseph E. Johnston brought his subordinate commanders General James Longstreet and General Gustavus W. Smith. After more than twelve hours of discussion and debate that lasted into the wee hours of April 15, Davis told Johnston to hold the approaches to Richmond at all costs. Johnston, not at all persuaded this was the appropriate plan of action, acquiesced reluctantly because, as he noted later, "events on the Peninsula would soon compel the Confederate government to adopt my opposing the Federal army" at the gates of Richmond.[18]

People in Richmond were only too aware that the enemy was on the move. The appearance of troop elements from the Manassas line in Richmond en route to the peninsula filled locals with both cheer and dread. Caroline Kean Davis wrote that the city was awash with rumors, but little else. "The cloud hanging over our Southern Confederacy," she admitted, "seems to grow darker—but I still cling to the hope that we shall yet be saved from our foes." Another Richmond woman found the soldiers of the various commands "cheerful," "but their appearance was enough to bring tears to one's eyes. Sunburnt, ragged, stained with clay as if they had been living in it, they presented a sad contrast to the time when clad in their uniforms . . . they left their happy homes." Perhaps more ominous on that Sunday was news that the men had had nothing to eat for more than twenty-four hours. "As soon as this was ascertained," wrote that same Richmond lady, "it was announced in several of the churches and persons without waiting for the services to close, got up and going home, sent whatever they could . . . for them to eat." Mary Taylor also observed "a large number of troops go off this morning to Yorktown. They had been marching and looked so worn and tired. Fannie and I bought crackers and distributed them among them." A Mississippi soldier summed up the situation when he wrote home that "Richmond is one living, moving mass of soldiers & to day [sic] the streets show nothing but a continuous stream on their way to Yorktown—infantry, cavalry and artillery."[19]

That the Confederate forces had not been fed underscored some of the challenges facing the Confederate army and capital early in the war. Provisions in the city had been scant throughout the spring. The hungry troops who filed into Richmond had watched in horror as tons of provisions and other supplies were put to the torch upon their withdrawal from Manassas. Now, Richmond was faced with the prospect of running out of food: many wondered if both the civilian population and the army could be fed. This problem in supply would continue to haunt Richmond and its defenders.[20]

As Confederate units shifted to the Peninsula, word reached Richmond that John B. Magruder's defenders at Yorktown were in desperate need of sandbags to shore up their fortifications. As one Richmond lady remarked,

"How strange! I never would at one time have dreamt that we would sit down on a Sunday to sew things for an army." Women gathered at their churches and met the challenge of sewing 30,000 sandbags in thirty hours. Additional requests for more sandbags—100,000 total—were quickly fulfilled.[21]

Meanwhile, the Richmond City Council resolved to work with the Confederate government to shore up the riverine approaches to the city. The council appropriated $50,000 to cover labor and materiel. Not surprisingly, both the council and the Confederate government relied heavily on slave labor. As one scholar has noted, "By drawing so many adult white males into the army . . . the war multiplied the importance of the black workforce." A British visitor observed, "The fine works of Yorktown are monuments to negro labor for *they* were the hewers and the diggers. Every slave owner in Eastern Virginia was obliged to send one half of his male servants between the ages of sixteen and fifty to the Confederate camps and they were organized into gangs and set to work."[22]

Those soldiers headed to Yorktown would not stay there long. General Johnston, convinced he could not sustain the line and defend against Federal gunboats and Union artillery, informed Lee on April 29 that he was evacuating his position and withdrawing up the peninsula. Johnston's actions forced the Confederates to hurriedly abandon Norfolk. Confederate flag officer Josiah Tatnall worked feverishly with his crew to save the ironclad *Virginia* but could not. Rather than allow the vessel to fall into Federal hands, Tatnall ran it aground and set it afire. When the flames reached the vessel's magazine, it blew apart. News of the ironclad's destruction shook Richmonders, who had believed it would aid in the defense of the capital. As Henry W. Smart wrote to his sister, the destruction of the ship "was unnecessary if not criminal [and] I see no good reason for so doing[.] [S]he could have laid at the mouth of the James River and protected it from the egress of the enemy Gunboats." He concluded his missive by stating, "There is something rotten in Denmark."[23]

Word of the evacuation of Yorktown and Norfolk caused ripples of anxiety in the Confederate capital. Robert Ritchie wrote to Belle Harrison, "I can't feel hopeful about Richmond, in spite of the natural advantages for defense from here to Rocketts." Samuel Mordecai penned a note to his brother George and admitted, "Since you left[,] our City has been quiet, but it was not the quiet of repose and comfort, but of apprehension." Kate Rowland confided to her diary, "The grand armies of the North and South are advancing nearer and nearer to Richmond. Even as I write they may be engaged in battle and the world will witness the most desperate contest of the campaign, for on its issue depends the fate of the Confederate Capitol."[24] The president's decision to send his family to Raleigh, North Carolina, and out of harm's way did nothing to allay Richmond's fears, nor did the various government bureaus' packing up of official documents for shipment south to Columbia, South Carolina. Indeed, there began a steady exodus of people from the Confederate capital out of fear McClellan's army would soon seize and occupy it much as the Federals had done in Nashville and New Orleans. Sallie Putnam observed, "Citizens were leaving by the hundreds in all directions, and in all measure of conveyances. Baggagewagons, heaped up with trunks, boxes and baskets, were constantly rattling through the streets. Houses were left deserted, or occupied by the more courageous refugees, who were glad to secure a temporary home. Business was suspended and the only consideration of the people was the means of flight if it became absolutely necessary."[25] The arrival of elements of Johnston's army after the fight at Williamsburg shattered the calm in Richmond on that Sunday. One spectator admitted, "The appearance of the army . . . did not cheer the inexpert." "First came the convalescent sick, barely able to march, who had been sent ahead to save the ambulances for those worse than they." Next came the weary veterans of Yorktown, "wan and holloweyed . . . weak—mud-encrusted and utterly emaciated." Once again, locals sprang into action to feed and care for the troops. "Few women dined in Richmond that Sabbath," the onlooker concluded, because all had sent whatever they possessed to Johnston's hungry soldiers.[26]

As T. C. DeLeon recalled, "It were impossible to describe accurately the state of the public feeling which now prevailed in the Southern Capital. Absolutely in the dark as to the [army's] actual movement and consequences [and] . . . hearing only the gloomiest echoes from the Peninsular advance . . . it was but natural that a gloomy sense of insecurity should have settled upon the masses, as a pall."[27]

Officials in Richmond acted quickly to stanch the rumors the city would be surrendered without a fight. Even as the various Confederate bureaus continued packing and the Confederate Congress voted to adjourn, the Richmond City Council and Virginia State Legislature met and resolved "that they were willing to stand any loss of property and life even the destruction of the city before giving it up to the enemy." J. B. Jones observed that the state legislature was especially adamant, "calling upon the C.S.

Government to defend Richmond at all hazards, relieving Confederate authorities in advance of all responsibility for any damage sustained." Sallie Putnam, who attended the public meeting where the resolutions were passed, recorded that the crowd cheered Mayor Joseph Mayo and Governor John Letcher. Mayor Mayo, whose great-grandfather had surveyed the site of the city with founder William Byrd, was especially eloquent, promising to resign his position "and . . . shoulder a musket himself in defence of the capital." "In the audience," Putnam added, "were some of the wealthy of our population, who declared they would fire their own beautiful residences, in preference to delivering up the city to our foes." All these sentiments were conveyed to President Davis, who responded to the crisis by assuring people in Richmond he would "defend the position while a man remained." Privately, Davis was less sanguine. He wrote to his wife, Varina, "There has arisen a desire to see the city destroyed rather than surrender. . . . [T]hese talkers have little idea of what scenes would follow the battering rows of brick houses. I have told them that the enemy might be beaten before Richmond or on either flank, and we would try to do it, but that I could not allow the Army to be penned up in a city."[28]

As Richmond prepared for the Federal onslaught, General Lee and Confederate engineers were busily shoring up the defenses at Drewry's Bluff on the James River. Critical to the city's defenses was the Tredegar Iron Works. From the beginning of the war, Joseph Anderson and his firm had contracted with the Confederate government to manufacture siege guns to be used along the coast. Now, with McClellan's army working its way up the peninsula, Tredegar turned to the production of artillery for the Confederate army. The results were decidedly mixed. One Confederate commander informed the War Department, "We are no match for the Yankees at an artillery play with our wretched ordnance, poor in quality and feeble in quantity." Confederate units also had problems with Tredegar pieces exploding, killing and wounding Southern gun crews. Some wondered if the absence of the firm's owner, Joseph Anderson, had affected the grade of pieces produced. Anderson had petitioned the War Department for a command in August and had received his wish in September 1861. Although he had assured the government that the Tredegar could function under the oversight of another, the poor showing in the spring of 1862 raised concerns; the imminent threat to the capital forced the firm to address issues of quality and quantity. The Tredegar's managers succeeded in getting artillery to Confederate forces at key junctures, while also shoring up the river

Tredegar Iron Works, 1865. Courtesy of the Library of Congress, Washington, D.C.

approaches to the city. But the issues raised would have to be addressed if the Confederates defending Richmond were to succeed in pushing back the Federal host.[29]

While Lee and his men worked, and as the Tredegar churned out artillery pieces, anxious residents could hear the Union gunboats shelling the batteries guarding the approaches to the city in mid-May. The *Daily Dispatch* wrote in an editorial titled "The Peril of Richmond," "The proximity of the gunboats of the enemy to this city places it in very great danger. A few hours will test the strength and efficiency of the obstructions placed in our river to prevent their passage." Many in the city were apparently concerned that "there have been gross derelictions with reference to the river defenses." Regardless, the *Dispatch* exclaimed, "the public are not willing to incur the disgrace of submitting to two or three Federal gunboats." The paper predicted locals would resist.[30]

In fact, the Federal ships that threatened Drewry's Bluff were the ironclads *Monitor, Galena,* and *Naugatuck* and the gunboats *Aroostook* and *Port*

Royal under the command of John Rodgers. His flotilla sailed within sight of the Confederate batteries on Drewry's Bluff, but Confederate artillery and sharpshooter fire from the bluff inflicted serious damage on the *Galena* and forced Rodgers to pull back. One cheeky Confederate sharpshooter yelled at the retreating gunboats, "Tell the captain that is not the way to Richmond!"[31]

Again, concern that the capital would be surrendered percolated up the chain of command. The War Department clerk J. B. Jones admitted to his diary that he had written "as strong a letter as I could to the President stating what . . . would be the consequences of the abandonment of Richmond. There would be demoralization and even insubordination in the army. Better die here!" More importantly, Davis's chief military adviser, Robert E. Lee, was committed to holding the city. When Davis suggested an alternative line be identified, the always composed General Lee exhibited raw emotion: "Tears rose in his eyes—'Richmond must not be given up; it shall not be given up!'" As one eyewitness recalled, "I have seen [Lee] on many occasions when the very fate of the Confederacy hung in the balance; but I never saw him show equally deep emotion."[32]

The pronouncements by city fathers and members of the high command apparently had the desired effect. Although many residents continued to leave the beleaguered capital, others resolved to stay and resist. Some locals questioned how wise it would be to torch the city, as many had threatened in public meetings. If the warehouses containing tobacco were burned, Samuel Mordecai wrote, "there is no telling what further injury it may cause." A Confederate soldier reported that when an officer from Richmond passed through his camp, he said "the people of Richmond has disided [*sic*] to burn the place if the Yankis [*sic*] get there. . . . [I]f they burn the place it will ruin so many thousand people and and [*sic*] not gain a thing for the Southern cause." Perhaps not surprisingly, the Richmond City Council weighed in on the matter of destroying stockpiled tobacco. The councilmen resolved "to prevent such burning by any means in their power," for they believed that action would "very likely result in great destruction of life in the present crowded condition of the City." Others in Richmond assured their loved ones, "We feel as cool & calm as if the enemy were 500 instead of 5 miles off from the city. We do not anticipate the city's being taken by the Yankees but should that dreaded event take place, we will not be at all fearful. I am as cool as a cucumber." Still more were disgusted by the Confederate army's inexorable retreat. As one Richmond gentleman wrote to his sister, "Johnston in my opinion is too fond of retreating and not fighting. [T]hat is the reason I believe the enemy is so close to us now at the very gates of the Capital. [I]t is a wonder they didn't evacuate Virginia altogether."[33]

The Battle at Seven Pines

The persistent sound of shelling and the reality that the Federal army could hear the church bells tolling in Richmond caused many to fear for the worst. As Sallie Putnam recalled, "Pale dismay sat on every countenance, and our hearts were well nigh bursting at the misery of our situation." Word that Johnston would attack McClellan's army on May 31, 1862, spread through town. War clerk Jones noted, "Everybody is upon the tiptoe of expectation. It has been announced (in the streets!) that a battle would take place this day, and hundreds of men, women, and children repaired to the hills to listen, and possibly see the firing." Judith McGuire recorded, "The booming of cannon, at no very distant point, thrills us with apprehension. We know that a battle is going on. God help us!" Henry Smart wrote to his sister, "We expect a terrible battle every day close to the city as they are not more than a few miles off[.] [T]here has been skirmishing already and the booming of the cannon is distinctly heard here indicating the storm that is approaching is about to burst upon us." People joined the exodus to the roof of the capitol and other high elevations around the city to catch a glimpse of the battle. The heavy cloud cover from a storm the day before could not disguise the smoke from artillery and rifle fire off to the east.[34]

Johnston's grand plan to attack McClellan ran afoul from the start. Complicating matters was the development of an acoustic shadow. This atmospheric phenomenon affected military operations more than once in the Virginia theater. In effect, low clouds and the humid aftermath of the heavy rains succeeded in muffling sounds over portions of the area. Hence, whereas people in Richmond could clearly hear the fight raging at Seven Pines, Johnston on the battlefield could not. Only in the late afternoon, when he was alerted that a battle was happening and the situation at Seven Pines was serious, did Johnston ride off in pursuit of more information. He arrived at Fair Oaks Station to watch a Confederate attack. Shortly thereafter, he took a bullet to the shoulder. Then a shell exploded, and he was severely wounded with a shell fragment to the chest.[35]

Anxious to learn what was transpiring on the battlefield, President Davis and several aides rode out to Johnston's headquarters. When they finally found the general, he was on a litter, in great pain, awaiting transportation to a Richmond hospital. Johnston's second in command, General Gustavus Smith, had succeeded Johnston after his wounding on June 1, 1862. But with McClellan still a stone's throw from Richmond, Davis had no choice but to select another commander. He turned to Robert E. Lee, who assumed command of the newly christened Army of Northern Virginia on June 2, 1862.[36]

As the fighting at Seven Pines petered out, ambulances and every conceivable form of conveyance began to transport the wounded to Richmond. T. C. DeLeon believed this "long parade of wounded men, more than [from the battle at] Manassas, forced the people of Richmond . . . to see the realities of war." "All day," he recorded, "the sad procession came in. Here a van with four or five desperately wounded stretched on its floor . . . [a] coal cart with the still, stiff figure, covered by the blanket and not needing the rigid upturned feet to tell the story." Sara Pryor was one of those who ventured out into the streets and noted "a strange scene—ambulances of wounded and dying men passed companies arriving on their way to the front, and cheered the other. Batteries of artillery thundered through the streets; messengers and couriers ran hither and thither."[37]

The sheer number of wounded soon overpowered the available hospital spaces. Confederate officials quickly converted tobacco warehouses, churches, and a hotel into makeshift infirmaries. "Dozens of surgeons," DeLeon added, "bare-armed and bloody flitted through [the warehouses], doing what man might to relieve the fearful havoc man had made." Constance Cary noted, "Night brought a lull in the cannonading. People lay down dressed upon beds, but not to sleep." At daylight on June 1, "the whole town was on the street. Ambulances, litters, carts, every vehicle that the city could produce went and came with a ghastly burden." That afternoon, "the streets were one vast hospital."[38]

The numbers of wounded and dying threatened to overwhelm the city. Sallie Putnam noted that more hospitals had been opened in the aftermath of Manassas, but after Seven Pines it was up to the private citizens of Richmond to tend to those in private hospitals "in which their [sic] was neither a bed, nor pillow, nor food, nor surgeons, nor nurse . . . nor anything but the bare floors." As Putnam acknowledged, Richmond's women once again met the challenge by nursing, cooking, and providing bandages and bedding.[39]

Sara Pryor was one of those women who made her way to one of the warehouses that had been converted hastily into a hospital. Pryor, whose husband, Roger, was a brigadier general and in the thick of the fighting, was unprepared for what she found. She convinced the matron at the make-shift hospital that she was dedicated to doing whatever needed to be done to alleviate the suffering. But as Pryor "passed by the rows of occupied cots, I saw a nurse kneeling beside one of them, holding a pan for a surgeon. The red stump of an amputated arm was held over it. The next thing I knew," Pryor admitted, "I was myself lying on a cot . . . I had fainted." She never-theless convinced the skeptical matron to give her a second chance. Time and, as she admitted, "a few drops of camphor on my handkerchief tided me over the worst."[40]

Like many other women in Richmond, Constance Cary and her sister set out to find a cousin who was reported to have been wounded in the fight at Seven Pines. Nothing could have readied them for what they witnessed as they trudged down Main Street in the stifling June heat: "Such a spec-tacle! Men in every stage of mutilation lying on the bare boards, with per-haps a haversack or an army blanket beneath their heads,—some dying, all suffering keenly, while waiting their turn to be attended to. To be there empty-handed and impotent nearly broke our hearts." "The impression of that day was ineffaceable." Cary later admitted, "There was not much going to bed that night either; and I remember spending the greater part of it leaning from my window to seek the cool night air."[41]

Lee Takes Command

Robert E. Lee lost no time in taking the initiative. Just two days after the command was turned over to him, he assembled his lieutenants to discuss the situation in front of Richmond. Solid engineer that he was, he also examined the defenses around the city and the approaches from the southeast. He accu-rately sized up McClellan's plans and conveyed his thoughts to President Davis on June 5: "McClellan will make this a battle of posts. He will take position from position, under cover of his heavy guns, & we cannot get at him without storming his works, which with our new troops is extremely hazardous. . . . It will require 100,000 men to resist the regular siege of Rich-mond, which perhaps would only prolong not save it. I am preparing a line that I can hold with part of our forces in front, while with the rest I will endeavour to make a diversion to bring McClellan out." Lee ordered all of the Army of Northern Virginia to dig trenches and build fortifications. That he was requiring them to do manual labor normally performed by slaves rankled and led to much opposition within the ranks, among the officer corps, and in the city proper. As Lee told the president, "Our people are opposed to work," and Davis agreed. In a letter to Varina, Davis wrote: "Politicians, newspapers and uneducated officers have created such a prejudice in our Army against labor that it will be difficult until taught by sad experience to induce our troops to work efficiently. . . . Caesar who revolutionized the military system of his age never slept in a camp without entrenching it." Not surprisingly, the Richmond press as well as many Southern citizens seized upon Lee's orders and ridiculed him as the "King of Spades"; others asserted that "gentlemen" did not dig ditches. The local newspapers also pointed out that Lee's career in the Confederate army had thus far been less than stellar. The editor of the *Richmond Examiner* drew attention to his lack of success in western Virginia in the fall of 1861 and argued, "The most remarkable circumstance of this campaign was, that it was conducted by a general who had never fought a battle, who had a pious horror of guerrillas, and whose extreme tenderness of blood [encouraged him] to essay the achievement of victory without the cost of life." Mary Chesnut spoke for many when she wrote that the evacuations and retreats were detrimental to the Cause: "Our chiefs contrive to dampen and destroy the enthusiasm of all who go near them. So much entrenching and falling back destroys [*sic*] the morale of the army."[42]

The battle for Richmond began on June 25, 1862, under clear skies at a place known as Oak Grove. Heavy fighting dominated the day and made Lee fear McClellan was anticipating his main offensive thrust at Mechanicsville the next day. Sporadic firing continued through the night, successfully unnerving the Federals in their ranks.[43]

The Battles of the Seven Days were not the Army of Northern Virginia's finest hour. Miscues and missed communications caused confusion, but Lee pushed his army to continue to press the Federals.[44] And the Army of Northern Virginia even had the advantage: George McClellan was psychologically a beaten general. He allowed Lee to seize the initiative, and Lee took full advantage of it. Although McClellan's army was still capable of inflicting serious damage on Confederate forces, McClellan was convinced he was outnumbered two to one. For him, there was only one recourse: withdraw his army to safety at Harrison's Landing, where Federal gunboats could protect him. Indignantly, he telegraphed Washington, "I have lost the battle because my force was too small."[45]

McClellan succeeded in getting his beaten army across the Chickahominy and safely ensconced behind the protection of the Union navy on

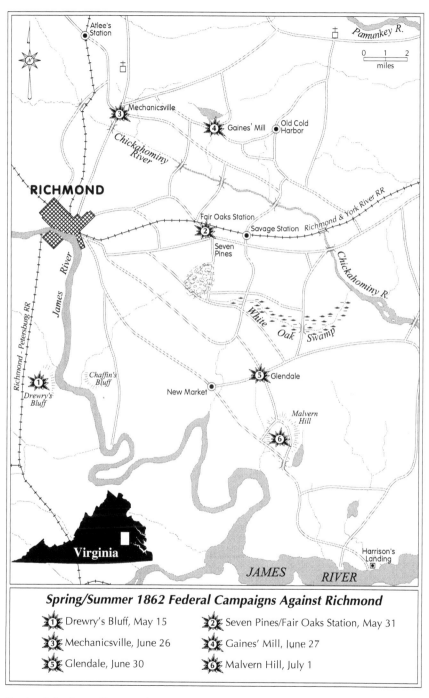

Battle of the Seven Days, 1862.

Harrison's Landing. But the Seven Days' Battles had undone him; his telegram to Lincoln and Stanton captured his mental state: "If I save this Army now," McClellan wrote, "I tell you plainly that I owe no thanks to you or any other persons in Washington—you have done your best to sacrifice this Army." Fortunately for McClellan, this insubordinate message never reached its recipients, for an amazed Union colonel in the War Department's telegraph office deleted the offensive lines before sending it on to the White House.[46]

"Never a Period of More Alarming Excitement"

People in Richmond could hear the sound of gunfire and cannon every day as Lee launched his army against the Federals. Sara Pryor noted, "The city was strangely quiet. Everybody had gone out to the hills to witness the aurora of death to which we later . . . [became] accustomed." Many flocked again to the grounds of the state capitol because it provided a clear view of the fighting raging around them. Civilians and government officials alike noticed the Federals were employing balloons to ascertain Confederate troop movements. As J. B. Jones observed, the balloons were "stationary, being fastened by ropes to trees; [but] they give us an idea of the extent of [the enemy's lines] . . . with glasses they can not only see our camps around the city, but they can view every part of the city itself."[47]

Meanwhile, people throughout the Confederacy awaited word on the fate of Richmond. Back home in South Carolina, Mary Chesnut received news that her husband James, an aide to Davis, was "Safe in Richmond." Wryly, Mary asked, "That is if Richmond be safe—with all the power of the U.S.A. battering at her gates." She also noted how people viewed such news differently now: "When we read of the battles in India, in Italy, in the Crimea—what did we care? Only an interesting topic like any other to look for in the paper. Now you hear of a battle with a thrill and a shudder. It has come home to us. Half the people that we know in the world are under the enemy's guns."[48]

Each day as the battle raged, one local noted, "The city waked up [sic] to a keen realization of the horrors of war." Each day "ambulances brought in the wounded—and open wagons were laden with the dead." The constant sound of artillery fire and the awareness that the Confederate army was trying to save the Confederate capital caused excitement—and anxiety—for many. "It is impossible to settle down to work of any kind," wrote one

Richmonder; "as long as this state of suspense continues . . . we spend our whole time in reading and re-reading the papers."[49]

A week of constant campaigning came with a heavy cost. Residents noted that gunfire sounded throughout the night, often keeping them awake. "But day by day as the red tide rolled back," recounted one local, "it swept into Richmond terrible fragments of the wreck it had made. Manassas had hinted the slaughter of a great fight; Seven Pines had sketched all the hard outlines of the picture; but the Seven Days put in all the dismal shadows, with every variation of grotesque horror." War clerk Jones noted that the city's fifty hospitals were "filling fast with the sick and wounded. I have seen many men in my office and walking in the streets, whose arms have been amputated within the last three days. The realization seems to give them strength." In many cases, the number of wounded exceeded the capacity of Southern doctors to treat them. To address this desperate situation, "a band was formed, consisting of nearly all the married women of the city, who took upon themselves the duty of going to the hospitals and dressing wounds from morning until night." The soldier who witnessed this also noted that when the hospitals were beyond the capacity to care for any more wounded men, women volunteered to take them into their homes. As one officer from the Deep South remarked, "God bless these Virginia women! [T]hey're worth a regiment apiece."[50]

As Sallie Putnam recalled, "The Seven Days' battles around Richmond left us enough to do. We had neither the time nor the inclination to make merry over the triumphs of our arms. There were no noisy jubilations . . . there were no bells rung, no cannon fired . . . no indecent manifestations of exulting victory over our enemies." Rather, locals tended to the sick and wounded and tried to care for the dying. Putnam, like so many others in the capital, realized few families in Richmond were left untouched by the week's bloodshed.[51]

Adding to the already overburdened mix in the city was the appearance of hundreds of Federal prisoners of war. According to J. B. Jones, June 27 was an especially busy day, "our streets . . . crammed with thousands of bluejackets." These unfortunates were taken to Libby Prison for incarceration. Among them were many high-ranking Union officers, including, according to Jones, several generals. One of those unlucky commanders was John Reynolds, a Pennsylvania brigade commander. While Reynolds waited to be transported to prison, he encountered a Confederate official whom he had known formerly in the U.S. Army and who greeted him

View of Libby Prison, 1865. Courtesy of the Valentine Museum, Richmond.

warmly, "'General, this is in accordance with McClellan's prediction; you are in Richmond.' 'Yes, sir,' responded the general in bitterness; 'and d—n me, if it is not precisely in the manner I anticipated.'"[52]

The weather conspired against the sick and wounded of both armies in the city. June and July were brutally hot, and as a result, according to Putnam, "death held a carnival in our city." Gangrene, erysipelas, malaria, and a host of other diseases swept through Richmond's various hospitals, adding to the misery of the wounded. The stench of death and dying was pervasive. As Varina Davis recalled, she returned to the Confederate capital "immediately after the seven days' fight, and the odors of the battlefield were distinctly perceptible all over the city." George Bagby, too, noticed "the odor of suppurating wounds" apparent from Manchester, across the river, and the pungent odor only intensified as he got closer to Richmond.[53]

As summer progressed, the city's cemeteries literally ran out of room, and gravediggers were forced to inter the bodies on the edge of town, dangerously close to Richmond's water supply. Fears that the hasty burials would contaminate the reservoirs, the city council directed the Committee on Oakwood Cemetery "to offer to the Secretary of War so much of the property under their charge as may be necessary for burying the soldiers dying in the service of the Confederate States."[54]

Some in the city wondered how with so many people there could be a shortage of gravediggers. One had only to be acquainted with the work to understand. As one unfortunate laborer told Sallie Putnam, "We could not dig graves fast enough to bury the soldiers. . . . Frequently we were obliged to leave them over night, when, sometimes the bodies would swell and burst the coffins in which they were placed. . . . Our work was a horrible one! The odor was stifling!"[55]

The casualty statistics told the tale. From Mechanicsville to Malvern Hill, the Confederates lost 20,141 killed, wounded, and missing; Federal losses totaled 15,849. While Richmond tended to its dead and wounded, many began to question how the South could have let McClellan escape.[56]

But most in Richmond would echo Ordnance Department chief Josiah Gorgas, who wrote, "[McClellan] has been driven from Mechanicsville . . . across the Chickahominy & thro' the marshes & thickets . . . to the James River . . . where he now lies under the cover of his gunboats. Where are now the brilliant hopes which centered in the possession of Richmond[?] McClellan was certain to be in Richmond. There was no doubt about it. He *was* 6 miles off. *Now* he is 25 miles away." Sallie Putnam recorded, "The clouds were breaking on all sides, they had been lifted from Richmond, and an incubus so heavy that it had well nigh crushed out the life of many of us, had been lifted from our hearts. . . . Great God! I thank thee! The Lord alone omnipotent reigneth!" Mary Chesnut was similarly jubilant: "Victory! Victory heads every telegram now." She went on to add, "For the first time since Joe Johnston was wounded at Seven Pines, we may breathe freely. We were so afraid of another general, or a new one. . . . Now we are throwing up our caps for R. E. Lee." Chesnut, like virtually everyone in the Confederacy, now viewed the "King of Spades" as the savior of Richmond. [57]

Aftermath of the Siege

Richmonders could not exult over their good fortune for long. McClellan and his powerful host were still within striking range. Moreover, Confederate casualties in the Seven Days had been very heavy—20,000, almost a quarter of all those engaged. Perhaps most ominous was the reality that the besieged capital was overtaxed with the dead, the wounded, and Federal prisoners. Mary Chesnut listened to a friend recount what she had witnessed in

Richmond: "McClellan is routed and we have 12,000 prisoners. Prisoners! My God! And what are we to do with them? We can't feed our own people."[58]

There was much truth in that exchange. The continued blockade of Southern ports and active military operations had seriously affected the food supply in the capital. Prices in the spring were high, but they would go even higher as the summer months turned to fall. T. C. DeLeon blamed the Confederacy's depreciated currency for the high prices. "Board at the best hotel in Richmond," he wrote, "was $20 per day—equivalent to $1 in gold, while it was $3 in New York or Washington." War clerk Jones found rents doubled from the previous year and prices for basic staples consistently on the rise. The price-setting policies of the provost marshal's office were, according to Jones, "keeping a great many things out of [the] market." Edmund Ruffin worried that the advent of colder weather would cause more hardship on the troops in the field. The army, he wrote, was "generally deficient in clothing & many destitute of blankets & shoes." He went on to note, "All the articles of prime necessity—as sugar, coffee, cotton & woolen cloths of all kinds, & especially shoes, leather & salt, & gunpowder—and latterly grain, forage, & all agricultural products—have risen to enormous and unprecedented prices."[59]

Once again, General Winder attempted to fix prices, and once again the result was less than successful. One grain manufacturer complained directly to Secretary of War Randolph concerning the deleterious effect Winder's price fixing was having on the commonwealth's farmers. By forcing Virginia's farmers to sell flour only in Virginia and at half the cost it would fetch in North Carolina and Georgia, the law was encouraging farmers to "refuse to sell at all until the order is cancelled, which will tend to advance prices both here and in the south much higher than they otherwise would have done."[60]

Farmers did withhold their crops from the market, and more shortages ensued as a result. Residents and the local press excoriated the "speculators" and "hucksters" who took advantage of the citizens. "It mattered not for themselves who suffered," wrote T. C. DeLeon. "Suffice it that the human hyenas of speculation did prey" upon the people of the Confederate capital. Speculators were gradually deemed synonymous with Jews. Sallie Putnam averred, "One could almost have imagined being in a strange city" because so many of the stores had names "innumerable of the Ancient People instead of the old Anglo-Saxon which had designated the most important business firms of Richmond." She went on to add, "The war was a harvest to that class of our population . . . [and] [t]hey were much abused for extortion." Thus began a wave of anti-Semitism that never really abated.[61]

Concomitant with rising prices was a dearth of housing. Refugees once more arrived in Richmond and burdened local hotels and boarding houses beyond their capacity. Resident Sallie Putnam observed, "From the first day that war was declared . . . Richmond was taxed to the utmost extent of her capacity to take care of the surplus population that accumulated within her limits." This reality was not lost on refugee Judith McGuire, who noted in her diary, "Spent the day in walking from one boarding house to another, and have returned fatigued and hopeless. I do not believe there is a vacant spot in the city." Mary Chesnut was similarly discouraged. After leaving the Ballard House Hotel, she and her husband "made our home with some 'decayed ladies' forced by trouble, loss of property, &c to receive boarders. A dreadful refuge of the distressed it was. . . . [Y]ou paid the most extravagant price, and you were forced to assume the patient humility of a poor relation." Yet as Chesnut readily acknowledged, "We had no right to expect any better lodgings, for Richmond was crowded to suffocation—hardly standing room left."[62]

No wartime census was taken in Richmond, but many commented on the growth of the population. Most of the newcomer refugees were women who had been forced from their homes by Northern incursions and by the need to attain some means of employment to support their families while their husbands served at the front.

One of the biggest consequences of McClellan's failed Peninsular Campaign was the formal creation of Richmond's Unionist underground. What had been a disparate group banded together and were led by Elizabeth Van Lew. Although the Unionist underground was dominated by the "old Whig elite," who financially supported it, its backbone comprised what one historian has described as "men of the commercial or laboring classes, predominately by non-slaveholders of immigrant or Northern background, who would bear the brunt of the physical dangers and risks in fulfilling the underground's missions."[63] They would be active to the very end of the war.

A New Threat

Even as Richmond struggled to regain some normalcy in the aftermath of the Battles of the Seven Days, the Federal government was planning yet another offensive against the Confederate citadel. McClellan remained ensconced behind the Federal gunboats at Harrison's Landing. But as the battles had raged around Richmond, Lincoln summoned General John Pope from the west, where he had won renown in Mississippi by capturing Island Number 10. Pope's force of 45,000, named the Army of Virginia, was poised to strike across the Rapidan River in July. To counter this threat, Lee dispatched Stonewall Jackson and 12,000 troops northward to protect the key rail line at Gordonsville.

The Confederate commander also directed that even more be done to shore up the Richmond's defenses. He wrote to General Gustavus W. Smith, in charge of the Division of Richmond, "I deem no instructions necessary beyond the necessity of holding Richmond to the last extremity." Lee also instructed Jeremy Gilmer, the chief engineer of the Army of Northern Virginia, "to use every exertion to perfect and complete the defences around and to the approaches of Richmond by land and water. I wish them in such a condition that troops can be withdrawn from them in safety to the city." In this way, Lee could ensure the mobility he would need in meeting Federal threats elsewhere in Virginia.[64]

While Lee kept watch on McClellan, Jackson marched and engaged Federal forces under General Nathaniel Banks at Cedar Mountain on August 9. By then convinced Little Mac would not advance against the Confederate capital, Lee sent Jackson 13,000 more reinforcements and encouraged him to outflank the Army of Virginia. Jackson did just that and set the stage for another clash on the Manassas battlefield.[65]

The Battle of Second Manassas thrilled the people of Richmond. Pope, whose arrogance and bombastic proclamations had not only infuriated and insulted his rebel foes but also his own army, was completely defeated on August 29–30, 1862. War clerk Jones spoke for many when he exulted, "When *Lee* says 'signal victory,' we know exactly what it means and we breathe freely." He concluded that the news from northern Virginia "is glory enough for a week."[66] By this time, McClellan had also withdrawn from Harrison's Landing. In the span of two months, the Union army, which had been only five miles outside of Richmond, was now back in the vicinity of Washington.

Just four days after the victory at Manassas, Lee wrote to President Davis, "The present seems the most propitious time since the commencement of the war for the Confederate Army to enter Maryland." But he also conceded, "The army is not properly equipped for an invasion of an enemy's territory. It lacks much of the material of war, is feeble in transportation . . . and the men are poorly provided and in thousands of instances are destitute of shoes." "Still," the general argued, "we cannot afford to be idle." He also asserted that Federal armies in Virginia "are much weakened and demoralized." For Lee, the advantages outweighed the risks: he had his eyes set on cutting the key Baltimore & Ohio Railroad and perhaps even destroying the Pennsylvania Railroad bridge at Harrisburg.[67]

That Lee would propose such a move with his army in such a deplorable condition was perhaps not as foolhardy as it might appear. Both Lee and Davis were only too aware of how ravaged Virginia and especially the areas around Richmond were in the aftermath of the spring and summer's fighting. Moving north and living off the land in Maryland would provide the Old Dominion's farmers a welcome respite during harvest season. It would also ease the strain on the food sources available for the ever-growing population of Richmond.

The Invasion of the North

Lee launched his invasion on September 4, 1862. The Army of Northern Virginia was in good spirits as it crossed the Potomac, singing "Maryland, My Maryland" as it advanced. Many of the men were barefoot, and they left bloody footprints on the hard roads of the state. People who watched the army march past were shocked by its appearance; had they known of Lee's missive to President Davis, they might have thought he understated the situation within the army. As a woman in Shepherdstown observed, "When I say that they were hungry, I convey no impression of the gaunt starvation that looked from their cavernous eyes. . . . [T]hat they could march or fight at all seemed incredible."[68]

People in Richmond knew the army was invading the North, and they waited anxiously for word of Lee's movements. Many expected the Confederates to move on Baltimore or Philadelphia, and some hoped the next dispatch from the Army of Northern Virginia would be from "conquered Washington." But if one sentiment dominated, it was relief: the Army of the Potomac had left Richmond and the Old Dominion. T. C. DeLeon voiced the sentiments of most Richmonders when he wrote: "Excitement reigned in the Rebel Capital, but it was joyous and triumphant. The people had long panted to see the theater of blood and strife transferred to the prosperous and peaceful fields of their enemy. They had a secure feeling that when these were torn with shell and drenched with carnage; when barns were rifled and crops trampled by hostile feet, the northern people would begin to appreciate the realities of war they had so far only seen by the roseate light of a partial press."[69] Davis proclaimed September 18 a day of prayer and thanksgiving in Richmond in recognition of the South's victories before Richmond and on the fields of Manassas. People willingly observed it, but with an anxious eye to the north. Divergent reports kept coming in regarding Lee's fight against McClellan. Judith McGuire wrote that "confused and contradictory accounts" in the newspapers made it difficult to discern exactly what was happening. For several days, conflicting rumors engulfed the capital, and no one could be certain what had transpired in western Maryland. On September 21, J. B. Jones noted sadly, "We have one day of gloom. It is said that our army retreated back to Virginia." Judith McGuire added that locals had the sense that "the most desperate battle of the war was fought [on September 17]."[70]

McGuire was more correct than she realized. The battle at Sharpsburg was the bloodiest of the entire war. More than 22,000 Union and Confederate soldiers were killed or wounded in what was essentially a tactical draw, for at the end of the day, after hours of bloodletting, the battle lines remained where they had been at dawn. For Lee, however, Sharpsburg was a strategic defeat: his invasion was halted, and he was forced to take his shattered army back to Virginia.

As reports from the army filtered back to the capital, people were stunned by the magnitude of the carnage. Equally distressing was word from the Northern press that Lincoln had issued a proclamation freeing all the slaves in the rebellious states effective January 1, 1863. Richmonders greeted this news with anger and contempt. President Davis declared the proclamation "the most execrable measure in the history of guilty man." He directed the state governments that any captured Northern African American troops were to be executed. J. B. Jones asserted that the emancipation decree "will only intensify the war, and add largely to our numbers in the field." Judith McGuire caustically noted, "The Abolition papers are in ecstasies; as if they did not know that it can only be carried out *within their* lines, and there they [the slaves] have been practically free from the moment we were invaded." Edmund Ruffin actually welcomed the proclamation because he believed it "will serve only to strip off all disguise from the established policy."[71]

Autumn of Uncertainty

The people of Richmond received more depressing news in October when they learned the Confederate invasion of Kentucky had been turned back at a place called Perryville. The Confederate commander, General Braxton Bragg, had withdrawn all the way to Murfreesboro, Tennessee. Federal forces were also operating in Mississippi in preparation for a campaign against the Confederate stronghold at Vicksburg. Meanwhile, Lee's army had retreated to the vicinity of Culpeper Court House, and McClellan appeared disposed to allow him to stay there untouched. For many in the Confederate capital, the high hopes of August seemed cruelly dashed as the weather grew cooler with the approach of fall.

During that autumn, Constance Cary observed "numbers of people swathed in black," but she believed that, given all the city had been through, "Richmond showed little trace of its battle summer." Although she admitted that she and her family did not feel "the pinch of the times," she realized that as refugees they were more than grateful for what they had. Others were not as optimistic as she. In early October, war clerk Jones worried about the continued high costs. "How shall we subsist this winter? There is not a supply of wood or coal in the city—and it is said there are not adequate means of transporting it hither." Jones went on to note, "Flour at $16 per barrel, and bacon at 75 cts. per pound threaten a famine. . . . Better [to] die in battle," he concluded, "than die of starvation produced by the enemy." Just a couple weeks later, Jones was "gratified" to find Richmond's markets with "the greatest profusion of all kinds of meats, vegetables, fruits, poultry, butter, eggs, etc. But the prices are enormously high." Even socialite Mary Chesnut reflected on the rising cost of food in the city. "Turkeys were thirty dollars apiece . . . but we lived well," she recorded, thanks to the monthly delivery of provisions—"wine, rice, potatoes, hams, eggs, butter, pickles"— from their South Carolina plantation.[72] Food might be available, but it came with a steep price. More and more in Richmond would discover they had to rely on friends and family in the countryside to augment their diet.

The situation worsened as more refugees continued to flood into Richmond to escape Federal forces elsewhere and to seek some means of employment. The population in the capital swelled to more than 70,000, a twofold increase from 1860. Prices continued to rise, and one government official predicted the state's wheat crop would be insufficient to feed Lee's army, let alone the civilian population of Richmond, during the winter of 1862–1863. Finally, one of the army's commissary officials announced Lee's army would be forced to go on half rations in the New Year. Some in the city believed the Commissary and Quartermaster Departments were "cheating the government." Regardless, it appeared famine was a real possibility.[73]

But it was the appearance of Confederate soldiers marching through Richmond "without shoes, *in the snow,*" that precipitated action: a citizen's committee petitioned the War Department to impress whatever shoes, boots, blankets, and the like could be found in Richmond's shops to outfit the army.[74] Governor Letcher went one step further and issued a proclamation urging the citizens of Richmond "to furnish such articles as they be able to spare for our troops." He went on to note, "Few of us, while seated around our own fires in winter well-supplied with comfortable clothing, can realize the situation of those who are exposed to the inclemency of the weather, without sufficient covering, without change of apparel, or with tattered and unclean underclothing. . . . Who can see the soldiers of Virginia marching with naked feet, in weather such as we have lately experienced, without feeling his cheek flushing with sensations of shame and mortification?"[75]

The Richmond City Council matched the local citizens' actions throughout the summer and fall of 1862. As early as mid-June, the council accepted a physician's offer to run a train from the countryside, where supplies were plentiful, to the city. The council also appropriated money to buy salt, a critical commodity, from Stuart, Buchanan & Company and to distribute it in twenty-pound increments to those in need. Fears of a harsh winter also prompted the city's fathers to appoint a committee to consider furnishing the poor with fuel to heat their homes. As prices for wood continued to climb, the council resolved to appropriate funds to purchase wood for the needy; it also directed the Union Benevolent Society to appoint an individual to distribute the wood.[76]

Richmond's solons did not neglect soldiers' families either. During 1862, the Soldier's Aid Fund and the Union Benevolent Society dispensed almost $150,000. City council minutes for each month in 1862 also show that the council voted unanimously to appropriate anywhere from $2,500 to $5,000 for the support of "families of volunteers now in service from this city."[77]

In spite of such activities, the city fathers realized the people's need was fast outstripping the resources at hand. In the council's report for December 8, 1862, the chairman of the Committee on Poor Relief, David J. Burr, stated the case unequivocally: "There can be no doubt that public charity will have a much larger field for its exercise this winter than heretofore and that the occasion calls for increased appropriations from the City Treasury. It is one of the highest duties of every community to see that the necessities of life are provided for its poor. And your committee are satisfied that the people of Richmond will cheerfully bear any additional burden incident to this object." The council agreed to appropriate an additional $20,000 and directed the YMCA and the Union Benevolent Society to dispense the funds in December 1862 and January, March, and April 1863.[78]

Despite these efforts, many in Richmond suffered at the end of 1862. As one refugee remarked, "Luxuries have been given up long ago. . . . Coffee is $4 per pound and good tea from $18 to $20; butter ranges from $1.50 to $2 per pound . . . corn $15 per barrel; and wheat $4.50 per bushel." Another resident observed, "A portion of the people look like vagabonds. We see men and women and children in the streets in dingy and dilapidated clothes; and some are gaunt and pale with hunger."[79]

The general situation grew even worse when an epidemic of smallpox broke out in mid-December. The city council moved quickly to have portions of the city quarantined in an effort to halt the disease's spread; in short order, yellow flags appeared outside residences denoting where smallpox had infected locals. The council also directed the city's health officer to vaccinate "voluntar[ily] or involuntary[ily] . . . all persons who are not able to pay for it themselves at the expense of the city." It also requested that hospitals be canvassed to ensure there were adequate beds for the victims. As one woman noted in her diary, "The smallpox it is said has become an epidemic, but so absorbed is the public mind with the battles, that it has hardly been realized."[80]

The city was also afflicted with outbreaks of measles and scarlet fever. Like smallpox, these diseases were no respecter of class. General James Longstreet hurried to Richmond from the front only to watch helplessly as three of his children succumbed to scarlet fever.[81]

Fredericksburg

The "battles" the Richmond lady referred to raged fifty miles to the north of the Confederate capital. Angered by McClellan's lack of pursuit after the bloodbath at Antietam, Lincoln finally relieved him of duty once and for all on November 7, 1862. In his stead, Lincoln appointed General Ambrose E. Burnside to command. Burnside's goal was to assault Richmond from the north along the Rappahannock River. His efforts to outflank Lee and the Army of Northern Virginia came to naught, however, when he reached Falmouth, across the Rappahannock from Fredericksburg, and discovered that the pontoon boats he needed to cross the river were nowhere in sight. While Burnside waited, Lee succeeded in establishing a formidable position along Marye's Heights.

The approach of the Federals and the threat that Fredericksburg would be shelled produced yet another wave of refugees, both whites and slaves, who descended on the Confederate capital. The plight of these poor souls moved Judith McGuire deeply. She noted one wealthy family had been forced to settle in "a damp basement-room in Richmond." "Another family," McGuire observed, "consist[ed] of a mother and four daughters, [who lived] in one room [and were] supported by the work of one of the daughters who has an office in the Note-Signing Department. To keep starvation from the house is all they can do." J. B. Jones recorded in his diary in late November that "women, children and negroes" had arrived in the city by train. "The benevolent and patriotic citizens here," he noted approvingly, "made some provision for their accommodation." Jones added mistakenly that the Federals had not yet shelled Fredericksburg, but as T. C. DeLeon later learned, that city "was a ruin, riddled with shot and shell, tenanted by only her poorest classes. Her once cheerful and elegant population were ruined and starving refugees in Richmond." Accounts of the poor refugees of Fredericksburg and their struggles in the capital were replicated in many Richmond households.[82]

Burnside launched the attack that began the Battle of Fredericksburg on December 13, 1862. Successive frontal assaults against the entrenched Confederates produced nothing but heavy Union casualties. By sundown, almost 13,000 Federals had been killed or wounded. As one war correspondent wrote, "It can hardly be in human nature for men to show more valor or generals to manifest less judgment."[83]

Once again, rail cars and other conveyances were pressed into service to carry the wounded to Richmond. Kate Rowland noted in her diary on December 15 that she and her mother "went yesterday evening to the cars on Broad St. and saw them bringing in the wounded. The street was thronged, and ambulances, hacks, omnibuses were all in requisition to carry the brave unfortunates to the various hospitals." Compared to other engagements in 1862, Confederate losses were comparatively light: approximately 5,000. Nonetheless, as Sallie Putnam observed, "the labors of benevolence that had been for awhile [sic] suspended, or less extensively exercised, were called into full action and the summer occupation of the inhabitants of Richmond was rehearsed in the cold of winter."[84]

As the army went into winter quarters, the people of Richmond prepared for the holidays. December was an especially cold month in the capital. Frigid temperatures and persistent snows found people scrambling to find fuel to stay warm. J. B. Jones worried about his family: "Wood is $18 a cord, and coal $14 per cart load." Food prices were also on the rise and forced Jones to sell his silver watch for $75 (he had paid $25 for it, which suggests again how inflated prices had become) in order to afford "fuel for a month and Christmas dinner." An English visitor to the capital remarked "that the merchants of Richmond were, like all their brethren in the Confederate States, put to great straits for goods to sell. Most of their stocks had been sold out long ago." That gentleman also noted that "provisions . . . were very dear, partly owing to the rush of visitors and partly to the lines being blocked by military stores." Many of the city's women devoted themselves to ensuring the Confederate wounded were suitably feted. Kate Rowland recorded that she and her sisters spent Christmas Eve with their mother at the hospital, where Mrs. Rowland had rendered extraordinary service since the very beginning of the war. "On Christmas Day, [we] helped to make things good for the soldiers; stewed oysters and made egg-nog and then superintended the Christmas dinner for the Convalescents. It was delightful to see their enjoyment. Four hundred men were served with chickens, ducks, pies and cider; and the wounded and sick in the wards had turkey, oysters, &c." Elsewhere in Richmond, "the boys are firing Chinese crackers everywhere and no little gunpowder is consumed in commemoration of the day." But for many "there was little to remind us of the festival of yore."[85]

Richmond and its people had weathered 1862. They had survived the siege of the city; they had struggled to meet the challenge of tending to thousands of wounded and dying soldiers; they had attempted to take care of the poor and the families of those defending them on the peninsula, on the plains of Manassas, and in Maryland; they had gone to work in the factories and the bureaus to support the Confederate war effort; and they had countered the threat of epidemic disease. But few in Richmond could know that the coming year, 1863, would tax them even more.

3

Hardship and Despair, 1863

"A General Gloom Prevails"

According to war clerk J. B. Jones, "This first day of the year dawned in gloom, but like the sun of Austerlitz, soon beamed forth in great splendor upon a people radiant with smiles and exalted to the empyrean."[1] For people in Richmond, the dawn of a new year brought hope and promise. Eighteen sixty-two had ended with Southern arms victorious at Fredericksburg, and the news from Tennessee appeared equally auspicious. But within days the hopes of January 1 faded as locals received less-encouraging word from the battlefront. Those tidings were duly noted, but for most in the city January brought cold, snowy weather, and empty market stalls. The winter of 1863 promised to challenge locals as never before.

Persistent Shortages and Few Remedies

Sara Pryor's good friend Agnes wrote her a chatty letter from the Confederate capital just after she attended a New Year's levee at the Confederate White House. Despite admitting "we shall soon be without a stitch of clothes" because there was but little fabric and "not a bonnet for sale in Richmond," Agnes managed to piece together some semblance of dress to accompany the Prince de Joinville to the Davises' reception. The conversation turned to the high cost of provisions in Richmond. Agnes relayed to Sara that the prince "calmly [told] people that rats, if fat, are as good as squirrels, and that we can never afford mule meat. It would be too expensive, but the time may come when rats will be in demand."[2]

Agnes and her foreign friend were not the only ones aware that the situation in Richmond was difficult. One needed only to read the local papers or converse with a neighbor or colleague to realize Richmond in 1863 still had some of the same problems that had dogged the city the year before.

Food was scarce, as were lodgings, and both commanded top dollar. Rebel war clerk Jones worried how he would support his family of six when board was commanding $60 a person per month. What troubled Jones most, however, was the reality that not all were suffering equally. "In these times of privation and destitution," Jones observed, "I see many men, who were never prominent secessionists, enjoying comfortable positions and seeking investments with their surplus funds. Surely there must be some compensation in this world or the next for the true patriots who have sacrificed everything and still labor in subordinate positions with faith and patient suffering." Jones concluded sadly, "These men [the patriots] and their families go in rags, and upon half-rations, while the others fare most sumptuously."[3]

War Department bureaucrat Robert Garlick Hill Kean was similarly concerned about the high cost of everything in the capital. "I recently made a rough calculation to compare the present currency with a sound one in the matter of my household expenses," Kean recorded. "The result is that my salary of $3000 will go about as far as $700 would in 1860." Kean went on to list how prices had skyrocketed: flour was selling for $28 (whether per pound or some other weight is not specified), tea for $15, and bacon for $1.25—goods that before the war would together have cost $9.50 a pound. Similarly, Ordnance Department chief Josiah Gorgas noted the Confederate Congress was debating a new tax bill, and although no one in the city had a sense of its provisions, "Every one prays it may be one adequate to sustain the war and remedy the deplorable currency." Scarcity ruled Richmond's markets, and prices continued their rapid advance. "Of course in this state of things many colossal fortunes will be made," Gorgas concluded. "But we salaried officers who do the work of the war are pinched."[4]

Gorgas's observation struck at the heart of the issue. Although no one, it appeared, was left unaffected by the shortages and inflated prices, there was a correlation between the ways in which the city's denizens coped and their class status. Those fortunate enough to have farms or plantations outside of Richmond could call upon family and friends to come to their assistance. Samuel Mordecai wrote to his brother George that the arrival of a large quantity of beef was a welcome gift: "I assure you . . . nothing could be more acceptable or claim warmest thanks." Mary Chesnut noted that her servant, Laurence, was without peer when it came to locating hard-to-find goods in the Richmond markets—so long as she provided him with a supply of ready cash. But she was also cognizant of the reality: "We had sent us from home wine, rice, potatoes, ham, eggs, butter, pickles. About once a month," Chesnut noted, "a man came in with all that the plantation could furnish us." Newlywed Lucy Chamberlayne was relieved she could honeymoon in the countryside at Farmville, where "the abundant food was a treat after our deprivations in Richmond."[5]

Others were not as fortunate as Mordecai, Chesnut, and Chamberlayne. Refugee families, government bureaucrats, and the city's working class found it increasingly difficult to make ends meet. J. B. Jones feared, "By degrees, quite perceptible, we are approaching a condition of famine." Confederate politician Clement C. Clay wrote to his wife, Virginia, that in Richmond "a general gloom prevails because of the scarcity and high price of food. . . . In this city the poor clerks and subaltern military officials are threatened with starvation, as they cannot get board with their pay. God only knows what is to become of us." Many were concerned—General Lee foremost among them—that there were not enough supplies to feed both the people of Richmond and the army in its winter quarters. Lee wrote to Secretary of War James Seddon that his army was on half rations, "consisting of 18 ounces of flour, [and] 4 ounces of bacon of indifferent quality [per day]." Despite such meager fare, Lee reported, "The men are cheerful and I receive but few complaints." But Lee warned that the men's general health would ill prepare the veterans of the army "to endure the hardships of the approaching campaign."[6]

Others in Richmond expressed similar worries. Christopher Tompkins despaired that "prices of every commodity are almost absurd." As winter progressed, there was little change. Continued cold temperatures and persistent snow falls made the situation even more critical. "Meanwhile things here are bad. Extortion & fraud pervade all class[es] . . . Oh my country!"[7] War clerk Jones was even more graphic. He wrote in his diary: "Some idea may be formed of the scarcity of food in this city, from the fact that while my youngest daughter was in the kitchen to-day, a young rat came out of its hole and seemed to beg for something to eat; she held out some bread, which it ate from her hand, and seemed grateful. Several others appeared and were as tame as kittens." Jones concluded his anecdote in language reminiscent of the prince de Joinville: "Perhaps we will have to eat them!"[8]

Several problems caused this state of affairs. The winter of 1862–1863 was unusually harsh. Locals noted more than twenty-two measurable snowfalls; indeed, in late February Richmond was buried in eighteen inches of snow from one storm. The frequent snows continued into March and were often accompanied by sleet and ice. Although some saw a silver lining in this snowfall—full ice houses boded well for the spring and summer—others realized that the inclement weather further interfered with efforts to supply the city with food. Locals tracked the weather religiously and worried what would happen, for even after the snow melted, the city's streets remained impassable due to mud. That reality, the local press argued, further discouraged farmers from bringing their goods to market. Many worried about the effect the frequent snows would have on those unprepared and caught unawares. J. B. Jones remarked, "There are some pale faces in the streets from deficiency of food," but surprisingly "no beggars, no complaints." Nonetheless, "we are all in rags. . . . This for our liberty," he wryly concluded.[9]

Even more ominously, the railroads serving Richmond were in a deplorable condition. Contemporaries noted that the government monopolized the lines that were running and ferried soldiers to the various camps instead of subsistence goods to the city. The Richmond press reported that the railroad superintendents were stymied in meeting the increased demands on their trains because they lacked the labor needed to keep the lines in "good running condition." The *Daily Dispatch* urged the Confederate Congress to detail some of the "hundreds of ablebodied [sic] men held in various civil and military prisons for trivial offenses" to be sent to the railroads to alleviate the "emergency." The vagaries of transportation succeeded in allowing "scurvy and starvation [to stalk] a land of comparative plenty."[10] Indeed, in some areas crops rotted by the side of the road while people in Richmond faced bare shelves and empty market stalls.[11]

Others in Richmond believed speculators and extortioners were the true culprits behind the high price of food. The *Richmond Whig,* among other city dailies, railed at those who profited amid such misery: "It is deplorable in times like these," the *Whig* exploded, "when the country is bleeding from every pore, when there is wailing in nearly every household, and when the energies of the best portion of us are taxed to the utmost for the bare necessities of life, that we should be gouged by heartless extortioners and robbed by official rogues." The *Daily Dispatch* was even blunter. It published a comparison of a grocery bill for a "small family" in 1860 and 1863. In 1860, that family could spend $6.55 altogether on butter, meat, flour, sugar, real coffee, and bacon as well as candles and soap. That same basket of goods commanded $68.25 in 1863. "So much we owe to the speculators who have stayed at home to prey upon the necessities of their fellow citizens," the *Dispatch* concluded.[12]

Richmonders also decried the spirit of "avarice" and the "mania for speculation and riches, which blinds their patriotism." Many worried aloud what impact accounts of popular suffering would have on the men in the ranks. The editors of the *Daily Dispatch* warned of the deleterious consequences such stories could have. They recounted the tale of a soldier who deserted from his unit in Alabama because he had received so many distressing and dispiriting letters from his distraught wife. That soldier was caught, tried, and executed for desertion. The *Dispatch* surmised that the widow had to be wracked with guilt "with the thought that her exaggerated representations of her trials and sufferings had caused her husband's death. Let this case be a lesson to all wives and mothers." Instead of dwelling on hardship and high prices, Southern women should "speak words of encouragement; cheer their hearts and souls, and arouse their patriotism."[13]

"The Ladies of Richmond"

The local press, public figures, and even the private diaries of the time expressed what the civilian population's attitude should be: people behind the lines, especially the women, should comport themselves as heirs of the revolutionary tradition of 1776 or as the selfless wives and mothers of ancient Athens and Sparta. Such sentiments had been prevalent since the first shots were fired but seemed to intensify as the conflict ground on. As enlistments proceeded and as the mobilization continued, women were expected to maintain their femininity but be strong and stoic in accepting the burdens the war would produce. Few in the halcyon days of 1861 could have anticipated how truly onerous those burdens would become.[14]

When the men went off to fight, they precipitated what some historians have termed a "family crisis." One scholar, for example, maintains that the men's departure for the front necessitated that women assume new roles that often created "sexual tension as the course of the fighting seemed to make hash of traditional definitions of female propriety." Another suggests, "Male prerogative and male responsibility . . . served as the organizing principle of southern households and southern society." However, secession and war produced family separations and placed new demands on Southern women, developments that "exerted significant strain on family relations." Part of this strain related directly to gender roles: war demands weakened significantly the patriarchal structure that had dominated the antebellum South. The absence of men forced women to become the heads of households, at least temporarily. Other women were driven out of their homes as the Federal armies advanced on all fronts. Thousands of those women made their way to Richmond, where they found safety as refugees. Finally, in many instances women were compelled to enter the workplace for the first time in order to support their families while their husbands were off fighting. The net effect of all these developments was a significant challenge to the notions of Southern womanhood.[15]

Initially at least, women welcomed the opportunity to participate in the war effort; indeed, many found the calls to be stoic an expression of patriotism. Women's diaries also reflect the reality that many of them regretted that their gender precluded them from the fight. Typical were the sentiments expressed by Lucy Breckinridge: "I wish the women could fight." Both yeomen and upper-class women bewailed their sex and earnestly desired they had been born male, so they, too, could go to the front. As Mary Chesnut wrote, "I think *these* times make all women feel their humiliation in the affairs of the world. . . . Women can only stay home, and every paper reminds us that women are to be violated, ravished and all manner of humiliation. To men—glory, honor, praise, power." Chesnut was even more graphic shortly thereafter. "If I had been a man in this great revolution—I should either have been killed at once or made a name and done some good for my country. Lord Nelson's motto would have been mine—Victory or Westminster Abbey." Such energies were channeled quickly into activities that were more fully in keeping with women's traditional roles.[16]

From the beginning of the war, women in Richmond and elsewhere banded together to form voluntary aid associations. In some respects, this was a novel development, for, unlike their Northern counterparts, most Southern women did not participate in such activities before the war. Geography played the key role here: the rural Southern population was physically dispersed, and elite women on the plantations saw no need for such organizations. In urban areas such as Richmond, however, these activities were more prevalent. After Fort Sumter, women came together in churches and other venues to sew everything from uniform garments to sandbags. Thomas Cooper DeLeon observed, "As Dickens made his *Madame Defarge* 'knit shrouds' before the greedy knife of the Terror, the sewing circles of Richmond stitched love and hope and sentiment into the rough seams and hems of nondescript garments they sent to the camps by the bales." The *Daily Dispatch* noted, "The ladies of Richmond belonging to the several denominations of Christians are particularly and earnestly requested to meet at the lecture rooms of their respective churches every day until further notice . . . to assist in making beds for the sick and wounded soldiers of our army." First Lady Varina Davis, among others, believed "our women knitted like Penelope, from daylight until dark. They did it, however, not as subterfuge, but to clothe their families and the soldiers." Everywhere one went, one saw knitting needles flying.[17]

To be sure, sewing was firmly in keeping with a woman's traditional role. But even here, again, class differences loomed large. Many upper-class women knew only fancy needlework—needlepoint and crewel, for example. Making a shirt or knitting socks often caused great consternation, if not embarrassment. Typical was the experience of a newlywed wife of a Confederate officer in Richmond. She ruefully admitted she was forced to rely upon neighbors to teach her how to sew her husband's shirts. Similarly, few elite women had ever had the need to spin their own cloth. Spinning wheels were hauled out of the attic or storage shed, but their presence was more symbolic than real. Over time, women did without new clothes, recycled items, or traded garments for food and other necessities. By the midpoint of the war, the always fashion-conscious Mary Chesnut averred, "We were all in a sadly molting condition. We had come to the end of our good clothes . . . and now our only resource was to turn them upside down or inside out—mending, darning, patching." One enterprising slave offered to sell "various articles of clothing for different ladies " among the middle- and upper-class whites to other white women who had the means. The ladies were undoubtedly embarrassed to be forced to sell their silk-and-lace dresses for money to buy food and other necessities, so this slave did it for them and charged them for her efforts.[18]

Other women in Richmond formed soldiers' aid societies. These groups were dedicated to raising money and supplies to assist the soldiers in the field and their families at home. Acknowledging "that we, as the weaker sex, [are] unable to join in the defense of our country," Richmond's women resolved to "encourage the hearts, and strengthen the hands of our husbands, brothers, fathers and friends by all means within our power." To that end, they established the Ladies Aid & Defence Society, promising they would donate what personal possessions would best aid the war effort. These Richmond ladies also resolved to raise all the necessary funds to lay the keel of a new Confederate gunboat. Maria Clopton, elected president of the society, was indefatigable in pressing forward its work. She wrote articles for the *Daily Dispatch* urging locals to "collect and send to the Tredegar

Works all the metals they can for the Gun Boat now to be built by the Ladies Defence Association." Clopton concluded one of her pleas by noting, "A poor widow came & offered to the Assoc [*sic*] a . . . metal kettle she had owned for forty years. I trust we shall have many such examples of self-denial." As one Richmonder observed, "The brave women of the city were a constant reproach, in their quiet, unmurmuring industry, to the not infrequently faint-hearted men."[19]

Clopton's activities led the ladies of Prince Edward County, Virginia (located in the Piedmont, slightly southwest of Richmond), to join in the effort. The president of the soldiers' aid society there, Cornelia Berkeley, wrote to Clopton that her "ladies" "wish to aid you in the noble enterprise of the Gunboat Association: during the past few days, we have collected articles of silver plate together with one hundred fifty dollars, several gold watches, chains, etc.," Clopton graciously accepted the donations. By late March 1863, the Confederates stationed at Drewry's Bluff wrote to Clopton to thank her and "the Ladies Gunboat Association" for all they had done and asking permission to christen the gunboat the *Lady Davis.* The men concluded their missive by noting that if the ladies were so inclined, they were "very much in want of clothing of all kinds."[20]

Even these activities, though they may have appeared traditional, gave birth to change: women became more conscious of their gender, "for they saw themselves in groups; here they explored the meanings of gender in a way they had not previously." Gathering routinely in associations such as the Ladies Aid & Defence Society, women may have affirmed a traditional role, "but by their very existence these organizations defined and empowered women as women, independent of men."[21]

Into the Workforce

The growth of women in the Richmond workforce paralleled the fortunes of the war. At the beginning, aid societies and sewing circles dominated as women worked to furnish their husbands, sons, and fathers with socks, shirts, and trousers. But other opportunities quickly presented themselves. Unlike in the North, men had dominated the teaching profession in the antebellum South. Yet as the men went off to war or after 1862 were conscripted, many women saw an opportunity to enter that field. In Richmond, there were few schools, but those private academies that did survive witnessed a shift from male to female teachers.[22] As with the aid societies, however, teaching—nurturing young people's minds—had fallen within traditional notions of what proper role women should play in society. Although many women welcomed the idea of replicating the positive experiences they had had as students, there was a stigma. In the fall of 1861, *De Bow's Review* would write that the South "must overcome its tendency to 'rank teaching among the *menial* employments' or to regard it as 'socially degrading' or 'fit for Yankees only.'" Although some people exhorted women to fill the void left by the absence of the men, they tempered their comments by reminding women of their proscribed spheres. Predictably, perhaps, many wondered if a woman's mind, especially for mathematics and science, might be inferior.[23] Some women found teaching exhausting and intimidating. One Richmond minister, Moses Hoge, went so far as to urge his daughter to seek a position in the Treasury Department instead. The women employed there earned $500 a year and labored only six hours a day. He concluded that such a position "is far less fatiguing & vexatious than teaching."[24]

Pastor Hoge was not alone in seeing government work as an attractive alternative. Sallie Putnam believed "no place in the Confederate Capital was more interesting or attractive" than the Confederate Treasury Department. There, "fair operatives were engaged and signing Mr. Memminger's Confederate bills. The duties were pleasant and profitable." Basically, the women signed a set number of notes and "trim[med] the edges with long shears." The work was so popular that applications usually outnumbered available positions. In fact, Secretary of the Treasury Christopher G. Memminger told an aspirant for such a position, Emma Read, "that one vacancy will bring a hundred applications." Hence, as Read observed, "it was not an easy matter to get an appointment, one must have influence." Read's application was typical of the hundreds Secretary Memminger received. Read had been a teacher in the city, but the "incursions of the enemy" had prematurely ended that employment. "I do not wish to be idle," she told Memminger, "& the claims of others dear to me, upon my earnings, are of a very pressing nature."[25]

Emma Read, Kate Rowland, and Lucy Chamberlayne also sought work as "Treasury Girls." Kate noted she and "L" hoped to obtain a position "gumming stamps" but were unsuccessful, and "we are now trying to get a position . . . signing Virginia notes." Lucy Chamberlayne was more fortunate. She garnered her plum job at the Treasury in the fall of 1862 and, along with "30 of us girls," occupied a room in the Treasury Department. According to Chamberlayne, "it was called 'Angel's Retreat.'"[26]

Women were soon found in the Confederate Post Office, the Quarter-master Department, the Commissary Department, and the War Department. But the Confederate Treasury would throughout the course of the war employ the most women in Richmond. This phenomenon was yet again directly related to the Southern class structure. As both Richmonders then and historians since have observed, "Ladies of the South's privileged orders who had fallen on hard times constituted the overwhelming majority of the women who received these desirable situations and the recommendations of well-connected friends exerted significant influence." Moreover, the women who worked in the Treasury and the Commissary Department in particular were required to pass examinations proving basic arithmetic skills and spelling ability. That necessarily excluded even those women who had a rudimentary education. Such employment was, concludes one scholar, "a form of government welfare distributed on the basis of gender and class."[27]

"A Woman *Must* Soar beyond the Conventional"

Wartime demands also compelled women to take up work that challenged both society's and their personal notions of propriety. Nowhere was this more apparent than in the hospitals, where the constant influx of the sick and wounded overwhelmed the existing staffs. The local papers were constantly advertising for slave men and women as well as free people of color to work in the hospitals as nurses, laundresses, cooks, and attendants.[28]

Despite the sterling example of Florence Nightingale in the Crimean War of 1853–1856, people in the South regarded nursing with apprehension if not disdain. Up to the outbreak of the war, hospital nurses were male, hailed from the poorer classes generally and the slave population. But with secession and the opening movements of the armies in the summer of 1861, popular attitudes appeared to change dramatically. Mary Chesnut observed in Richmond, "Every woman in the house is ready to rush into the Florence Nightingale business."[29]

The reality that the war would not be over quickly and bloodlessly was brought home to Richmonders as the first casualties arrived in the city after First Manassas. From the Seven Days' Battles through Fredericksburg, Richmond became the hospital center of the Confederacy. At first, individuals opened their private homes to tend to the never-ending stream of wounded and dying Confederates. But then the Confederacy gradually opened hospitals throughout the city. In 1862, the Confederate Congress endeavored to bring some further order to the system when it passed legislation detailing the various positions women could assume within the hospitals as well as the salaries they would receive.[30]

The largest Confederate hospital, Chimborazo, was located in Richmond. During the spring campaigns of 1862, Chimborazo's surgeon, Dr. James B. McCaw, wrote to Surgeon General Samuel P. Moore that "it will be utterly impossible to continue to operate Chimborazo without the 256 nurses and cooks employed to take care of the nearly 4,000 sick and wounded." This would not be the first time McCaw would ask for or advertise for black nurses. According to one scholar, "in no other Southern city were so many negroes employed in the Medical Corps congregated as in Richmond, the South's chief hospital center." McCaw would go on to make Chimborazo a totally self-sufficient hospital, with living quarters, laundries, kitchens, and bakeries. It also had one of the lowest mortality rates of any hospital in the Confederacy.[31]

Employing white women in Richmond's hospitals challenged the nineteenth-century South's notions of propriety. The idea that women would tend to men in various degrees of undress and would be exposed to any number of bodily fluids unnerved many. One Southern woman who overcame her misgivings was Phoebe Yates Pember.

Pember was born to a prominent Charleston family and was well educated. Widowed early, she was an unhappy refugee in northern Georgia when she received an invitation from Mrs. George Randolph, wife of the secretary of war, to apply to be one of the matrons at Chimborazo Hospital in Richmond. Pember recalled Randolph's "graphic and earnest representations of the benefit a good and determined women's rule could effect in such a position." Pember admitted she had her reservations: "The natural idea that such a life would be injurious to the delicacy and refinement of a lady—that her nature would become deteriorated and her sensibilities blunted was rather appalling." But Randolph's entreaties allayed her fears, and she journeyed to the capital to take up her new role.[32]

As Pember told her sister, "I am to have board and lodging in the Hospital and at a boarding house adjacent and forty dollars a month, which will clothe me. I have entire charge of a department, seeing that everything is clean, orderly, food prepared and so on." Interestingly, Pember declined a position at another hospital because one of the doctors was "a friend, very pleasant, handsome and intelligent, and as we would be comparatively alone and eat together, *that* would not do." Apparently, it was better to risk one's delicacy than to mix promiscuously with an attractive male physician.[33]

Pember's experiences at Chimborazo underscore how gender and class roles clashed in wartime Richmond. Her arrival coincided with the Confederate Congress's action stipulating the role that female matrons would play in the Confederacy's hospitals. She noted that the surgeons in the hospitals worried excessively about the effect of "petticoat government." That view was further borne out when Pember overheard the surgeon in her unit tell a colleague "in a tone of ill-concealed disgust that *one of them had come*."[34] To her credit, Pember prevailed and managed to win several skirmishes with the doctors over such matters as the distribution of the whiskey ration. She was less successful in hiring women who would assist the doctors and nurses in the wards.

Pember needed a "corps" of people who would provide food, drink, and other services to the never-ending stream of wounded that poured into Richmond. She admitted that "there was no lack of applications" from interested women, "but my choice hesitated between ladies of education and position . . . and the common class of respectable servants." Pember opted to hire the "respectable servants," and her reason is telling: "it was supposed they would be more amenable to authority." Pember discovered to her dismay how wrong she was. The first woman hired refused to tend to men who were not fully dressed. Two other women insisted on seeing Pember and informed her they "were not satisfied, for I had not invited them to call upon me." According to Pember, "they considered themselves quite as much ladies as I was" and hence were dissatisfied with the rough quality of their accommodations. When Pember went to "inspect" their quarters, she was chagrined to find these women dipping snuff—a clear indication, at least for Pember, that they were not in her class. The final straw came when one of those women, who arrived with seven huge trunks, insisted on creating her own "private quarters." She was unceremoniously evicted and loaded into an ambulance, "very drunk by this time and sent away." On the whole, the hiring of this lower class of women was, according to Pember, "a very disappointing experiment."[35]

That Pember believed less-educated women would be more "amenable" to taking orders and being subordinate to their more well-to-do supervisors indicates that class status continued to exert a large influence in the Confederate South. As elite women became nurses or government clerks, they strived to keep the antebellum era's social stratification in place. Even when privileged women were driven out of their homes as refugees and forced to seek remunerative employment, the war "made [them] more insistent about their rank and position even as it drew the bases for such distinction increasingly into question."[36]

Pember was one of the few upper-class women who maintained her position at the hospital throughout the war, perhaps because her duties as matron more closely resembled those of an administrator or because as a widow she was deemed more "independent." Regardless of her status, Pember did tend to the wounded and admitted that she witnessed many things she never could have imagined before 1862. One of her more poignant accounts describes "Fisher," a twenty-year-old soldier severely wounded during one of the battles in 1863. According to Pember, "sedulous care" on the part of the entire ward proved effective, for Fisher seemed to recover. But then Pember was summoned to his cot one evening after a nurse noticed some blood. Fisher's efforts to walk with the aid of a crutch had apparently severed an artery. "I instantly put my finger on the little orifice and awaited the surgeon," Pember wrote. The doctor's news was grim. According to Pember, the much-beloved Fisher could survive only while she held the artery. When informed of this, Fisher "broke his silence at last. 'You can let go—.'" "But I could not," Pember recorded, "not if my own life had trembled in the balance." As she noted later, "The pang of obeying him was spared me, and for the first and last time during the trials that surrounded me for four years, I fainted away."[37]

Pember's activities and her willingness to tend to soldiers such as Fisher made her a role model of sorts. Not surprisingly, she addressed directly the notion "that a woman must lose a certain amount of delicacy" if she took up nursing. According to Pember, "There is no unpleasant exposure under proper arrangements, and even if there be, the circumstances which surround a wounded man . . . suffering in a holy cause . . . hallow and clear the atmosphere in which [a nursing woman] labors." Pember asserted, "A woman *must* soar beyond the conventional modesty considered correct under different circumstances."[38]

Another educated, prominent woman who made a significant contribution to Richmond's nursing community was Sallie Tompkins. Born to a wealthy family in Virginia's Tidewater region, Tompkins journeyed to Richmond shortly after the outbreak of the war. The Battle of First Manassas spurred Tompkins to action. She prevailed upon Judge John Robertson to give her his home on Third and Main (he and his family had left the city for the safer environs of the countryside) so she could turn it into a private hospital. Tompkins dedicated all her efforts and her personal money to out-fitting the hospital and tending to the thousands of wounded who poured into the city throughout the war. She was such a fixture in the community that President Jefferson Davis commissioned her a captain in the Confeder-ate cavalry on September 9, 1861. That captaincy allowed her to continue to operate her independent hospital after the Confederate government man-dated all hospitals be placed under the purview of the War Department in 1862. Tompkins treated more than 1,300 wounded soldiers; she lost less than a hundred before the hospital closed in June 1865.[39]

Sadly for the wounded in Confederate Richmond, few women were able to duplicate Pember and Tompkins's willingness to tend to the sick, wounded, and dying of the city. Many women tried but found the hospitals more than they could bear. Mary Chesnut wanted to tend to the sick and wounded but found it challenging on multiple levels. She determined to dedicate her time to assisting the sick and wounded in Richmond, but again class and gender issues intruded. Chesnut made her way to Sallie Tompkins's hospital. When she asked Tompkins if she could tend to the wounded and ill hailing from her native South Carolina, she was, as she admitted, "rebuked. I deserved it." Tompkins told Chesnut, "I never ask where the sick and wounded come from." Perhaps that exchange convinced Chesnut to offer her services at another hospital. Shortly thereafter, she visited the Sisters of Charity Hospital and was impressed by what she saw. But when she arrived at the St. Charles facility, she reacted with repugnance: "Horrors upon horrors . . . want of organization. Long rows of them dead, dying. Awful smells, awful sights." Chesnut admitted that she recalled little of the conversation with a nurse, "for I fainted. The next that I knew of, the doctor and Mrs. Randolph were hav-ing me, a limp rag, put into the carriage at the door of the hospital."[40] Ches-nut would eventually become more accustomed to the hospital wards and continued to volunteer in Richmond and back home in South Carolina, but she admitted that doing so tried her sensibilities and her resolve.

Chesnut was not unique in her reaction to the horrors of Richmond's hospitals. Other women in the city never passed through the doors of the various establishments. Whether because they feared such duties were not suited to their notions of propriety or because the men in their lives disap-proved of such activities, many of Richmond's elite women never "soar[ed]" above convention as Phoebe Pember had so earnestly hoped. Even the press's exhortations failed to rouse some Richmond women. While the *Daily Dispatch* noted with pride "the kind attention shown the [wounded] by our citizens," it also beseeched "every mother and sister of Richmond to contribute their aid in alleviating the distress of our wounded." Ultimately, Richmond's slaves, free blacks, and convalescent whites would bear the burden of tending to the tens of thousands of sick, wounded, and dying Confederates who moved through the city's wards from 1861 until the end of the war. They served as nurses, cooks, laundresses, stretcher bearers, and maids. All were employees of the Confederate government.[41]

The Brown's Island Girls

Perhaps not surprisingly, upper-class women were even more conspicuously absent in the city's factories. As noted, the Confederate government hired women in many of its branches. Although ladies may have signed the nation's rapidly depreciating currency and worked in the Confederate Post Office, it was largely lower-class women who joined the ranks of Richmond's workforce in the factories that churned out the materiel of war.

Visitors to Richmond noted the streets were thronged with women heading to and from the various factories and government works from dawn to dusk. One of the largest employers of women was the Ordnance Department's laboratory located on Brown's Island in the James River, just south of the Tredegar Iron Works. The *Richmond Daily Dispatch* noted approvingly that a "village has sprung up on Brown's Island, where over 300 girls are daily employed." The *Dispatch* went on to describe this "village": "a dozen large warehouses" maintained several different branches of manufacture. In fact, the Brown's Island "girls" worked on everything from manufacturing percussion caps, primers, and signal rockets to packing ammunition and making small-arms cartridges. Despite shortages of some needed raw materials, "The works never failed to respond to a call."[42]

The young women and girls who labored at Brown's Island had fathers and brothers serving at the front, which necessitated their work on behalf of the Confederate cause. Their daily wage varied from $1.50 to $2.40, which was actually more money than the substantial salaries the Treasury girls commanded for merely signing their names to the increasingly worthless Confederate notes. Their toil in an enterprise that arguably contributed more to the Confederate war effort led sadly to tragedy.

On March 13—Friday the thirteenth to be exact—Christopher Tompkins heard "a heavy explosion not unlike an earthquake" in his office at the Tredegar Iron Works. Tompkins and his coworkers were "perplexed, but concluded it was the explosion of a gun." Just a few minutes later "a man rushed in stating that the Laboratory had exploded." The office quickly emptied as the men hurried outside to see what had transpired. What they saw was horrifying: dozens of girls dazed and badly burned by the explosion. "Some of them . . . in their fright, ran from adjacent buildings and plunged into the river" to extinguish the flames.[43]

Confederate Ordnance Department chief Josiah Gorgas, stunned by the casualties, ordered an investigation. Apparently one of the older laborers, teenager Mary Ryan, had been attempting to dislodge a primer that was "stuck on the varnishing board. And [so] she struck the board three times very hard on the table." Ryan told Gorgas that after the last strike, "she was immediately blown up to the ceiling and on coming down was blown up again," for the initial explosion set off the gunpowder in the room. Of the sixty-nine killed or wounded in the blast, sixty-two "were females and chiefly girls & children." Mary Ryan lingered for four agonizing days before she finally succumbed to her burns. Three of her female coworkers also died. Gorgas worried that the severity of the burns would produce more casualties. "It is terrible to think," admitted Gorgas, "that so much suffering should arise from causes possibly within our control."[44]

Gorgas's fears were well founded. The *Richmond Daily Dispatch* reported on March 16 that "the loss of life . . . proves far greater than was first supposed." Eyewitnesses recorded that after the explosion "many of the poor creatures who were enabled to rescue themselves from the debris of the building ran about the island shrieking in their anguish, the[ir] clothes in flames . . . while others who were too far disabled to move were stretched on litters." Judith McGuire recorded in her diary that "Richmond was greatly shocked on Friday by the blowing up of the Laboratory, in which women, girls and boys were killed on the spot." War clerk Jones was similarly struck by the "great calamity" that occurred at Brown's Island. What troubled Jones most was the reality that "most of them were little indigent girls!" Ultimately, thirty-four girls would die of their burns.[45]

Jones's observation focused on the heart of the tragedy. The victims of the Brown's Island accident were poor, illiterate girls and teenagers who had few skills but desperately needed the meager pay the laboratory provided. Because they were illiterate, they were unable to obtain safer, better-paying positions in the Treasury and Post Office. Once again, class mattered in wartime Richmond. Many of those who managed to survive the blast were left permanently disfigured—and unemployed. Interestingly, one girl who did survive and was forever scarred told a Northern visitor after the war, "There was five weeks nobody thought I would live. But I didn't mind it . . . for it was for a good cause." Despite the obvious danger, when the laboratory reopened, young girls and teenagers lined up to obtain positions.[46]

Adding to the woes of the survivors of the blast and other working-class Richmonders was the ongoing spiral of inflation. Locals noted that prices continued to rise unabated during the month of March, with cornmeal commanding $17 a bushel and potatoes $16. Meat could not be found in the city's markets, and vegetables were scarce. Residents in the city were also buffeted by March's capricious weather. Between February 22 and March 22, Richmond was pounded by heavy snows. Several of the storms dropped more than a foot on the capital, which, according to J. B. Jones, "laid an embargo on the usual slight supplies brought to market." The *Richmond Daily Dispatch* reported that supplies were desperately low because the "country people" faced "acres of mud and slush" in trying to get their produce to the city. "The prices now asked for all articles for the table are beyond all precedent," the *Dispatch* noted gloomily. Moreover, the continued inclement weather often delayed the shipment of coal and wood to the city. Even when these fuels were available, locals had to scramble to collect the $20 or $30 needed to buy a ton of coal or a cord of wood. In the midst of what many believed one of the worst winters on record, President Davis issued a call for a national day of fasting and prayers. Jones's reaction to this news epitomized the feelings of most residents in the cold, starving capital: "Fasting in the midst of famine! May God save this people!"[47]

As if the specter of famine were not enough, the city was also afflicted with epidemic diseases throughout the winter of 1863. The outbreak of small pox in 1862 continued to affect the capital through the early months of 1863. The disease tended to concentrate in the poorer, working-class sections of the city. And it was not the only scourge. Samuel Mordecai wrote to his brother that outbreaks of measles and scarlet fever also affected locals. "This state of things cannot continue," Mordecai warned, "without producing something of [a] civil commotion."[48]

"We Celebrate Our Right to Live"

Mordecai could not have been more prescient. Richmond's working class was hit hard by the high cost of food and fuel during the winter of 1863. Although wages did rise, they could not keep pace with inflation.

Fearing starvation, a group of working-class women gathered at the Belvidere Hill Baptist Church in the Oregon Hill neighborhood on April 1. Located at the western end of the city, Oregon Hill was an enclave of working-class Richmonders, many of whom labored in the Tredegar Iron Works. By the end of that meeting on Maundy Thursday, the women had resolved to petition Governor John Letcher for food; if refused, they determined to seize it forcibly.[49]

On April 2, the women assembled and wended their way to Capitol Square. They were joined by many other working-class people. Such a gathering was not out of the ordinary. Throughout the war, Capitol Square served as a great meeting place where Richmonders would flock to exchange information, watch military parades, and generally enjoy the parklike expanse. As one local described it, "The public square is a famous place of rendezvous [where] . . . gentlemen and ladies, gaily attired officers and war-worn soldiers [congregated]. . . . Around the Washington Monument . . . the little girls jump rope or play 'hide and seek.'"[50]

Those who gathered that morning selected a delegation to meet with the governor. The women apparently never met Letcher, only an aide, so they carried out their threat to seize food.[51]

Contemporary accounts of what happened next vary but contain common elements. J. B. Jones encountered the mob on his way to the War Department. "Not knowing the meaning of such a procession, I asked a pale boy where they were going." An "emaciated" young woman answered that "they were going to find something to eat." Jones's response was blunt: "I could not, for the life of me, refrain from expressing the hope that they might be successful; and I remarked they were going in the right direction to find plenty in the hands of the extortioners."[52]

Ordnance chief Josiah Gorgas was not as charitable. He recorded that "a crowd of women assembled on the public square and marching thence down Main, sacked several shoe, grocery and other stores." According to Gorgas, "their pretence [sic] was bread, but their motive was really license. Few of them have really felt want." Sallie Putnam found the rioters a "heterogeneous crowd of Dutch, Irish, and free negroes." They were armed and looted whatever they could. Putnam admitted there was "*want of bread* at this time . . . but the sufferers for food were not to be found in this mob of vicious men and lawless viragoes." First Lady Varina Davis noted that her husband received word of the disturbance at his office, and "he at once proceeded to the scene of the trouble in the lower portion of the city." According to Mrs. Davis, the rioters "were headed by a tall, daring, Amazonian-looking woman, who had a white feather standing erect from her hat, and who was evidently directing the movement of the plunderers."[53]

The mob made its way down Ninth Street to Main and then to Cary Street, attracting more participants and spectators to its ranks as it went. As the assemblage proceeded, they attacked various establishments in Shockoe Slip, loading food, shoes, and other goods into wagons as they proceeded. One eyewitness was struck by "a pale emaciated girl, not more than eighteen. . . . As she raised her hand to remove her sunbonnet," this observer noted, "[she] revealed a mere skeleton of an arm." When asked what was happening, the gaunt teenager replied, "We celebrate our right to live. We are starving."[54]

As word of the riot spread, shopkeepers and merchants did what they could to protect their establishments from the fast-moving mob. On Franklin Street, several merchants barricaded themselves within their stores, while others met the group with firearms. By this time, local officials had gathered, and someone had summoned the Public Guard; the mob was far too large to be contained by Richmond's miniscule police force—only eleven daytime officers.[55]

Perhaps one of the fullest accounts of the riot came from Confederate soldier Hal Tutwiler, who wrote to his sister Nettie of what he saw that fateful April Day. Tutwiler noted that he proceeded to his office, but he had barely entered the building when he "heard a most tremendous cheering." He and others proceeded to go back down to the street, where they noticed "that a large number of women had broken into two or three grocery establishments, & were helping themselves to hams, middlings, butter, and in fact everything they could find. Almost every one of them were [sic] armed. Some had a belt on with a knife, while some were only armed with a hatchet, axe or hammer."

Tutwiler went on to observe the men who joined the throng and, "instead of trying to put a stop to this shameful proceeding[,] cheered them on & assisted them all in their power." According to Tutwiler, the efforts of Mayor Joseph Mayo and Governor John Letcher did little to disperse a crowd he estimated at 5,000. He went on to say that "Gov. Letcher told them . . . to disperse & if they did not . . . he would have them fired on by the city guards."[56]

A local woman wrote to her son, "We had a terrible row here yesterday[.] [A]bout six hundred women started out *impressing* [*goods*]. They knocked down the men in the stores—took wagons in the streets & put the things in—They went on Cary[,] Main[,] Broad & to the Market—such a terrible mob and howling."[57]

Others who saw the riot unfold recorded similar accounts. Christopher Tompkins recorded "a *riot* today—a regular riot and a mob of females." He also argued that "Irish" were responsible for much of the looting. Kate Rowland maintained the riot was "probably instigated by the Yankees." She, too, noted that Mayor Mayo and Governor Letcher had little success in dispersing the mob. Rowland also mentioned that President Davis appeared and made an impassioned speech to the looters.[58] Eyewitnesses estimated the crowd numbered between several hundred to at least a thousand people. The havoc arguably drew more and more spectators into the streets, adding to the general confusion.

Perhaps one of the more ominous accounts of the incident came from George M. Waddy, who wrote to his aunt about the riot. After describing what he witnessed, Waddy concluded: "God only knows what will become of the people[.] I do not wonder at what has occured [*sic*] and I am afraid it will be even worse that thare [*sic*] will be war with the poore against the rich[.] [F]or my part I do not blame the mob for what they did." Many in the beleaguered capital probably shared Waddy's sentiments. Though some middle-class Richmonders recorded their outrage about the incident, others supported the rioters. The foremost student of the riot finds that the participants included some "who were quite respectable and solidly middle-class [*sic*]." That some rioters might have been better off than the "less-genteel" types the press and other locals tended to blame for the disturbance indicates that many in the capital were feeling the pinch of war. The once prosperous middle class was slowly sinking into poverty as a result of high costs and stagnant wages. As if to underscore the class divisions Waddy discerned, Lucy Chamberlayne, one of those fortunate "genteel" Treasury girls who earned significantly more in the pleasant confines of "Angel's Retreat," was busy signing notes when she heard the clamor in the streets. "[B]ut," she noted with some aloofness, "we worked on tranquilly."[59]

The Public Guard finally did restore order, but the situation in Richmond remained tense. Local officials placed cannon on Richmond's streets to discourage any further incidents, and Department of Richmond commander General Arnold Elzey notified General James Longstreet that his men in the department had been placed on alert due to "the continually threatened riots in Richmond." More women gathered again the next day but were quickly dispersed.[60]

Many city residents decried the violence and argued that it was unnecessary and ill advised. Josiah Gorgas recorded, "There is scarcity but little real want." He went on to add, "Laborers earn 2½ to three dollars per day, and women and children can earn 1½ to 2½. With such wages and flour at even $30 they cannot starve." Samuel Mordecai was equally incensed. He wrote to his brother George, "The mob was an outrage, unpardonable, not got up by those who were suffering but a concerted plan for general pillage." Sallie Putnam, too, was convinced that "the real sufferers were not of the class who would engage in acts of violence to obtain bread." All who remarked upon the incident blamed the poor, immigrants, and other undesirables in the community.[61]

One wonders how the poor workers would have responded to Gorgas's allegation that they could afford food on their meager wages. That the rioters were aided by sympathetic soldiers and convalescents indicates that many believed the situation intolerable. Ultimately, about seventy people were arrested, and many were tried in the Richmond Hustings Court throughout 1863.[62]

Margaret Wight spoke for many when she wrote that she was convinced the events of April 2 "will injure us more in the eyes of the Yankees than anything that has occurred."[63] Perhaps that sentiment explains the relative absence of local news accounts of the riots. Confederate and city officials appealed directly to the Richmond press and asked them to refrain from reporting the incident. In each petition, leaders argued that such stories would add fuel to the North's propaganda campaign. The Richmond press largely acceded to the requests, though they did cover the arrest and trials of the riot's ringleaders. Despite these efforts to conceal the event, the *New York Times* ran a front-page story, "BREAD RIOT IN RICHMOND. Three Thousand Hungry Women Raging in the Streets," on April 8. The *Times* story was based on an eyewitness account by a Colonel Stewart, a member of an Indiana regiment who observed the fracas from the windows of a Confederate prison in Richmond before he was exchanged as a prisoner of war.[64]

The Richmond Bread Riot was not an isolated incident. In the spring of 1863, similar demonstrations rocked High Point and Salisbury, North Carolina; Atlanta and Augusta, Georgia; and Mobile, Alabama. Nonetheless, the Richmond incident was, as one historian has observed, the "most serious" and indicated how critical the situation was in the capital. With the city's population swelling to almost 100,000 and with inflation seemingly out of control, locals leaped into action. Two days after the riot, on April 4, the Richmond City Council adopted a resolution to appoint a committee from each ward "to enquire and report some plan for the relief of the meritorious poor of the City, and for excluding from such relief all who render themselves unworthy of it by riotous and disorderly conduct." The council did not mince words: it stated bluntly that in the aftermath of April 2, it would distinguish between those "worthy" to receive aid and those "unworthy." It also officially condemned the riot and all its participants: "The said mob or riot was uncalled for and did not come from those who are really needy but from base and unworthy women instigated by worthless men who are a disgrace to the city and the community."[65]

The council's language was repeated publicly and privately, and the council apparently played a role in the severity and length of sentences handed down to those arrested in the aftermath of the riot. According to one historian, "What might appear to be a double standard of justice seems to have been applied in the cases of a fair number of rioters." Those women who were better dressed and who were "genteel looking" were often released. Others, characterized as "Amazonian" or as "public women"—euphemisms for prostitutes—were vilified in the press, fined, and imprisoned, in some cases up to five years.[66]

After their meeting on April 4, the city fathers convened in secret session and ordered Richmond's Overseers of the Poor to investigate more closely the living conditions of the city's indigent. What they discovered apparently led to the passage of an ordinance, "For the Relief of Poor Persons Not in the Poor House," on April 13. This legislation directed the Overseers of the Poor to establish a city store, open every week, where those deemed "meritorious" could obtain free food. The overseers were further instructed to meet weekly "to hear and determine applications for relief." The ordinance went on to state, "No further relief shall be given unless the applicant is unable to procure subsistence or fuel . . . nor shall it be given to any able-bodied man, nor any person who has participated in a riot, rout, or unlawful assembly." Section 8 of the ordinance stipulated, "Relief shall only be afforded in provisions or fuel and shall not be given in money." The city council assumed that local charitable organizations and Richmond's tax assessors would verify the applications of those requesting relief.[67]

The city council's actions were not unusual. Richmond had a long tradition of tending to the poor dating back to the 1820s. Local organizations such as the Male Orphan Asylum and the Union Benevolent Society had distributed relief throughout the antebellum era. Moreover, the city had an almshouse, though, interestingly, it had been turned over to the Confederate government to use as a hospital in 1861.[68] Where the council did diverge from its past actions was in detailing specifically who could and could not receive aid. Although Richmond's solons had always differentiated between "worthy" and "unworthy" poor, in the aftermath of the riot they wanted even closer oversight and a clearer sense of who the real sufferers were. Finally, they wanted to ensure that poor relief was being used as it was intended—the distribution of food and fuel instead of cash, which might find its way to a tavern or a faro (gambling) house.[69]

The city fathers also allocated money for soldier's families, as they had done from the beginning of the war. All these actions elicited praise from the Richmond press. The *Examiner* editorialized, "The City Council has certainly done its duty well in providing for the poor—not only well but generously." Some funds remained unexpended, and the *Examiner* argued, "If the poor have suffered it is because they have not applied for relief. . . . [I]f the poor had applied for relief, it would have been cheerfully extended."[70]

In some respects, however, the city council's actions ushered in a new phase in Richmond's poor-relief efforts. After the Bread Riot, the city embarked upon an extended relief effort that can be understood as the beginning of total municipal government activism. In effect, from the spring of 1863 until the end of the war, relief in Richmond was institutionalized: it became a major part of council deliberations—and expenditures—and was a source of ongoing interest as city leaders and private citizens grappled with the situation that the war had created.

Equally significant is the reality that the Confederate government did not adopt similar measures. Despite becoming a large, centralized state that controlled mobilization, instituted conscription, and enacted sweeping tax laws, the Davis government did not pass any type of relief legislation for its citizens. As one scholar has shown so effectively, Davis's inability to meet the needs of the common folk made the Confederate government appear indifferent to their plight. Perhaps Davis, a member of the privileged elite, believed such actions were better suited to private organizations. Whatever the reason, the City of Richmond's decision to expand its assistance to its less-fortunate citizens reinforced local loyalties to the city and eventually to the state of Virginia at the expense of loyalty to the Confederate States of America.[71]

In general, the Confederate government's economic policies exacerbated the situation in the capital and elsewhere in the Confederacy. During

the severe winter of 1863, Congress passed an impressment act that empowered Confederate Commissary Department officials to take food and other
goods to supply the army. As one historian has observed, the March impressment act "merely legitimized the existing practice." The War Department
did reimburse farmers and other producers for the provisions it seized, but
it paid in inflated currency and according to a price list that was well below
what the market would bring. These factors, coupled with the persistent
snow and ice, discouraged Virginia's farmers from supplying Richmond's
market stalls. "Richmond lacked food not because of scarcity in surrounding counties but because farmers feared that Confederate agents would
impress their produce as it was being transported to the city and because
city buyers risked being charged for interfering with the effort to feed
the army."[72]

As if to add insult to injury, just a few weeks after the Bread Riot the
Confederate Congress enacted a new tax law on April 24, 1863, that one
scholar has deemed "stern to the point of being confiscatory": the legislation
included everything from an income tax to a license tax. But the section of
this tax law that caused the most outrage was the tax-in-kind, wherein Southern farmers were required to pay a 10 percent tithe on "everything grown or
slaughtered in 1863."[73] That legislation led to hoarding and a singular
unwillingness among local farmers to supply Richmond's empty markets.

Many in the city protested that the tax-in-kind was illegal and derided
the "TIK men," the tax-in-kind agents, as little better than "licensed
thieves." But the reality was the government had to do something to gener-
ate food for the army in anticipation of the spring military campaigning
season. General Lee had warned the administration for months that his
battle-hardened veterans were weakened and many in ill health because of
the scarcity of provisions. When Lee dispatched General James Longstreet
to Suffolk, Virginia, to parry Federal movements along the North Carolina
coast, the Confederate commander became aware of massive quantities of
fish, bacon, and other provisions in the Carolina countryside. Longstreet
thus fulfilled two key assignments from February to May: he defended
Richmond's southeastern flank, and he garnered badly needed supplies
for the army.[74]

The spring of 1863 witnessed another disaster: the burning of the Crenshaw Woolen Mill, which spread to the Tredegar Iron Works. The blaze
started in the picking room of the mill. According to the *Richmond Daily
Dispatch*, "although [the fire] made but little headway when discovered,

Haxall Mills ruins, 1865.

such was the combustible nature of the material in the room that the flames spread with a rapidity that soon enveloped the whole building." The *Dispatch* went on to state that the loss of yarn, woven goods, and 30,000 pounds of wool and machinery "at the present time is irreparable."[75]

Equally disastrous was the reality that the fire spread to the neighboring Tredegar Iron Works. The *Dispatch* noted the flames reached the "machine shops, boring mills, pattern shops, blacksmith and carpenter shops." Although the fire was a tremendous setback, the *Richmond Examiner* reported that the owner of the Tredegar, General Joseph R. Anderson, assured the paper that normal operations would be resumed in a few days. Although Anderson remained optimistic and confident, he was only too aware of the challenges the firm faced: he needed laborers and materials to rebuild, things the firm lacked. This loss would play a key role in the spring and summer military campaigns.[76]

A Week of "Unexampled Disaster"

The warm weather of April and May succeeded in drying out the roads in and around Richmond. But spring's advent also meant the renewal of military conflict. On April 30, J. B. Jones recorded in his diary that the Federal

Army of the Potomac, now under the command of Major General Joseph Hooker, was crossing the Rappahannock; it was yet another "On to Richmond" campaign. Lee's Army of Northern Virginia was again outnumbered two to one. As Jones observed, "The awful hour when thousands of human lives are to be sacrificed in the attempt to wrest this city from the Confederate States has come."[77]

As Lee battled Joe Hooker in the Wilderness near Chancellorsville, Richmond was threatened by Federal cavalry under the command of George Stoneman, which, according to Josiah Gorgas, came within four miles of the Confederate capital. With all the army engaging Hooker, it was up to locals to take up arms, which they did on May 4. Despite their attitude of defense, according to Gorgas, "people were frightened and indignant at such Yankee impudence."[78]

The day after Richmonders repelled the "impudent" Yankees, the city received word of Lee's great success against the "finest army on the planet." But rejoicing over this resounding victory was tempered by the news that the famed Stonewall Jackson had been seriously wounded by his own men and his left arm amputated. People in the city followed Jackson's recovery anxiously and were devastated to learn their esteemed warrior succumbed to pneumonia on May 10. As Kate Rowland observed, "The city is one house of mourning; the stores closed and crape hanging from each door and window." War clerk Jones recorded, "The flags are at half-mast. . . . A multitude of people, mostly women and children, are standing silently in the streets, awaiting the arrival of the hero, destined never again to defend their homes and honor."[79]

Jackson's body was brought to the capitol, where it lay in state. Hundreds of mourners filed past their hero "for three days and until late in the night," according to Varina Davis. Davis went on to observe, "When at last the beloved form was taken to its last resting-place, the streets, the windows and the house-tops were one palpitating mass of weeping women and men." The Stonewall Brigade served as honor guard and on May 14 escorted Jackson's remains to Lexington.[80]

Jackson's death, coupled with the arrival of yet another stream of seriously wounded Confederate soldiers, cast a pall over the city. Constance Cary recalled, "Outside in the soft spring air, a tumult of war sounds continually distracted our thoughts and racked our nerves. The marching of armed men, the wheels of the wagons containing shot and shell, the clash of the iron gates in the Capitol Square . . . went on without ceasing." Ellen

Mordecai was even more emphatic in her descriptions of the city in the aftermath of Chancellorsville: "Of all heartrending places on this continent poor melancholy Richmond is now the greatest."[81]

As locals tended to the wounded, many in the city worried about the state of its defenses. After all, Stoneman's cavalry had advanced almost into town. Josiah Gorgas noted "rumors" of Federal incursions throughout June and fears of the Union navy's renewed attacks via the James River. "Our local troops were gotten into readiness," Gorgas recorded, and "we have organized our workmen into companies and armed them, making 10 companies altogether of 800 men." Robert Kean was less confident regarding local efforts. Although "great efforts" were launched, they met "with very indifferent success." Kean, too, noted that clerks and workers had been organized into a local defense force. But despite the governor and the mayor's "inflammatory appeals to the citizens," the force's numbers remained rather small.[82]

Gorgas and Kean's concerns were well founded. Fresh from his stunning victory at Chancellorsville, Lee had convinced Davis and his cabinet that the time was propitious to launch another invasion of the North. Lee reasoned such a bold stroke would relieve Federal pressure on the besieged garrison at Vicksburg, the key to the Mississippi. Moreover, advancing into the lush farm country of Pennsylvania would allow his army to subsist off the land, giving the desolated Virginia countryside around Richmond a much needed respite. However, while Lee marched north, Richmond was vulnerable. As one local wrote, "Are you not afraid for Richmond while Genl Lee [sic] is so far away with his army? I hope he has made his calculations for the protection & safety of our capital."[83]

Richmonders waited expectantly to learn what was happening in the Mississippi Delta and in the rolling country of south-central Pennsylvania. Word from the west reached the city first and was greeted with despair. Sallie Putnam noted, "The news to us in Richmond" detailing the surrender of the Vicksburg garrison "was astounding and . . . paralyzing. . . . The sun of hope had receded many degrees on the good fortune of the Confederacy." Christopher Tompkins remarked, "People are decidedly blue as to the homefront—Port Hudson has followed Vicksburg—of course Natchez will go next." Sara Pryor wrote that news of the fall of Vicksburg descended heavily on the capital. "Surely and swiftly the coil was tightening around us. Surely and swiftly should we, too, be starved into submission." Heavy rains added to the gloomy atmosphere in the capital. Josiah Gorgas recorded that steady showers plagued Richmond for almost four weeks straight. Vicksburg's surrender and the growing realization that Lee's invasion had been turned back at Gettysburg forced Gorgas to wonder if God had turned against the South: "Can we believe in the justice of Providence, or must we conclude that we are after all wrong? . . . It appears we are not yet sufficiently tried." Shortly thereafter he concluded, "Yesterday we rode on the pinnacle of success—to-day [sic] absolute ruin seems to be our portion." Robert Kean echoed Gorgas's despair on July 10: "This week just ended has been one of unexampled disaster since the war began."[84]

"Misfortunes Come in Clusters"

The heavy rains of July continued into August, and many feared it would doom both the wheat and corn crops in Virginia. Once again, as fall neared, people in Richmond worried about famine. The *Daily Dispatch* found markets fairly well supplied at the time, but all produce commanded "exorbitant prices." Of equal concern were reports of extortioners preying on the public. The *Dispatch* threw down the proverbial gauntlet:

Again the money worshippers are at work for the defeat of our cause and the destruction of our hopes. Not satisfied with clutching in their grasp all the sugar, molasses, bacon and lard to be found in Virginia they have fastened upon all the flour in the markets, stored [it] away in secret places, and are now demanding exorbitant prices for it. Can the people bear these impositions longer? Will not the government come to their relief and demand a disgorgement? Or must the masses, to avert starvation, take the law into their own hands, and by force and violence, drag from the basements and garrets of their worse than Yankee enemies the stock of flour now concealed? We are opposed to mobs in every shape and form, but unless the Government comes in at once to the rescue of the people, they may be expected to rise in their might and take by force that which nature demands. The man that buys and hoards up for speculation and extortion the necessaries of life is not only an enemy but a traitor to his country and no punishment, however cruel, that can be inflicted upon him is too severe.[85]

The editors' words are especially striking when one realizes the city had been rocked by such a riot just four months earlier.

The Richmond City Council apparently took note of this editorial, for it embarked upon renewed action. In August 1863, it again instituted relief measures when it passed an ordinance that prohibited the buying and reselling of foodstuffs in Richmond's markets. It also created legislation that clamped down on "huckstering." By October, the tax-in-kind and impressment laws had so discouraged farmers from going to the city's markets that the council's Committee on Supplies recommended that the city buy foodstuffs in bulk and sell them at reduced prices to needy Richmonders at a city depot. That committee felt compelled to recommend such action because scarce goods and high prices continued to threaten many with starvation. A city depot, council members concluded, could eliminate the extortionate middlemen who seemed to prey on the neediest. Moreover, such a depot would encourage local farmers to come to Richmond with their goods because the city offered prices that were more competitive than those of the "TIK men."[86]

The city council's decision—made in secret session—to exercise control and oversight of city markets and to establish a food depot marked a drastic departure from its other relief practices, but it signaled the desperate nature of the situation. Richmond, like other Southern cities in 1863, was feeling the effects of total war. Real income was down almost 40 percent, whereas the Consumer Price Index rose on average 10 percent per month from 1861 to 1865. Between January and November 1863, the general price index hovered between a low of 700 times and more than 2,200 times the rate in 1861. As one local remarked, "Somebody says that one goes to market with their money in their pocket & a basket for the marketing. [N]ow you must take your money in a basket & bring home your marketing in your pocket."[87]

The Virginia General Assembly was not idle during this time, either. Also in October 1863, it passed an act that required the state's railroad companies to transport all fuel supplies to the Old Dominion's cities. Further, it outlawed the use of foodstuffs for distilling purposes. The state government also debated a bill that would fix prices throughout Virginia. Perhaps predictably, Richmond's citizens were deeply divided over that measure: they had endured real hardship when John Winder, the provost marshal, had implemented price fixing in the city in 1862.[88]

It is no coincidence that Richmond's working class as well as its salaried government workers followed the developments in the city council and the state General Assembly closely. On October 10, 1863, a general workers meeting convened in response to word that Richmond's Confederate state senator, the former secretary of war and Richmond native George Randolph, had vowed to vote against the bill unless advised otherwise by his constituents. These laborers unanimously adopted eight resolutions, and the language they employed is telling. They urged Governor Letcher not to allow the assembly to adjourn until it took action on pending matters. Further, the workers stated "that as freemen we abhor and detest the idea that the rich must take care of the poor, because we know that without the labor and production the man with his money could not exist, from the fact he consumes all and produces nothing, and that such dependence would tend to degrade rather than elevate the human race." Finally, they resolved "that it is the duty of the Government to take care of the unfortunate, and not the rich."[89] Once again, issues of class percolated up, as the workers' resolutions make clear. Their language clearly differentiated between those who produced and hence contributed to the common good and those who merely "consumed." This producerism ideology would continue to dominate the thinking of Richmond's laboring classes.

Members of the city's working class were not the only ones to perceive that the conflict was increasingly a "rich man's war and a poor man's fight." The Richmond City Council, by virtue of its assistance to soldiers' families and its expansion of poor relief, acknowledged that many were bearing heavier burdens than others. Government bureaucrats and other members of the Richmond middle class increasingly found they were hard-pressed to provide for their families and worried about the prospect of another harsh winter. Even the local press sensed deepening class divisions. Typical of editorials was one in the *Daily Dispatch*: "The large number of ladies employed in Government service must find it very difficult to support themselves on their limited salaries. Some of them are wives of soldiers in the army, with small children to take care of and heavy house rent to pay. Ought not their more wealthy neighbors look after them this winter and see that they have food and fuel? And will not the public stores supply them with necessaries at modest prices?" The *Dispatch* went on to note that some of these "ladies" had been thrust on hard times but were loath to ask for assistance. But others were "Soldiers' wives" who "must be provided for, and every benevolent association should see to them first of all."[90]

City leaders worked assiduously through the fall and early winter to tackle the issue of food and fuel for those "worthy" poor. But prices continued to soar. Robert Kean admitted that even with the aid of his father-in-law, he and his family were forced to subsist on "two meals a day (since May last) and they are of the most plain and economical scale." J. B. Jones went so far as to write to President Davis, "suggesting that the perishable tithes (potatoes, meal, etc.) be sold at reasonable rates to the civil officers of the people, when in excess of demand of the army . . . and that a government store be opened in Richmond. I told him plainly," Jones continued, "that without some speedy measure of relief there would be much discontent, for half the families here are neither half-fed nor half-clad." One needy Richmond woman was stunned to see how high the price of a barrel of flour had become. "'My God!' exclaimed she, 'how can I pay such prices? I have seven children; what shall I do?'" The merchant's reply chilled those who learned of the incident: "I don't know, madam, . . . unless you eat your children." J. B. Jones, who relayed this incident, concluded, "Such is the power of cupidity—it transforms men into demons."[91]

People in the capital especially feared another harsh winter. Josiah Gorgas recorded in late October, "I look forward to mid-winter with anxiety. There is not food enough to sustain the population here, and although there is abundance in the country the limited means of transportation and the unsettled state of the markets prevents food from reaching here." J. B. Jones wondered, "How long will the people suffer this? This community is even now in an inflammable condition, and may be ignited by a single spark." Both the *Whig* and the *Daily Dispatch* predicted a famine in the city if governmental policies were not amended. "*Impressments* by the Government agents are doing more to starve the people of Richmond and the Army . . . than all the Yankee invasions can ever accomplish," thundered the *Dispatch*. The situation continued to deteriorate through the fall. Perhaps predictably, there was an increase in crime in the city—especially robberies of food. The *Daily Dispatch* noted that farmers approaching Richmond on the Charles City and Williamsburg roads "constantly complain of the robberies committed on their property." It reported that one man had sixty shad stolen, while another lost his sturgeons. What made the robberies so "reprehensible," according to the *Dispatch,* was that some of the robbers were disguised as Confederate troops. As war clerk J. B. Jones concluded, "Many are desperate."[92]

A group of ministers made "an appeal in behalf of the poor" in the *Richmond Daily Dispatch* on October 14, 1863. They noted that "the poor residing on Union and Church Hills, and the adjacent localities outside the corporate limits of the city . . . are cut off from the appropriations made by the city authorities for the assistance and relief of indigent and dependent families." They went on to note that the money Henrico County had appropriated "[is] altogether inadequate to meet the urgent demands of this class of our population." As a result, the clergymen formed a "Humane Association" and urged locals to donate "a large amount of money, or its equivalent in fuel, clothing and provisions." Too many of those afflicted by want were soldiers' families who, the ministers claimed, were "on the verge of starvation."[93] Entreaties such as this would continue to appear in Richmond's press until the end of the year.

The approach of the holidays merely added to local concerns. In December, the women at the Brown's Island laboratory went on strike for better wages. The issue, those women argued, was equity: single women were paid $5 a day, while those married with children received $7. Interestingly, the married female workers supported their single counterparts. Unwilling to countenance labor unrest—it smacked of "Yankee innovations"—the Confederate laboratory closed, fired the strikers, and issued a call for 300 replacements.[94]

Christmas dawned cold in the capital, and snow appeared likely. Again ominously, celebrations varied by neighborhood and social class. J. B. Jones noted several days before the holiday that "pound cakes, size of a small Dutch oven, sell at $100. Turkeys from $10 to $40." While he greeted the day with sadness, his children had "decked the parlor with evergreens, crosses, star, etc. They have a cedar Christmas-tree," Jones recorded, "but it is not burdened [decorated]. Candy is held at $8 per pound." Josiah Gorgas did not even make an entry in his diary. Three days after Christmas, he wrote, "Christmas was not a merry one to me, & I passed it quietly, almost sadly at home." The *Daily Dispatch*'s Christmas Day editorial was more biting than usual: "We can scarcely bring ourselves to wish our readers a merry Christmas in such an era of selfishness and coldness of soul." Castigating the "Confederate Scrooges," the *Dispatch* argued, "The face of nature itself is not as dreary, the frozen streams not as cold as the hearts of men have been rendered by the absorbing thirst of gain and gold."[95]

Not all people in Richmond were as dismayed and discouraged as Jones, Gorgas, and the editors of the *Dispatch*. On Clay Street in the Chesnut household, a guest probably noticed little difference from before the war. Mary Chesnut wrote, "We had for dinner oyster soup, soup à la reine. It has so many good things in it. Besides boiled mutton, ham, boned turkey, wild ducks, partridges, plum pudding." Chesnut and her guests also enjoyed "sauterne, burgundy, sherry, and Madeira wine. There is," she declared airily, "life in the old land yet!"[96]

Most in the Confederate capital did not share Chesnut's optimism or the bounty of her family's repast. The acerbic editor of the *Richmond Examiner,* John Moncure Daniel, captured popular sentiment well in his year-end editorial. "Today closes the gloomiest year of our struggle," Daniel wrote. "What was once competence has become poverty, poverty has become penury, penury is lapsing into pauperism. . . . The cry of scarcity resounds through the land, raised by the producers in their greed for gain, re-echoed by the consumers in their premature dread of starvation and nakedness." Unbelievably, "a nation of farmers could indeed go hungry."[97] Few could find reasons to celebrate in the New Year.

4

The Overcrowded and Hungry City, 1864

"We Are in a Sad and Anxious State Here Now"

Richmond in 1864 was a city of contrasts. Letters, diaries, and newspaper editorials decried the scarcity of food and high prices, while others, as one historian has written, noted the capital city was teeming with "refugees and revelers."[1]

The new year found little changed in the Confederate capital. Several residents reflected on the city's "dingy," "dilapidated," and "war-worn" condition. Others remarked that Richmond had become the "Hub of the Confederacy" and that its citizens were confident that the army would protect and defend the capital against the anticipated Federal onslaught. In fact, certain locals believed the city had become "invulnerable" because it had resisted capture repeatedly. All those sentiments would be tested in 1864.[2]

Yet beneath this facade of bravado, many in Richmond were deeply worried. By 1864, Richmond's population had swelled to more than 100,000, and some believed the number was closer to 130,000. Refugees continued to flock into the capital because they knew it would be defended at all costs. One refugee admitted to another, "Oh we are too happy in getting to Richmond! It is after all the safest place in the Confederacy!" Locals were not so gleeful. Emma Mordecai wondered in her diary, "I can't think how people are to be fed and lodged." Ordnance chief Josiah Gorgas echoed Mordecai's concern: "There is much anxiety on the subject of food for the capital."[3]

In many ways, the situation in Richmond in 1864 was little different from that of 1863. Once again, the city and state suffered an unseasonably cold and snowy winter. Many of the snowfalls averaged eight to ten inches and discouraged farmers from bringing their crops to the Richmond markets. Moderating temperatures caused melting, which merely exacerbated the situation: the dirt roads leading to the city became quagmires of mud. The railroads running into Richmond also caused problems. Federal raids, the dearth of equipment, and broken tracks militated against getting goods to the capital. The net results were empty markets and concerns that people in the city would starve.[4]

Indeed, one need only peruse the abundant diaries, newspaper articles, and private correspondence of this period to see how desperate people in Richmond viewed the situation throughout 1864. Unionist Elizabeth Van Lew surveyed the setting from her home on Church Hill. "There is a starvation panic among the people," she wrote in January 1864. Underscoring her Unionist sympathies, Van Lew added, "Women are begging for bread with tears in their eyes, and [are] a different class from ordinary beggars. . . . The peace, plenty and freedom of the whites under the old government stands in strange contrast with the scarcity and apprehension of the Southern Confederate government." War clerk J. B. Jones was gravely worried that a bread riot would erupt among the Union prisoners held at Belle Isle. He recorded that all 8,000 of them had been on reduced rations and had not been fed meat in eleven days. "The Secretary [of War] says the Commissary-General informs him that they fare as well as our armies . . . so he refused . . . to buy and bring to the city cattle he might be able to find. An outbreak of the prisoners is apprehended: and if they were to rise, it is feared some of the inhabitants of the city would join them, for they, too, have no meat—many of them—or bread either." The situation was so extreme Jones doubted the city battalion would do anything to quell such a disturbance.[5]

Circumstances did not improve as winter progressed. Clara Minor Lynn wrote that she and her family "lived mostly on corn bread, sorghum and beans, the latter often so old and hard, that no amount of boiling tendered them." Another woman noted that "as a general rule a Richmond dinner . . . consisted of dried Indian peas, rice and salt bacon and corn bread." John Godwin wrote to his wife that "times have come to be so hard, and provision so scarce and high that even the wealthy have fears of suffering."[6] Josiah Gorgas dutifully recorded prices in his diary. On March 23, 1864, he observed, "Flour $300 the barrel; a shad costs $35; turkey, $5 to $9 per pound; beef, $5 to $6; Eggs, $7 and so on. . . . Even meal sells at $30 per bushel." Samuel Mordecai wrote to his brother George that a barrel of flour commanded $150. He also stated that the impressment law allowed the army to seize what little beef was available. Virtually everyone who left a record echoed Gorgas when he observed, "How the poor live is incomprehensible."[7]

Even those prisoners who Jones feared would rise up in fury over their short rations were struck by how dismal the situation was. Prisoner of war F. F. Cavada, who was held in Libby Prison, wrote of the hungry local children who always gathered outside the prison: "Every afternoon I note in the street beneath my window, a group of ill-clad juvenile beggars, of both sexes. They hold up their little red hands to us, as they stand there shivering in the cold. We throw to them spare fragments of corn bread, and occasionally a macerated ham bone, which they scramble for greedily."[8] For some locals, the only answer was planting gardens and relying upon friends and relatives who lived outside the city. As early as New Year's Day 1864, war clerk Jones was skipping a holiday reception at the White House of the Confederacy to tend to his "lettuce plants, which have so far withstood the frost, and a couple of fig bushes I bought yesterday. I am also breaking up some warm beds, for early vegetables, and spreading manure over my little garden: preparing for the siege and famine looked for in May and June when the enemy encompasses the city." What struck Jones the most was the reality *"And yet no beggars in the streets."* Lucy Chamberlayne noted that all those who lived on Gamble's Hill shared whatever provisions they received from friends outside the beleaguered city. John Godwin, who boarded in Richmond, wrote to his wife that he helped the owner of his boardinghouse to plant a garden that included cabbage, potatoes, cucumbers, butter beans, corn, and tomatoes. Judith McGuire was grateful that friends in Essex County "sent over a wagon filled most generously with all manner of necessary things for our larder." She noted, "The clerks' salaries, too, have been raised to $250 per month, which sounds very large." McGuire then added that $250 "sinks into insignificance" "when we remember that flour is $300 per barrel."[9]

To add to the misery, clothing, boots, and shoes during that harsh winter were also in short supply. Sallie Putnam noted that when the war began, calico sold for twelve and half cents a yard; by 1864, it cost between $30 and $35 a yard. Boots routinely commanded $250 a pair. One Confederate officer captured the plight of Richmonders during the winter of 1864 when he wrote, "People without overcoats met one another upon the streets and talked over prospects of peace, with their teeth chattering, their thin garments buttoned over their chests and their shoulders drawn up, their gloveless hands sunk deep into their pockets for warmth."[10]

And yet, as the *Richmond Enquirer* pointed out, the suffering was not universal. On February 12, 1864, the *Enquirer* railed against the "reckless frivolity" that marked Richmond during that winter: "While General Lee's army was on short rations, and often without meat—while the doors of Colonel Munford's office were daily crowded with starving women, there have been those in Richmond who were spreading sumptuous suppers before their already well-fed neighbors and dancing with joy and delight, as though no want and famine were in the land; consuming the meat so much needed by the soldiers, and depriving the famishing poor of the little that came to the city." The *Enquirer* ended its blistering editorial by asking, none too rhetorically, "Is our National Independence to be disgraced by an imitation of the manners, customs and society of that fashion of strumpet-cracy from which our people are struggling with such giant efforts to free ourselves?"[11]

J. B. Jones was also aware that privations in the capital city were not being shared equally. He noted, "I saw a note of invitation to-day from Secretary Mallory to Secretary Seddon, inviting him to his house at 5 p.m. to partake of 'pea-soup' with Secretary Trenholm. His 'pea-soup' will be oysters and champagne, and every other delicacy relished by epicures. Mr. Mallory's red face and plethoric body, indicate the highest living." Jones went on to write, "His party will enjoy the dinner while so many of our brave men are languishing with wounds, or pining in cruel captivity."[12]

The *Richmond Whig* was similarly dismayed by the "prevailing mania and frivolity in this city. There has never been a gayer [*sic*] winter in Richmond. One night last week there were *seven parties*." The *Whig* concluded its editorial with biting sarcasm that some of its more well-off readers may have been oblivious to: "Go on, good people. It is better to be merry than sad. The wolf is far from your doors, and it signifieth nothing to you that thousands of our heroic soldiers are shoeless and comfortless; or that a multitude of mothers, wives, and children of the gallant defenders of our country's rights are sorely pinched by hunger and want."[13]

Many ignored such opprobrium and carried on as before. Sarah Pryor's friend Agnes was one of those who enjoyed the social scene. She wrote to Sarah, "President and Mrs. Davis gave a large reception last week, and all the ladies looked positively gorgeous. . . . We should not expect suppers in these times, but we do have them! Champagne is $350 a dozen, but we sometimes have champagne! The confectioner's charge $15 for a cake, but we have cake!"[14]

The irrepressible Mary Chesnut was also a frequent partaker in the Richmond social scene in 1864. In January, she informed a friend she planned to reciprocate some of the hospitality she had enjoyed in the Confederate capital: "Just think of the dinners, suppers, breakfasts we have been to," Mary told her friend. But she went on to complain about the lack of "variety" in the food her hosts had displayed, though she conceded it was wartime. Her friend was incredulous: "Variety! You are hard to please." He rattled off a sample of the *table d'hote* they had enjoyed: "Terrapin stew, gumbo, fish, oysters in any shape, game, wine as good as wine ever is. I do not mention juleps, claret cups, and apple toddy, whiskey punches, and all that." He concluded, "I tell you it is good enough for me."[15]

A little more than a week later, Mary recorded that she had attended Varina Davis's "luncheon for the ladies." "Many more persons there than at any of those luncheons which have gone on before," Mary observed. But, again, the menu would have stunned, if not sickened, the vast majority of Richmonders, who were so terribly pinched and would be shocked by the extravagance. Mary airily wrote in her diary, "[We had] gumbo, ducks and olives, supreme de volaille, chickens in jelly, oysters, lettuce salad, chocolate jelly cake, claret soup, champagne, &c,&c,&C."[16]

Such excess was not lost on the fast-declining middle class, let alone the poor, in Richmond. People walking about in the evening could hear the music and laughter as the wealthy ate and drank as if there were not a war raging around them. Mary Chesnut received a jolt of reality when she and a friend stopped in to visit Mary Lee, the invalid wife of the general in command of the Army of Northern Virginia. "Her room was like an industrial school—everybody so busy. Her daughters were there, plying their needles, [with] several other ladies. . . . 'Did you see how the Lees spend their time!'" Mary asked her companion. Obviously humbled, if not momentarily contrite, Mary admitted, "What a rebuke to the taffy parties!"[17]

Many members of the elite, such as refugees Constance and Hetty Cary, sought to buck this frivolous trend by becoming the "founders" of the Starvation Party. In essence, individuals who hosted these gatherings issued invitations to all their friends and whatever officers were nearby. No refreshments were served, "save the amber-hued water from the classic James." Constance Cary claimed she had General Lee's approval of her entertaining because it gave his men a lift to their spirits. One wonders, however, how many ate something before venturing out to attend a Starvation Party.[18]

But as Richmonders struggled to survive what appeared to be, if it not already was, approaching famine, they were soon shook by news of a daring escape of more than one hundred Federal officers incarcerated at Libby Prison. The Union men had secretly dug a tunnel under the basement. The tunnel was three feet wide and about fifty feet long and ended outside of Libby. The Richmond press was both outraged and impressed with the Yankees' ingenuity, if not audacity. The *Examiner* was certain the men broke off singly or in pairs or were "laying up in the houses or hiding places, provided by the disloyal element to be found in and around Richmond."[19] The *Examiner* was prescient. The Richmond Unionist underground had taken in many of the escapees and helped them return to the Northern lines.

Locals had barely digested the news of the prison break when they were stunned by a daring Federal cavalry raid that penetrated the inner defenses of the city. On March 1, two columns of Union cavalry led by Brigadier General Judson Kilpatrick and Colonel Ulric Dahlgren attacked local defense units and the city battalion. Thinking they could easily brush off these untrained clerks and artisans, the Union troops were surprised by General Wade Hampton and his veteran Confederate cavalry. What was planned as a daring stroke and approved by Lincoln and Union secretary of war Edwin Stanton became a comedy of errors that left Dahlgren dead and 350 of the combined forces prisoners of war.[20]

Thirteen-year-old William Littlepage's scavenging eclipsed press coverage of the raid. Littlepage was a member of the Home Guard unit sent out to repulse the Federals. After the fight, he set out to look for some souvenirs to give to his schoolteacher, Edward Halbach, who was also a member of the Home Guard. Littlepage came across the dead body of a Federal officer and began rifling through his pockets, hoping to find a gold watch. He instead found a cigar case, but it was the contents of the cigar case that created the subsequent firestorm. In that case was an address Colonel Dahlgren had delivered to his men outlining the goals of the raid: "We hope to release the prisoners from Belle Isle, first, and having them fairly started, we will cross the James River into Richmond, destroying the bridges after us and exhorting the released prisoners to destroy and burn the hateful city; and do not allow the Rebel leaders Davis and his traitorous crew to escape."[21]

Locals were outraged. Mary Chesnut mused, "Once more we have repulsed the enemy. But it is very humiliating indeed that he can come and threaten us at our very own gates whenever he so pleases." She went on to add, "If a forlorn negro had not led him astray . . . unmolested he would have walked into Richmond." War clerk J. B. Jones wrote in his diary that "some extraordinary memoranda [sic]" had been taken from Dahlgren's body, and he noted that the Richmond press was arguing for swift retaliation in the form of executions of the prisoners. Josiah Gorgas deemed the raiders "outlaws—bandits . . . beasts and murderers." Virtually everyone in the city was calling for the hanging of those captured. But General Lee had the final word. He wrote to Secretary of War Seddon that all the papers confiscated be formally published so "that our people & the world may know the character of the war our enemies wage against us, & the unchristian [sic] & atrocious acts they plot & perpetrate." Lee continued, however, "I cannot recommend the execution of the prisoners that have fallen into our hands." The general reasoned that because the plot had been foiled, executions were out of the question, though he admitted, "I presume that the blood boils with indignation in the veins of every officer & man as they read of the account of the barbarous & inhuman plot." Lee's caution, however, may have been attributed to the fact that his second son, General W. H. F. "Rooney" Lee, was still held in a Federal prison camp.[22]

On March 8, 1864, the *Richmond Daily Dispatch* reported that officials in the capital city had decided to bury Dahlgren's body secretly so as to end the matter. But the *Daily Dispatch* suggested that the dead cavalryman "be buried in a prominent place, and that a stone should be set up over it. . . . It would be a monument of infamy—a beacon to warn all of the fate of one so execrable. The youth of Richmond, when passing the spot, would derive fresh courage and renewed determination to defend their country and their homes as they contemplated the last resting place of a man who led a band that came to burn their city and butcher their people."[23]

The local press seized on the raid as evidence of Union perfidy. The *Dispatch* thundered, "The miserable wretch whose orders to hang Jeff. [sic] Davis and burn and sack the city, have brought down a storm of deserved execrations upon his head. . . . The misfortune of Dahlgren was that he was found out." The *Dispatch* also suggested that women in Richmond "provide [themselves] with the protection of a revolver, or some defensive weapon, to keep at bay ruffians." The paper argued that because their husbands, sons, and fathers were at the front, the "women of the Confederacy" needed to be safeguarded from "the brutes who are invading us."[24]

Dahlgren's body was ultimately interred at Oakwood Cemetery in Richmond. Determined he should be returned to his family and receive a decent burial in keeping with Victorian customs, Elizabeth Van Lew and her Unionist underground located the burial site, exhumed the body, cut locks of hair for his family, and prepared to send Dahlgren's remains north. Van Lew also sought out Union general Benjamin Butler to alert Dahlgren's father, Admiral John Dahlgren, that his son's remains were "in the hands of devoted friends of the Union who have taken possession of them in order that proper respect may be shown to them."[25]

"The FAMINE Is Still Advancing"

Spring brought warmer temperatures but also new challenges. Heavy rains throughout April disrupted transportation, menaced crop land, destroyed bridges over the James River, and threatened to overwhelm the James River and Kanawha Canal. Although this weather delayed the spring campaigning season, it did little to alleviate the food shortages in the Confederate capital.[26]

Once again, the Richmond City Council and neighboring Henrico County stepped in to aid the poor. On March 23, 1864, the council voted to appropriate $25,000 for the Overseers of the Poor. The Overseers of the Poor also set aside funds for the Female Orphan Asylum and the Female Humane Association. The city council then passed a resolution that the Overseers of the Poor "be authorized to charter cars and engines of the Virginia Central and the Richmond, Fredericksburg & Potomac Railroads and send to the South and obtain corn for the support of the poor and needy of the City." Henrico County officials authorized $50,000 in bonds for relief purposes and appropriated $40,000 to buy corn. It also raised the levy of $10,000 for soldiers' families to $40,000 and began attempts to obtain free wood for the poor.[27]

The *Richmond Enquirer* noted that "the city supply depot continues to furnish large numbers of the needy with the necessaries of life. The officers of the depot say that every applicant has been supplied and the distribution continues with regularity and satisfaction." The *Richmond Daily Dispatch* reported on March 26, 1864, that the firm of Haxall & Crenshaw was offering food to the needy at reduced prices. It argued that the "timely charities of Haxall & Crenshaw entitle the firm to a prominent place amongst those who deserve to be held in grateful remembrance for their deeds during this trying period of the war."[28]

Despite all these efforts, there were deep concerns among the populace. Josiah Gorgas recorded in his diary, "There is much anxiety on the subject of food for the capital. It is said—on the authority of the assessors—that the population of Richmond is now 130,000 against the 50,000 three years ago." He went on to aver that with "proper energy in the use of the Rail Roads," food supplies could be procured. J. B. Jones noted, "The FAMINE is still advancing." More troubling still was the rash of food robberies: "The pigeons of my neighbor have disappeared. Every day we have accounts of robberies, and the preceding night, of cows, pigs, bacon, flour—and even the setting hens are taken from their nests!" Almost daily the *Dispatch* reported that homes were "forcibly entered and robbed of a large lot of bacon, soap, &c."[29]

Not even the elderly were immune from such thefts. "An aged colored couple['s] shanty was broken into, and in their presence, a small stock of provisions, which they had just laid in, was carried off." The *Dispatch* went on to report, "The perpetrators of this outrage were black skins, but it is believed they were white persons in disguise."[30]

The army protecting Richmond was also suffering. As one resident noted, Lee's Army of Northern Virginia was subsisting on half rations, and that sacrifice had "infused its spirit into the whole nation."[31] General Lee was less enthusiastic. On April 12, 1864, he wrote to President Davis a letter bluntly expressing his concerns and outlying an alternative that must have made Davis blanch:

> My anxiety on the subject of provisions for the army is so great that I cannot refrain from expressing it to Your Excellency. I cannot see how we can operate without present supplies. Any derangement in their arrival or disaster to the railroad would render it impossible for me to keep the army together, & might force a retreat into North Carolina. There is nothing to be had in this section for man or animals. We have rations for the troops today & tomorrow. . . . Every exertion should be made to supply the depot at Richmond & at other points. All pleasure travel should cease, & everything devoted to necessary wants.[32]

Lee's missive apparently had the desired effect because J. B. Jones noted that Lee again alerted the secretary of war, who agreed to move a large portion of the civilian population into the countryside "to accumulate supplies for the army." Lee also urged Seddon to relocate "all the population whose presence would impede or endanger our efforts . . . especially that part of which increases the consumption of public stores." He went on to suggest that Northern prisoners of war and paroled Confederates be the first to be relocated. Lee's entreaties accelerated the transport of Federal prisoners from Libby Prison to a new prison erected in southwestern Georgia: Andersonville.[33]

One reason for the overcrowded conditions in Richmond's prisons was the breakdown of the prisoner exchange that had been in place since the beginning of the war. With Lincoln's Emancipation Proclamation, the Federal War Department had begun the enrollment of African Americans into United States Colored Troop units. In response to the preliminary Emancipation Proclamation, Davis ordered Confederate units to treat captured Colored Troop units as "criminals engaged in inciting servile insurrection."[34] Because the Confederacy would not recognize the black troops in these units as legitimate prisoners of war, the exchange system broke down.

Confederate cabinet officials examined their staffs to see who could be sent away from the overcrowded and hungry city. Secretary of War James Seddon argued that he had to have his full staff in place in Richmond, so he ordered the Treasury Department to relocate all its female clerks to Columbia, South Carolina. One woman wrote to her mother that a friend went down to the station to see them off. "She says she never imagined such confusion talking—laughing—crying, screaming and everything else going on all at once." Noting how grateful she was not to have landed a job signing notes, she admitted, "I feel so sorry for the girls." Eighty of the young women, unwilling to leave their families, resigned, thus depriving their families of much needed wages.[35]

But those measures had little effect. The *Richmond Enquirer* noted, "The evil effects of a superabundance of population in Richmond, by reason of which the price of every perishable good is rendered so enormous," were causing surrounding towns, such as Ashland, to mirror the costs of food in Richmond. One local resident was forced to send his wife and two children to visit relatives in "King & Queen Co [*sic*] . . . for the past two weeks. More in the capacity of *commissary* for our larder than for pleasure. Provisions are so high in Richmond and none to be had here [in Ashland] that this was absolutely necessary."[36] The local YMCA made an urgent appeal in the pages of the *Richmond Daily Dispatch*. Noting that since 1861 "Richmond has been a refuge for those who have been driven from their homes by our ruthless enemies" and that the organization had labored diligently to supply the wants of all "our soldiers and their families," the YMCA acknowledged it was dangerously short of provisions. It urged all Rich-monders to donate desperately needed food and clothing for those impoverished in the capital. It concluded, "Let those soldiers not be discouraged now, upon the eve of our severest and as we trust, our last and most glorious campaign."[37]

But white residents and refugees were not the only ones suffering from high prices and limited goods. Richmond's slave and free black populations were also seriously affected. Most were employed by the Confederate government, but many were "lent out" to other factories in the city. Indeed, both slaves and free people of color dominated most of the Tredegar's workforce. Not only was the work dangerous, but also wages could not keep pace with inflation. Slaves also dominated all conveyances with regard to military transportation and were often impressed to build fortifications.

Slaves and free blacks also saw their ability to move around the city and to live where they pleased affected by the war. Now, slaves and free blacks needed passes, signed by their owners or employers, to walk to work, to market, or to home. Passes had been required in the antebellum era, but that law was never enforced. With concerns about slave insurrections and spies, locals were vigilant in checking slave passes. If one was caught without a pass, he or she could be "immediately [impressed] for public defense work."[38]

Finally, "just living in Richmond, which was overrun by armed, drunken soldiers, proved fairly hazardous." The local press reported countless stories involving altercations between soldiers and civilians, white and black.[39]

"On to Richmond": The Overland Campaign of 1864

In early March 1864, Abraham Lincoln asked the U.S. Congress to resurrect the rank of lieutenant general and recommended that the hero of Vicksburg, Ulysses S. Grant, be promoted to that rank and become overall commander of all Federal forces. Grant was summoned to Washington to meet with Lincoln and discuss his plans for the campaigning season that year. The *Richmond Daily Dispatch* greeted the news with a yawn. Deeming McClellan the greater intellect, it averred, "Whatever [Grant] has accomplished has been the result of overwhelming numbers and the weakness and imbecility of our own resistance. Did he ever defeat a Confederate army except by three to one?"[40]

Grant's strategy was simple. Instead of Union armies "act[ing] independently and without concert, like a balky team, no two ever pulling together," he suggested coordinated campaigns throughout the Confederacy. He would travel with the Army of the Potomac, still under the command of Major General George G. Meade; General William T. Sherman would succeed Grant as head of the Army of Tennessee; General Benjamin Butler would advance with the Army of the James on Richmond via Fort Monroe; General Nathaniel Banks and the Army of the Gulf would move against Mobile; and General Franz Sigel would clear the Shenandoah Valley of Confederate troops using Union units from West Virginia and the valley. Of particular interest to the armies, especially the Army of the Potomac, was the destruction of key railroad lines linking Richmond to the rest of the commonwealth as well as to North Carolina. As General Meade noted, "Until that railroad [the Virginia Central] is destroyed, we cannot compel the evacuation of Richmond, even if we succeed in seizing and breaking the Southside [sic] and the Danville Roads."[41]

Grant launched the combined campaigns on May 4, 1864, by crossing the Rapidan River. The next day, Lee's army surprised the Federals in the overgrown territory near Fredericksburg dubbed the Wilderness. A savage, two-day fight ensued, made all the more horrific because rifle fire set the woods ablaze, and many a wounded soldier, Union and Confederate, burned alive waiting for aid to come. Casualties were heavy; Grant lost 17,000 to Lee's 11,000. In the past, such bloodshed induced Federal commanders to pull back. Grant instead swung south toward the vital crossroads at Spotsylvania. Once again the fighting was deadly and the casualties enormous, and once again Lee stymied Grant's offensive, but at a terrible cost. Grant could replace his losses; Lee could not.[42]

Grant was undaunted—and determined. He wired Chief of Staff General Henry W. Halleck on May, 11, 1864: "I am now sending back to Belle Plain all my wagons for a fresh supply of provisions and ammunition, and propose to fight it out on this line if it takes all summer."[43] Lee apparently anticipated this possibility because he confided to General Jubal Early as he moved his army south to thwart Grant's next advance, "We must destroy this army of Grant's before he gets to the James River. If he gets there, it will become a siege, and then it will be a mere question of time."[44]

People in Richmond could hear the sounds of battle raging to the north. Unionist Elizabeth Van Lew noted in her diary, "Awakened by the cannon. The firing has been uninterrupted all day, and so loud as to jar the windows. Much of the day passed on the housetop. Who can sit still . . . ?" Henri Garidel, a refugee from New Orleans, went to morning mass and then to his office as he always did. "The city was in a state of panic," he wrote. "People were expecting attacks from all sides, and everyone was flying to arms." Sarah Lawton wrote to her sister that no mail was being delivered and most of the stores were closed because the militia and Home Guard units had been sent out to guard the approaches to the city. Although her husband, the Confederate quartermaster general Alexander Lawton, wanted her to leave, she refused. "I am . . . very unwilling to leave my 'things' to the mercy of the negroes and the fortunes of a disorganized city."[45]

The *Daily Dispatch* gloated over Butler's failure to advance up the James River and Grant's inability to outflank Lee. In an editorial titled "Richmond Not Taken," it wrote, "The capital is safe. The Government is determined to defend it, and the army and its heroic leaders are competent to the task." Although the *Dispatch* grudgingly admitted that "the suspense and agony of the struggle tries [*sic*] the spirit of the people," it asserted with hope that "a short time of this painful ordeal will bring relief—the sweet repose of quiet and security, and the joy that the capital of our beloved mother Virginia has again been saved from the ruthless invader."[46]

Rebel war clerk Jones was not as sanguine as the *Dispatch*. He wrote in his diary on May 13, 1864, that the president and secretary of war had met in closed session. "It is now too late for the evacuation of Richmond," he despaired, "and a *desperate* defense will be made. If the city falls, the consequences will be ruinous to the present government."[47]

By the beginning of June, locals knew the Federal juggernaut was at the gates of Richmond. Henri Garidel wrote, "There is no news today, only rumors. The enemy is at peak strength and prevailing. Who knows how this will end?" The *Richmond Enquirer* was more optimistic: "While everyday [*sic*] the booming of death-dealing ordnance peals on the ears of the metropolis, what a singular aspect does the city afford? Utterly regardless of the fact that within a few miles of their homes a foe, fiercer and more barbarous than even the cohorts of Bonaparte, the citizens of Richmond pursue their daily avocations with the calmness of the palmiest days of peace."[48]

Most people in Richmond would not have agreed with the *Enquirer's* sunny outlook. Indeed, many were more worried about the specter of famine than about Grant's approaching legions. Sallie Putnam averred, "So enormous had become the expenses of living that the question had grown to be . . . 'On what can we subsist that will furnish the greatest amount of nutrient for the least amount of money?'" Clara Minor Lynn recorded that over the spring and summer "we were limited to two meals a day, vegetables and corn bread washed down with our multifarious coffee, now made of rye and okra." Gottfried Lange echoed Lynn's comments: "Everything [is] so expensive that one could hardly make ends meet—Usually we had corn bread and coffee 3–4 times a week for dinner and I often think that if one looked into my mouth, he'd still have some of it in my gullet."[49]

Lange was especially disgusted that the high prices and food shortages that dominated the spring and summer in Richmond were caused by the local merchants' hoarding of food and speculating in supplies. "Ask our merchants," Lange contended, "who knew how to evade the army with their money [and] were the biggest usurers. When one asked them, 'Do you have any meat?—No. Do you have any flour?—No. Always—No, and yet, through the windows one could see the kegs of flour on the 4th & 5th floor of the Warehouses.—The rich man could get what he wanted. The middle class had to do the dirty work and pay the most taxes; and in recent months that caused great discontent in many families."[50]

J. B. Jones was struck by the increasingly widening gap between the rich and poor in Richmond. "I wrote a letter to the president to-day, urging the necessity of preventing the transportation of any supplies on the railroads except for the distribution at cost, and thus exterminating the speculators." Jones went on to argue to Davis that "the poor must be fed and protected, if they be relied upon to defend the country. The rich bribe the conscription officers, and keep out of the ranks, invest their Confederate money and bonds in real estate, and would be the first to submit to the United States government." Jones completed his missive to Davis by stating, "The poor, whom [the rich] oppress, are in danger of demoralization from suffering and disgust, and might also embrace reunion rather than a prolongation of such miseries as they have so long experienced. The patriotism of 1861 must be revived," Jones warned, "or independence cannot be achieved."[51]

Sara Pryor's friend Agnes echoed Jones's comments: "The President likes to call attention to the fact we have no beggars on our streets, as evidence that things are not yet desperate with us." Agnes went on, "He forgets our bread riot which occurred such a little such a little while ago." J. B. Jones thought along lines similar to the president: "Still, in this hour of destitution and suffering among certain classes of people, we see *no beggars* in the streets."[52]

Although Davis appeared oblivious to the plight of the people in the Confederate capital, the Richmond City Council was not. In May 1864, the council passed a resolution to give the Union Benevolent Association $5,000 for "charitable purposes." It also asked the Overseers of the Poor to convey to the council how much more money needed to be allocated for Richmond's poor who were "not in the Poor House."[53]

In June, George Randolph noted that the Overseers of the Poor requested a hearing regarding "urgent business." William F. Taylor, the president of the Board of Overseers, read a partial report indicating that the firm of Haxall & Crenshaw had furnished meal to the poor and needed $56,440 to cover that donation. The council agreed to appropriate $35,000 to the Haxall & Crenshaw account. Meanwhile, city employees petitioned the city council "to purchase provisions from the supply store according to the size of their respective families, at the same rates at which sales are made to other persons." Local citizens also requested the council to regulate the price of bread. As the *Richmond Dispatch* noted, "Our citizens will be enabled to purchase for fifty cents the same size loaf of bread that now sells for one dollar." The *Dispatch* went on, "A careful estimate has been made as to the number of loaves the size of which is now the standard a barrel of flour will yield, and it has been ascertained that the net profits on each barrel cannot be less than four hundred dollars; so it will therefore be seen that should the weight system be adopted, the bakers will still make from fifty to seventy-five dollars on every barrel of flour they bake into bread." Perhaps not to be outdone, the Twenty-Sixth Mississippi, aware of the privations in the city, "unanimously offered to give one half of their rations for the next two days to be distributed among the poor women and children of Richmond. Mayor Mayo accepted the generous offer of these brave and noble soldiers and returned to them the thanks of the city."[54]

Sadly for Richmonders, such efforts, although prodigious, were not enough to end the real prospect of starvation. Now the culprit was not the speculators or the Union army, but the weather. Robert Kean noted in his diary that "a grievous drought lasting six to eight weeks has afflicted the country. . . . The corn crop has already been materially shortened. There has been some advantage in the early maturity and dryness of the wheat, which has thereby been made available for the army much earlier than usual." J. B. Jones observed, "The drought continues; vegetation wilting and drying up. . . . The [Union] raiders have caused many who were hiding and hoarding their meat and grain to bring them to market for fear of losing them." Jones went on to note, "This has mitigated the famine, and even produced a slight reduction of prices." But, he conceded, "the gardens are heavily ruined, and are only kept alive by watering freely. Mine has repaid me." According to Jones, "The tomatoes are growing apace, and seem to endure the drought pretty well; also the lima beans. We are now eating the last of the cherries."[55]

Some of the Northern press were apparently aware of the famine haunting Richmond. The *Philadelphia Inquirer* wrote that wheat prices in the Old Dominion were climbing and urged its readers to "cheer up, the Confederacy is about 'going up; they can't stand it another year.'" To that the *Daily Dispatch* responded, "The Yankee war of starvation has reduced us all to a state of gauntness that foretokens a nation of skeletons." It went on, "[The] well-fed hordes of Northern barbarians and plunderers will meet a Southern army of fleshless men, who will so resemble the escaped tenants of the grave-yards that their adversaries . . . will deem the day of judgement come" and flee. The *Dispatch* concluded, "Even Famine we will endure rather than submit to Yankee domination."[56]

Sensing the situation in the Confederate capital was desperate, General Grant decided to tighten the screws. In August, he ordered Major General Philip Sheridan to devastate the Shenandoah Valley: "Do all the damage to railroads and crops you can. Carry off stock of all descriptions, and negroes, so as to prevent further planting. If the war is to last another year, we want the Shenandoah Valley to remain a barren waste."[57]

Sheridan carried out Grant's orders with brutal efficiency. Writing from Woodstock, Virginia, in the valley, he informed Grant, "In moving back to this point the whole country from the Blue Ridge to the North Mountains has been made untenable for the rebel army." Not only would the Confederate armies suffer, but so, too, would the civilian population in Richmond.[58]

But still there were those who seemed unconcerned by either the Federal army or the dearth of food. Sallie Bird wrote to her friend Sarah Hamilton Yancey that "there has been considerable depression here and yet people have dances and weddings and bands . . . and ladies dress and walk the streets as if there was no war." She concluded, "Only the soldiers, the full hospitals and the wails of the bereaved tell us constantly of this dreadful war."[59]

For others, the lack of morals and the general debauchery in Richmond were a grave concern. Congressman Warren Akin wrote to his wife, "From what I hear this city must be very immoral. There are a great many women of ill-fame here, and many who keep up appearances are not as good as they appear to be." Akin admitted that part of the problem was the high cost of living: "Husbands and fathers are in the army, food difficult to obtain, temptation great and opportunity abundant." Because of that, "the simple hearted go down to ruin." He added that with the gas works shut down, walking at night in the capital was both frightening and dangerous. "I have not been out at night . . . since I have been here, and then I had two members of Congress to come home with me. I am afraid to walk the streets at night." Again he mentioned the large number of women parading the sidewalks, but he also reported that a man had been beaten, robbed, and eventually killed. He reassured his wife, "I shall be prudent and cautious."[60]

Henri Garidel was also appalled by the number of prostitutes he saw wandering about Capitol Square. Their appearance merely added to his distaste for the Confederate capital. Walking back to his office after yet another atrocious meal at his boardinghouse, Garidel stumbled in the dark. "The moon hadn't come out. I have never seen anything darker than the streets of Richmond when there is neither gaslight nor moonlight." Out of that darkness, "one of them [prostitutes] asked me if I hadn't picked up her veil. I answered her politely that I hadn't: I knew what she was getting at, but she was wasting her time. I hurried off so that I wouldn't have to spend any longer in their company."[61]

The local press bemoaned the number of bawdy houses and gambling establishments that flourished in Richmond, while the army—and the local population—struggled to find something to eat. The *Richmond Sentinel* reported on a raid local police made on a house on Wall Street. They arrested fourteen women and three men. "Ten women were under thirty and were of the vilest character"; one was deemed "the dirtiest person . . . [with] the most brazen face." The others were between forty-five and sixty years of age. The *Sentinel* went on to observe, "The women, during the day, exposed their persons in the windows and hallocd at[,] threw at, and spit upon all passersby. But when the sun went down arrived the time for the exercise of their most disagreeable practices. They got drunk and made the night hideous with their maudlin revelry." One scholar has noted, "The high class [*sic*] harlots lived up stairs [*sic*], above the gambling dens, and along Locust Alley, a narrow street that ran from Main to Franklin, in the block bounded by 14th and 15th streets." Their residence must have caused grave consternation, if not outright horror, to the residents of Franklin Street because that thoroughfare was considered the best address in Richmond.[62]

THE FALL OF RICHMOND,V.^a ON THE NIGHT OF APRIL 2nd 1865.

The Fall of Richmond, 1865. Currier and Ives.

The local press urged Mayor Joseph Mayo to do something about the licentiousness in the capital. The *Richmond Enquirer* wrote, "Never was a place more changed than Richmond. Go on the Capitol Square any afternoon, and you may see these women promenading up and down . . . jostling respectable ladies into the gutters." A relatively new publication in Richmond, *Southern Punch,* was similarly outraged by the state of the capital: "It has been asked, was there ever since the days of Sodom and Gomorrah, such a state of society as exists at present? Rogues, gamblers, swindlers, cutthroats infest us on all sides. Extortioners swarm at every turn. . . . [T]he Devil stalks at broad daylight in open view of everyone, without the care or precaution of dressing himself. In fact, cheating, swindling, garroting is [*sic*] the order of the day."[63]

Rivaling debauchery as a source of concern was the continued increase in robberies. The Richmond press daily reported robberies of everything from wood and soap to food and clothing. Sallie Putnam noted that virtually everyone in Richmond feared they would be targeted: "In addition to our other miseries, robberies were fearfully on the increase. The fortunate possessor of a well-stocked larder or coal house was in constant danger from burglary. It became an almost universal fashion in Richmond to permit 'every day to take care of itself.' It was useless to lay up for the morrow, or anticipate the rise in prices, and provide against it, for the cunning housebreakers were still better at calculation, and would ever upset the best laid schemes by their successful midnight depredations." The city council was well aware of the rise in crime in overpopulated Richmond. As early as January 1864, the city fathers passed a resolution creating the Committee on Police to investigate the problem and make recommendations to correct it. Despite the augmentation of the night watch, robberies continued to plague the city until the Federal army took control in April 1865 and declared martial law.[64]

The Confederate Army of Northern Virginia in the trenches at Petersburg was suffering through one of the coldest winters of the war. Everywhere, it seemed, there was hunger. J. B. Jones noticed that his daughter's cat could barely move because there was no cat food. Jones admitted, "Sometimes I fancy I stagger myself. We do not average two ounces of meat daily; and some do not get any for several days together. Meal is $50 per bushel. . . . Bacon brought $7.75 per pound." Things did not improve. Jones wrote barely a month later, "*It is now a famine,* although I believe we are starving in the midst of plenty, and if it were only equally distributed. But the government will not, it seems, require the railroads to bring provisions to the exclusion of freight for the speculators."[65]

The Federal high command was also cognizant of Richmond's plight. General Grant commented later in his memoirs, "Supplies were growing scarce in Richmond, and the sources from which to draw them were in our hands. People from outside began to pour into Richmond to help eat up the little on hand." He concluded, "Consternation reigned there."[66] He was confident that as he squeezed Lee, he could force the Confederates out of their lines.

J. B. Jones was only too aware of the military situation and confided to his diary, "At 2 p.m. the President's papers came in. Among them was one from the Commissary General stating that the present management of railroad transportation would not suffice to subsist the army." Lee realized the army was in extremis and informed the president that he might have to pull his army out of Petersburg and head to North Carolina, where supplies might be more readily available.[67]

Adding to Lee's anxiety was the reality that his once formidable army was melting away. Every day, cold, hungry veterans of the Army of Northern Virginia were deserting to the Northern lines because they were slowly starving to death. Lee pleaded with Davis repeatedly that he required a steady supply of rations because his men were malnourished and he feared for their ability to be an aggressive fighting force when the spring campaigning season opened in March and April. According to war clerk Jones, the commissary general, Colonel Lucius Northrop, estimated he had only fifteen days' worth of rations. The problem was the want of transportation. Northrop apparently told his superiors they may be forced to decide who got fed: the city of Richmond or the army defending it. Robert Kean had noted a year earlier that "the alternative was between the *people* and the army, that there is *bread* enough for both but not *meat* enough, and that we had to elect between the *army* and the *people* doing without."[68]

On the Petersburg Lines

The monotony of life in the trenches was momentarily interrupted in late July. Commander of the Union Ninth Corps, Ambrose Burnside, at the behest of a company of Pennsylvania coal miners, convinced Grant that the Pennsylvanians could dig a tunnel beneath Confederate lines and detonate a mine that would break the Confederate defenses. Grant acquiesced, but at the eleventh hour General George G. Meade ordered Burnside to change which division did the assault: U.S. Colored Troops were shifted in favor of a white division. Meade feared if the assault did not go according to plan, the army would be blamed for using the Colored Troops units as cannon fodder. The Battle of the Crater became a Federal disaster. The mine was detonated, but the Federals climbed into the crater instead of maneuvering around it. The Confederate lines reformed and had a field day firing into the crater, where Union troops were trapped. "It was the saddest affair I have witnessed in the war," Grant wrote to Halleck. "Such opportunity for carrying fortifications I have never seen and do not expect again to have."[69]

Grant's promise to "fight it out on this line if it takes all summer" had seen summer pass and autumn and early winter descend. The Federals and Confederates continued to face each other along almost thirty miles of trenches. Rations for the Confederates continued to be a thorny problem, and desertions reached epic proportions. Lee estimated that 100 of his men were deserting every day. Lack of food, inadequate clothing, a dearth of shoes, and heart-wrenching letters from Georgia pushed men to leave, to head to Federal lines, or to move south to protect their families in Sherman's wake as he maneuvered toward Atlanta.

But many in the beleaguered capital saw glimmers of hope as the summer turned to early fall. Sallie Putnam captured the spirit of many when she wrote, "When midsummer came on, it was obvious that an unmistakable check had been given to the concurrent operations intended for the destruction of the Southern Confederacy. General Grant had been brought to a 'stand still' before Petersburg, and General Sherman before Atlanta." Like Putnam, other Southerners were aware that the Northern public was experiencing extreme war weariness as the conflict appeared hopelessly stalemated. The Peace Democrats were clamoring for an armistice. Even the Northern president entertained doubts as to the outcome of the upcoming presidential election. On August 23, 1864, Lincoln presented his cabinet with a sealed memorandum and asked each man to sign it without reading it. The memorandum was most significant: "This morning, as for some days past, it seems exceedingly probable that this Administration will not be re-elected. Then it will be my duty to so co-operate with the President-elect, as to save the Union between the elections and the inauguration."[70]

Putnam's and other Richmonders' hopes that the stalemate would cripple Lincoln's reelection were devastated by the news that Atlanta fell to Sherman on September 2. That communication was a "severe blow to the Confederacy and was received in Richmond with unconcealed distress." Worse information was yet to come, for Sherman's Atlanta campaign virtually ensured that Lincoln would be reelected and hence the war would be waged until Union victory.[71]

The *Richmond Examiner* admitted the loss of Atlanta would "render incalculable assistance to the party of Lincoln, and obscures the prospect of peace, late so bright." So the editor hoped the Davis administration would make some move to restore popular confidence. But the *Examiner* voiced its doubts: "[I]t is difficult still to hope anything wise, or magnanimous, or unselfish, from the administration."[72]

Despite military setbacks, Richmonders plodded on. Empty market stalls and soaring prices continued to dominate locals' conversations. Ongoing concerns of how the poor would survive the coming winter prompted Reverend Charles Minnegerode, rector of St. Paul's Episcopal Church, to establish the Richmond Soup Association. According to the *Richmond Whig*, the Soup House would be located in the basement of the Metropolitan Hall on Franklin Street. It was expected to open on December 1. The organizers urged contributions until the association was up and functioning. Tickets for twenty-five cents could be purchased from the association's treasury, and the organization would be "under the control of the ladies of the Union Benevolent Society." All those deemed in need would receive a quart of soup. The Soup Association was apparently quite a success, and the Soup House was open daily at noon. According to the *Whig*, "The arrangements of the association are perfect, and the soup turned out delicious. The same article sold by them for 25 cents a quart could not be made by an individual for less than five dollars."[73]

Christmas 1864

As the Christmas holidays approached, most tried to make it as festive as they could, despite a continued dearth of food and a deteriorating military situation. In an effort to bolster morale in the trenches, the ladies of Richmond issued a call for locals to donate food so they could prepare a Christmas feast for the brave soldiers protecting the Confederate capital. The Richmond press, too, exhorted Richmonders to do their part for the men in gray. The *Daily Dispatch* noted approvingly, "The proposition of providing a sumptuous repast, on Christmas day, for all the gallant soldiers attached to the Army of Northern Virginia, seems to meet with universal approval. Besides liberal contributions from private citizens, the . . . Confederate Congress and the General Assembly of Virginia, in session . . . voted one day's compensation . . . for that purpose. Already upwards of fifty thousand dollars have been raised." The local press and firms pledged to aid in the effort to give Lee's army a memorable Christmas. But on December 23 a group of the organizers held an "impromptu meeting" and decided that with Christmas but two days away, "it was best to postpone the affair till New Year's day," but to continue planning and soliciting contributions. Sadly for Lee's starving army, when New Year's Day arrived, the "feast was "one small sandwich made up of two tiny slices of bread and a thin piece of ham! A few men ventured to inquire, 'Is this all?' After the 'meal' was finished," one Confederate reported, "a middle-aged corporal lighted his pipe and said: 'God bless our noble women! It was all they could do; it was all that they had.'" Truer words had never been spoken.[74]

Despite shortages and the high cost of provisions, and despite the sorry result of the women's best efforts to feed Lee's troops, Richmonders were determined to celebrate Christmas. J. B. Jones wrote, "We have quite a merry Christmas in the family, and a compact that no unpleasant word shall be offered." He noted that his wife and children were baking cakes and pies, "and to-day we shall have *full* rations." He observed that outside "there is much jollity and some drunkenness in the streets, notwithstanding the enemy's pickets are within an hour's march of the city."[75]

Sallie Putnam's celebration was much more muted. She noted, "The festivities of Christmas were rendered mournful by the fall of Savannah," and stated, "our praise and thanksgiving was [*sic*] blended with fasting and prayer, with deep humiliation and earnest contrition." After attending church services, Putnam and her family gathered for dinner: "Instead of the sumptuous banquet, around which we were wont to gather, we sat down to a poverty-stricken board."[76]

Judith McGuire, still a refugee in Richmond, dreaded Christmas because of all the deaths her family circle had suffered in the past year. Nevertheless, they attended church services and returned home to eat Christmas dinner. "We had aspired to a turkey," she wrote in her diary, "but finding the prices range from $50 to $100 in the market . . . we contented ourselves with roast beef and the various little dishes which Confederate times have made us believe are tolerable substitutes for the viands of better days." She went on to note that in the evening "I treated our little party to tea and ginger cakes—two very rare indulgences; and but for sorghum, grown in our own fields, the cakes would be an impossible indulgence." McGuire planned a gathering for New Year's, but, as she reflected on 1864, she was filled with grief: "What calamities and sorrows crowd into its history, in this afflicted country of ours! God help us, and guide us onward and upward, for the Saviour's sake!"[77]

The Fall of Richmond, 1865

"We Slept, as It Were, over the Heaving Crater of a Volcano"

The winter of 1864–1865 was once again harsh, and the people of Richmond found it increasingly difficult to survive. The loss of Savannah on December 20, 1864, and the Federals' seizure of the Saltville salt works in the Kanawha Valley only deepened the gloom. Christmas, usually celebrated with "sumptuous banquet[s]," was now [a] despondent" holiday. According to Sallie Putnam, "The New Year was ushered in with no better prospects."[1]

Throughout the Confederacy, but especially in the Confederate capital, the situation seemed desperate. Fort Fisher and with it the last blockade-running port of Wilmington, North Carolina, fell to Federal forces on January 15. Shortly thereafter, Congress elevated Robert E. Lee to overall command of the Confederate armies. His first act was to recall Joseph E. Johnston to active duty and to order him to try and assemble as many soldiers of the Army of Tennessee as possible to stave off Union general William T. Sherman in the Carolinas.[2] On the Virginia front, Lee's Army of Northern Virginia was starving in the trenches at Petersburg as General Ulysses S. Grant relentlessly extended his lines and thus forcing Lee to do the same—but with many fewer troops. Confederate desertions were on the rise as soldiers from Georgia and the Carolinas received tearful entreaties to come home because their families were frightened of Sherman and had nothing to eat.

Prices in the Confederate capital continued to spiral upward. Sallie Putnam noted, "Day by day our wants and privations increased. The supply of our provisions in the city of Richmond was entirely inadequate to the demand." War clerk J. B. Jones noted, "Flour is $700 per barrel to-day; meal $80 per bushel; coal, wood, $100 per load." Congressman Warren

Akin wrote to his wife in Georgia, "The poor here have a hard time always; but at present their condition is terrible. The suffering for food, clothing and in the cities, for want of fuel, is awful. Women and children are often seen on the streets begging for a little change to buy bread."[3]

Others reflected on how gloomy and dismal the capital city had become. Henri Garidel, a refugee from New Orleans who obtained a government position, noted in his diary, "I desperately need to wash myself. Everyone lives in filthy conditions here in Richmond. I have never been so filthy in all my life. They wash their feet when it rains because they don't have a tub. God, when will this end?" Irish visitor Thomas Conolly found that "the aspect of Richmond at this time is wretched[.] Shops with nothing in them except to show how miserably they are run[.] Stores with open doors & empty bales & broken up packing cases & dirty straw[.]" Even members of the Confederate Congress suffered. Warren Akin told his wife, "I am doing what I never did at home. I wear but two shirts a week, and my drawers and flannels and night shirts two weeks, a pair of socks a week, and therefore have but a dozen pieces washed in two weeks. I carry and use my handkerchiefs until they are soiled so much, I am ashamed sometimes to use them. But I feel it necessary on account of the state of my finances. It is absolutely necessary to be as economical as possible."[4]

Locals looked for a source of the myriad problems that afflicted the capital. Perhaps not surprisingly, they focused on the Confederate government and especially its president. Ordnance Department chief Josiah Gorgas noted, "In this dark hour of our struggle there is of course strong feeling against the administration for having mismanaged our affairs. This must be expected in adversity." Warren Akin, like Gorgas, lamented the situation but defended the much maligned president: "Were [Davis] removed today we should be *ruined* in a few months, and I fear we shall be anyway. . . . We are in a deplorable condition—standing on the verge of an abyss, the bottom of which no one can see."[5]

Others were not so charitable. War clerk Jones observed that the winter was bitterly cold and people were starving, "while Congress and the Executive seem paralyzed or incapable of thought or action." Thomas Chester, an African American reporter for the *Philadelphia Press* traveling with the Union's Army of the James, stated that the Richmond press "assure me that . . . the daily papers in no way represent the feelings of the people or the editors themselves but are conducted wholly with a view of keeping up the spirits of the rebels in arms." Chester went on to note, "The poorer class has

Richmond panorama, 1865. Courtesy of the Valentine Museum, Richmond.

long since given up all hope of succeeding and now the F.F.V.s [First Families of Virginia] are conscious of, and in their drawing rooms admit the impossibility of Southern independence."[6]

As early as February, locals began to talk about rumors of evacuating Richmond. Josiah Gorgas reported, "Here there is a good bit of consternation lest Richmond be evacuated. An order has been given to remove all cotton and tobacco preparatory to burning it. All the departments have been notified to *prepare to move.*" President Davis told Gorgas he worried about the impact such an order would have on the city, state, Confederacy—and Europe. Despite the dire situation, Davis still held out hope for European intervention. Gorgas went on to note, "[Davis] afterwards caused the Virginia legislature to be assured that in no event would Richmond be evacuated." On February 18, Henri Garidel recorded the fall of Columbia, South Carolina, to Sherman's forces on February 17 and stated, "The Yankees are closing in on us. Every day I await the order to evacuate Richmond." Ten days later he wrote, "Richmond is topsy-turvy. People speak of nothing but the immediate evacuation. All the bureaus are preparing for it." Judith McGuire reflected on the combined forces of Grant and Major General Phillip Sheridan that were pressing all around them and declared, "Oh, I would that I could see Richmond burnt to the ground by its own people, without one brick left upon one another, before its defence-less [sic] inhabitants should be subjected to . . . degradation!"[7]

The Cleburne Memorial

It was against this backdrop that Davis went to the Confederate Congress and asked for legislation to conscript 200,000 slaves and arm them to fight for the Confederacy. It was not a new idea. In January 1864, Major General Patrick Cleburne, a divisional commander in the Army of Tennessee, had proposed that because the Confederacy lacked manpower, it should avail itself of a great untapped resource: slaves. Cleburne argued to his superiors, "As between the loss of independence and the loss of slavery, we assume every patriot will freely give up the latter—give up the negro slave rather than be a slave himself [to the North]." Word of Cleburne's proposal reached Richmond, and Davis ordered it suppressed.[8]

But the proposal would not die. Confederate armies in both theaters were hemorrhaging. By 1865, Davis was willing to sacrifice the institution of slavery to achieve Southern independence. His speech to the Confederate Congress sparked intense and heated debate. Howell Cobb of Georgia spoke for many when he wrote to Secretary of War James Seddon, "Use all the negroes you can get, for all the purposes you need them, but don't arm them. The day you make soldiers of them is the beginning of the end of the revolution. If slaves will make good soldiers our whole theory of slavery is wrong." Only General Robert E. Lee's endorsement of the bill allowed it to be debated. Lee convinced the Congress that slaves would fight because they were accustomed to following orders.[9]

Public reaction was mixed. The *Richmond Daily Dispatch* carried an editorial on February 20, 1865, that urged its readers to "leave the solution to the sound, practical judgment of General Lee." It added, "He is known to be earnestly in its favor." The editors concluded, as did General Cleburne, "It is better to liberate two hundred thousand negroes, and to put them in the army than to run the risk of losing all. We would rather sacrifice them all, and make emancipation universal, than hazard the independence of the Confederate States." The *Richmond Enquirer* reported that along the Petersburg lines, where Lee's army was entrenched, morale was high: "It is cheering to know that the spirit of enthusiasm which pervades our army is now greater than at any time since the spring of 1861." It went on, "The soldiers, to a man, are braced for the pending issue. . . . Appreciating fully the situation of affairs, they, with but few exceptions, agree upon the practicality of introducing the negro" into the army.[10]

Others echoed the Richmond press. Kate Rowland of Richmond wrote in her diary, "People are willing—if it comes to the alternative—to give up slavery, if as is rumored, the European powers will acknowledge our Independence on that condition. Anything—everything we will sacrifice rather than come again under the same government with the hated Yankee! Such are the sentiments of everyone I have seen."[11] What Rowland was alluding to was a last-ditch effort by the Confederate government to obtain British and French recognition. In 1864, Davis and Secretary of State Judah P. Benjamin prevailed upon wealthy Louisiana slaveholder Duncan F. Kenner to run the blockade to Europe. Kenner's efforts were stymied by the strength of the East Gulf Blockading Squadron, which forced him to travel north in disguise and to board a German vessel in New York to sail to Europe in January 1865. He managed to meet with Confederate commissioners James Mason and John Slidell and to present to British and French leaders the Confederacy's plan to emancipate its slaves in return for European recognition. Neither Emperor Napoleon III nor British prime minister Lord Palmerston would accept this proposal, thus ending all of the Confederacy's hopes of European recognition and support.[12]

Meanwhile, the debate to arm the slaves continued to roil and dominated most conversations in the Confederate capital. Many were not as sanguine regarding the efficacy of drafting slaves as soldiers. In Richmond, George Patterson wrote to George Mordecai, "The spirits of the people are brighter now . . . tho' I cannot imagine what the feeling will be respecting making soldiers of negroes. My own opinion is, that they will not fight." Patterson added, "Our colored . . . do not fancy violent or sudden deaths. They do not endure pain well.—I do not think they would fancy long forced marches, just for the sake of purchasing freedom by marching or killing a few Yankees at the risk of their own life or limb." Patterson did concede, however, that "since Gen Lee thinks they will make efficient soldiers . . . I say let him try." J. B. Jones also chronicled the tortured path of the slave conscription bill in the Confederate Congress. On February 24, 1865, he recorded in his diary that the Confederate Senate voted down "the bill to put 200,000 negroes in the army" by one vote. He went on to note, "The papers to-day contain a letter from Gen. Lee advocating the measure as a *necessity.*" According to Jones, it was the large slave owners in the Senate—specifically Senator Robert M. T. Hunter—who opposed the measure. Nonetheless, on March 17, 1865, Jones wrote, "We shall have a negro army. Letters are pouring into the department from men of military skill and character, asking for authority to raise companies, battalions, and regiments of negro troops." He concluded, as did many others in the capital city, "It is the desperate remedy for the very desperate case."[13]

The Confederate Congress and Virginia General Assembly ultimately passed a watered-down version of the bill that expressly ignored the provision to emancipate the slaves upon winning independence. Davis and the War Department acted unilaterally and on March 23, 1865, promulgated General Orders No. 14, which called for raising black units and intimating that those who served would attain freedom upon independence. Shortly thereafter, Sallie Putnam noted, "Recruiting offices were opened in Richmond and soon a goodly number of sable patriots appeared on the streets clad in the grey uniform of the Confederate soldier. Their dress-parades on the Capitol Square attracted large crowds of all colors to witness them." War clerk J. B. Jones was less enthusiastic: "A parade of a few companies of negro troops yesterday was rather a ridiculous affair." As he well knew, "The owners are opposed to [the slaves' conscription]."[14]

Meanwhile, Francis Preston Blair pressured Lincoln to allow him to travel south to mediate a peace conference between the Union and the Confederacy. Davis, hoping to achieve independence at any price, dispatched Vice President Alexander Stephens, Senate president pro tem Robert M. T. Hunter, and Assistant Secretary of War and former associate justice of the U.S. Supreme Court John A. Campbell to meet with Lincoln and Secretary of State William Seward. The meeting took place on the U.S. vessel *River Queen* on February 3, 1865. Perhaps predictably, President Lincoln would accept only an unconditional surrender and Southern ratification of the recently passed Thirteenth Amendment abolishing slavery. With the parties agreeing to disagree, the Peace Conference ended after only an hour, and Stephens, Hunter, and Campbell returned to Richmond to report the negative result of the negotiations to Davis. Confederate War Department chief Robert Garlick Hill Kean recorded, "This ends this peace *fiasco* which must satisfy the most sceptical [*sic*] that we have nothing whatever to hope or expect short of the exaction of all the rights of conquest, whether we are overrun by force, or submit." Josiah Gorgas also noted, "The 'peace com-missioners' returned on Sunday, & with the answer I expected—no terms save Submission will be listened to." Two days later, Gorgas wrote that on February 9, 1865, "there was an enthusiastic meeting on the war, at the African Church [First African Baptist Church]. Mr. Hunter, Mr. Benjamin & others spoke. The war feeling has blazed out afresh in Richmond, & the spirit will I hope spread thro' the land." Local Caroline Kean Hill Davis wrote in her diary, "It seems our Peace Commissioners have accomplished nothing—& wonder if the Yankee government thinks we are *fools!* To accept such terms of peace as they offer us & think it is adding insult to injury." She went on to note, "I am glad the President sent the Commission-ers however for it must satisfy the weakened croakers that he is willing to try every means to stop this awful war—except to compromise our honor & integrity & our independence." Sallie Putnam was not as impressed as the others. She admitted, "Eloquent addresses were delivered; patriotic appeals were made; [and] a spasmodic enthusiasm was enkindled. But despondency rested too heavily on the hearts of many to permit more than a momentary and convulsive effort to shake off the incubus."[15]

The spring campaigns and constant fighting caused serious problems. The Shenandoah Valley was Virginia's and especially Richmond's bread basket, but it had been ravaged. The consequences for the Confederate cap-ital were extremely serious for an already overcrowded and starving popula-tion. Mary Chesnut noted from South Carolina, "Jack Middleton writes from Richmond: 'The wolf is at the door. We dread starvation far more than we do Grant or Sherman. Famine—that is the word now." Robert Garlick Kean recorded in his diary that four months after Major General Philip Sheridan turned the Shenandoah Valley into a "barren waste," the city was still reeling: "Through the effect of Sheridan's raid Richmond [in October] is rapidly approaching a state of famine. Bacon is $20 a pound, flour $1200 a barrel, butter $25 a pound, beef and that the worst, $10 to $12 [a pound], wood, $200 a cord, etc, and the supply exceedingly meager." He went on to observe, "The country, however, i.e. Virginia, is responding nobly to the appeal of General [Isaac M.] St. John, commissary general[,] . . . and if the communications are kept up [through the railroads,] he has no doubt of feeding the army." Mrs. William Simmons made similar notes in her diary. She revealed that all conversations in Richmond revolved around food—or the lack thereof: "The empty stomach makes itself felt everywhere; one sees now and then a man stagger in the street from sheer faintness. Our landlady[, who] has been shivering with her babe [in] the chill weather over a half dozen precious coals, and whose four little boys have been on half rations for weeks past, says 'If the Yankees *are* going to take the city I want them to hurry and get here before we are all starved.'"[16]

As shortages became endemic, crime, especially thefts of food and clothing, were on the rise. Returning from a Starvation Party, where the only refreshment was water from the James River, Constance Cary noticed a set of "black fingers" clinging to the window sill by her kitchen. "I reflected that the town was full of half-starved marauding negroes, and that in any case I would get nothing by crying out. So . . . I pulled down the window with a slam." Henri Garidel recorded, "A lot of people are stopped in the street at night. They beat you and knock you down in order to rob you." J. B. Jones noted in his diary, "My woodhouse was broken into last night, and two (of the nine) sticks of wood taken. Wood is selling at $5 a stick this cold morning."[17]

Not even the first family was immune from the famine. Varina Davis recorded in her memoir of her husband's life, "During the stringent period of our war I was obliged, through a tradeswoman, to sell my carriage, and horses, my handsome articles, jewelry, etc., to get the necessaries of life."[18]

The *Richmond Daily Dispatch* and other local newspapers daily reported thefts, but the local police force—miniscule in a city teeming with up to 130,000 people—was entirely inadequate to take measures against the thieves. The *Dispatch* especially condemned those who bought up scarce goods and then resold them for higher prices. In one editorial, the *Dispatch* excoriated "free negroes and unrefined foreigners [who] occupy most of the [market] stands and, like the leech, which is never satisfied till it gorges itself to death . . . continue to add to their prices each successive day." The editor finished, asking when the city council would expand its poor-relief efforts.[19]

The Richmond City Council was not unaware of the situation. Throughout the winter, it increased poor relief, provided low-cost fuel and salt to locals, and took special care to look after widows and orphans. Even Governor William "Extra Billy" Smith, who took office on January 1, 1864, became involved. In order to bolster local defenses, Smith organized two regiments of exempts and outfitted them with uniforms and arms. As Smith wrote later in his memoirs, "These regiments were organized shortly after my inauguration. They rendered frequent and valuable service. . . . They disappeared from the scenes of their patriotic services when the fall of Richmond rendered them no longer necessary."[20]

The governor next tackled the food-shortage problem. Tapping civil and military contingency funds and requesting a loan of $30,000 from the Farmer's Bank of Virginia, Smith collected $110,000. He hired an agent to run the blockade for supplies and "also organized a railroad train—obtained from the government a formal protection against all interference on the part of its subordinates—placed it in charge of an efficient agent, with the necessary funds, with instructions to proceed South and purchase corn, rice and other needful supplies." The agent was quite successful, and Smith was able to offer citizens of the capital food at much reduced prices. He later summed up his efforts: "I had supplied a large amount of public and private wants, controlled to a considerable extent the rapacity of private traders; kept Lee's Army in the field as before, and at the collapse, had cleared for the state the large debt due by the Confederate Government."[21]

A Season of "Gayety"

What struck many Richmonders in the winter of 1864–1865, despite inflation, the specter of famine, and the Federals besieging Petersburg, was the city's social scene: there was an explosion of parties, fancy balls, weddings, and general socializing. Judith McGuire mused, "Some persons in the beleaguered city seemed crazed on the subject of gayety [*sic* passim]. In the midst of the wounded and dying, the low state of the commissariat, the anxiety of the country . . . I am mortified to say that there are gay parties given in the city." One evening, as she returned to her rented lodgings after a long day of nursing the Confederate wounded, "I passed a house where there were music and dancing." McGuire wrote in disgust, "The revulsion of feeling was sickening. I thought of the gayety of Paris during the French Revolution, of the 'cholera ball' in Paris, the ball at Brussels the night before the battle of Waterloo, and felt shocked that our own Virginians, at such a time, should remind me of scenes which we were wont to think of only belonged to the lightness of foreign society. It seems to me that the army, when it hears of the gayety of Richmond, must think it heartless, particularly while it is suffering such hardships in her defense." What troubled McGuire most were the "suppers," where "cakes, jellies, ices, . . . and meats of the finest kinds [were] in abundance, such as might furnish a meal for a regiment of General Lee's army."[22]

Phoebe Yates Pember, the matron of Richmond's massive Chimborazo Hospital, was equally dismayed. She, too, was shocked at the Richmond social scene. "Besides parties, private theatricals and tableaux were constantly exhibited." She went on, "Wise and thoughtful men disapproved openly of this mad gayety." For Pember, "There was certainly a painful discrepancy between the excitement of dancing and the rumble of ambulances that could be heard in the momentary lull of the music, carrying the wounded to the different hospitals."[23]

T. C. DeLeon also noted that "the winter was passing in Richmond in most singular gayety." Officers on liberty from the Petersburg trenches routinely journeyed to the Confederate capital to attend these parties. According to DeLeon, "Parties were of a nightly occurrence. Not the brilliant and generous festivals of the older days,"—a marked difference from McGuire's observations—"but joyous and gay assemblages of a hundred young people who danced . . . who chatted, who laughed as if there was no tomorrow." Malvina Gist, a "Treasury girl" who was forced to leave Columbia, South Carolina, because of Sherman's advance, found herself a refugee in Richmond. She was amazed at what she saw in the capital city. "Oh! The seduction, the novelty, the fascination of this life in Richmond! If patriotism is its master-chord, pleasure is no less its dominant note." She, too, delighted in the robust social scene in the city, where parlors nightly "[were] full of visitors . . . officers, privates, congressmen, senators, old friends, and new ones, from all parts of the country." Although Richmond was "crowded to suffocation," she asked, none too rhetorically, "Are there great and somber tragedies going on around us? Is there a war? I thought so before I reached Richmond."[24]

Kate Rowland was similarly impressed by the partylike atmosphere. She recorded in her diary that she "accepted an invitation to the R[andolph]s and got a glimpse of the gay world of Richmond. The supper was as elegant & profuse as in good times, & must have cost an immense amount of Confederate scrip." Rowland also noted that among those in attendance were Lieutenant General James Longstreet and Captain Raphael Semmes of C.S.S. *Alabama* fame.[25]

T. C. DeLeon tried to downplay the charges of debauchery in Richmond. He wrote, "But the short spasm of gayety [*sic*] . . . was only the fitful and feverish symptom of the deadly weakness of the body and the impenetrable gloom." He went on to note, "The desertions of the army were assuming fearful proportions. . . . [S]upplies of bare food were becoming frightfully scarce and even the wealthiest began to be pinched for necessaries of life."[26]

Besieged at Petersburg

Meanwhile, the situation in the trenches before Petersburg was growing more difficult by the day. Grant continued to extend his lines, forcing Lee to spread his dwindling army even farther. The Confederate general was well aware of the impact this forced maneuver was having on his cold and starving men. Lee wrote to his wife in Richmond to send him the last batch of socks she and her daughters had been knitting for his troops "and bring your work to a close, for I think General Grant will move against us soon— within the week if nothing prevents—and no man can tell what may result. . . . I pray we might not be overwhelmed."[27]

Because of the deteriorating situation, the Richmond City Council convened a meeting on February 24, 1865, to discuss a message it had received from Lee's assistant adjutant general to General Richard S. Ewell, who had been named commanding general of the Department of Richmond.[28] In effect, Lee ordered Ewell to destroy all cotton and tobacco in the city, which could not be removed. As might be expected, this order set off a lively debate in the council chambers regarding the effect such an order would have on private property. Ultimately, the council concluded it had no authority to countermand the order. But it did pledge "to take precaution as circumstances permit against the destruction of property not included in the order." The city fathers also passed the following resolution: "That a company of six members, consisting of the President of the Council and five others appointed by him shall confer with the Mayor and aid him in his effort to see that the destruction of the cotton and tobacco be effected by the military authorities with as little damage to the city and other property as possible."[29] That order, to torch the cotton and tobacco stored in the capital city, came to be very controversial and was to have grave consequences.

For the vast majority of Richmonders, the threat of famine seemed more imminent than the arrival of the dreaded Yankees. At the end of March, William Brown wrote to his mother that if she believed prices were high when she left the city, she would be even more shocked now. He concluded his missive by observing, "It seems to be the universal opinion in Richmond that the Government will be compelled to leave this city in order to feed the army." Sallie Putnam noted, "In Richmond we had never known such a scarcity of food." Stalls were largely empty, and the city's fish supply was cut off by military operations. According to Putnam, an average

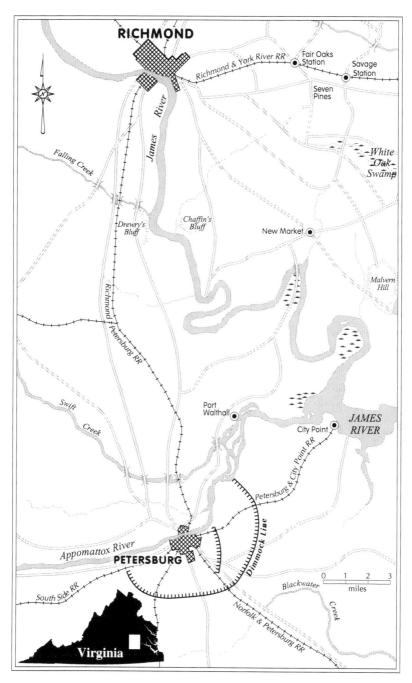

The Richmond–Petersburg, Virginia, theater of war, 1865.

citizen's dinner was extremely meager, and many did without meat for days. Robert Kean remarked on a letter from General Lee informing the War Department that his men in the trenches at Petersburg—barefoot, with limited blankets and scanty uniforms—had not had a meat ration in three days. As Lee said to his eldest son, Custis, "Well Mr. Custis, I have been up to see the Congress . . . and they do not seem to be able to do anything except to eat peanuts and chew tobacco while my army is starving.'"[30]

By late March, Grant's continued movements threatened the Southside Railroad and therefore Lee's escape route. On March 25, 1865, Lee ordered General John B. Gordon to launch an assault against Fort Stedman. The offensive—to punch through Grant's lines—was successful, but a Union counterattack reclaimed all territory the Federals had lost initially and forced the Confederates to fall back. Lee then moved to counter Sheridan at Dinwiddie Court House. Fierce fighting and the Confederate collapse at Five Forks on April 1 convinced Grant to order an all-out attack along Lee's front. Grant's offensive broke Lee's lines in three places. Lee had no choice but to withdraw from the Petersburg trenches. He wrote to the newly appointed secretary of war, General John C. Breckinridge, that he had to move "north of the Appomattox [River] if possible." He concluded, "I advise that all preparations be made for leaving Richmond tonight."[31]

The Evacuation

April 2 was a bright, warm Sunday, and President Davis was sitting in his pew at St. Paul's Episcopal Church when the sexton handed him a telegram. Mrs. William Simmons watched as Davis read the telegram, rose, and walked out of the sanctuary. "An ominous fear upon all hearts . . . seemed to spread itself to all churches, services were hastened to a close, and as we walked home, the very air seemed heavy with impending ill." Sara Pryor's friend Agnes was also at St. Paul's. She wrote to Pryor, "I was at St. Paul's Sunday . . . when the note was handed to President Davis. He rose immediately, and walked down the aisle—his face set, so we could read nothing." Fannie Taylor Dickinson noted on that Sunday that after attending church and eating dinner, "my sister came in asking, 'have [sic] you heard the news?. . . . the Yankees will be here tomorrow and Richmond will be evacuated.'"[32]

Breckinridge also relayed Lee's message to a stunned Jefferson Davis as he walked back to his office. Although Lee had been warning the administration for months that Richmond might have to be evacuated, Davis still received the missive in disbelief. He telegraphed Lee, "To move to-night [*sic*] will involve the loss of many valuables, both for the want of time to pack and of transportation. Arrangements are progressing, and unless you otherwise advise, the start will be made." Lee's reply was blunt: "I think it absolutely necessary that we should abandon our position to-night. I have given the necessary orders on the subject to the troops, and the operation, though difficult, I hope will be performed successfully."[33]

Confederate captain Clement Sulivane recorded, "About 11:30 a.m. on Sunday, April 2d, a strange agitation was perceptible on the streets of Richmond, and within half an hour it was known on all sides that Lee's lines had been broken below Petersburg; that he was in full retreat . . . that the troops covering the city at Chaffin's and Drewry's Bluffs were on the point of being withdrawn, and the city was forthwith to be abandoned."[34] Davis quickly summoned his cabinet, and they began to make plans to pack up all the government records and to relocate the Confederate capital. After agreeing to meet at the train station to head to Danville, Davis headed back to the executive mansion to collect some things. Fearing the military situation in front of Petersburg, Davis had sent Varina and his children away a week earlier, giving her a $5 gold piece and a pistol. Varina and the children begged to stay, but Davis was insistent: "If I live you can come to me when the struggle is ended, but I do not expect to survive the end of constitutional liberty."[35]

Meanwhile, Mayor Mayo asked the Richmond City Council to meet at 4:00 p.m. Mayo also requested further clarification from Governor Smith, General Lee, and Secretary of War Breckinridge. One councilman, James Alexander Scott Sr., "moved that a committee be appointed to wait upon the Governor and request of him two City regiments . . . to be retained in the City for the protection of the City." The council also resolved, "It is the imperative duty of this Council, in case of the evacuation of the City by the Government and the Army to provide, as far as it can, for the immediate destruction of the stock of liquor in the City." Lest local tavern owners protested, the council promised to reimburse them for all of the liquor destroyed.[36]

Sallie Putnam noted that as word spread about the Army of Northern Virginia's withdrawal from the Petersburg trenches, locals scrambled to find any type of conveyance they could. To add to the approaching chaos and confusion, according to acerbic editor E. A. Pollard, General Ewell, "obeying to the letter of his instructions, . . . issued orders to fire the four principal tobacco warehouses in the city." Pollard went on to observe, "In vain did Mayor Mayo and a committee of citizens . . . remonstrate against this reckless military order. The warehouses were fired . . . [and] the conflagration passed rapidly beyond control." Ordnance Department chief Josiah Gorgas had also implored Ewell not to fire the tobacco but rather to ruin it by dumping turpentine in the barrels. But Ewell went ahead as Lee had instructed.[37]

The flames spread quickly and soon reached the Confederate Armory. Lucy Chamberlayne noted, "At daybreak began the awful explosions—the Powder Magazine near the Poor House and the gunboats in the [James] river were blown up—Soon the Armory was fired." John Gottfried Lange, who had witnessed the Prussian bombardment of Erfurt in 1813, wrote, "Fire, fire, fire in all the streets. There was no end to the explosions. On top of it there was a light south wind which blew the flames still more toward the city. From the Armory to Rocketts [Wharf], a mile long, the lower part of the city was in flames. . . . The bursting of the grenades, the collapse of the houses, the sinister hissing of the flames, the screaming and lamenting of the homeless—it is impossible for my pen to describe."[38]

Irishman Thomas Conolly also witnessed the anarchy of the night of April 2: "I went out & what a sight at that hour, the streets filled with all the ragamuffins, chiefly niggers running and hurrying about & then another crash, another explosion & all the windows of the Spottswood [sic] are rent asunder as also all the stores in Main Street & now the plundering begins, men & women grabbing more than they can carry." Emmy Lightfoot also saw the bedlam. "We could see the fire from the front of our house raging on Main Street and the smoke was so dense the sun looked as if in eclipse; numbers of people were coming by laden with spoils from the burning stores." Lightfoot observed the roof of their home catch fire several times, but neighbors and "servants"—the family's slaves—were able to extinguish the flames.[39]

James W. Llewellen wrote to a friend that he and his family lost everything except the clothes they were wearing: "As the last of the Army moved out, the tobacco warehouses & depots & public stores were fired," and "as the wind blew fresh from the south . . . the flames spread rapidly, and enveloping the heart of the city soon destroyed." Sadly for Llewellen, "Besides our office which was valued at $100,000 before the war, we had a very large stock of pen, ink, and other materials, all of which were consumed." He concluded his missive by stating he was "penniless."[40]

Ruins of the Confederate arsenal, 1865.

In a letter to her mother and her brother, Constance Cary reported she sought shelter with her aunt. Although the house was full with other relatives and refugees, Cary was taken in. That night "the town wore the aspect of one in the Middle Ages smitten by pestilence. The streets filled with smoke and flying fire were empty of the respectable class of inhabitants, the doors and shutters of every house tight closed."[41]

The initial explosions came from the James River, where Raphael Semmes, newly promoted to rear admiral and given command of the James River fleet, was given a message from Secretary of the Navy Stephen Mallory: "General Lee advises the Government to withdraw from this city, and the officers will leave this evening accordingly." Mallory went on to inform Semmes that "unless otherwise directed by General Lee, upon you is devolved the duty of destroying your ships, this night, with all the forces under your command, [and to join] General Lee." Semmes decided to wait until night to fire the three ironclads and five wooden gunboats, but then he noticed "on the north side of the James, glowing with the fires of burning quarters, *materiel,* &c, lighted by our own troops . . . ! Concealment on my part was no longer necessary or indeed practical." The explosion that rocked the city the most, according to Semmes, was "the blowing up of the *Virginia II,* my late flag-ship. . . . Her shell-rooms had been full of loaded shells. . . . The explosion shook the houses in Richmond, and might have waked the echoes of the night for forty miles around."[42]

Emma Mordecai informed Edward Cohen that when she ventured out toward Broad Street, "the pavement was covered with plate glass from the fine doors & windows, reduced to powder by the explosions. . . . All stores were closed and the street *filthy.*" She went on to observe, "As I turned the corner of 9th Street from curb to curb was ankle deep with the fragments of Confederate printed blanks & other papers . . . Everything looked full of rubbish and disorder bespeaking ruin."[43]

Myrta Lockett Avary, whose husband served in Lee's army, noted that up until that fateful April day, most in Richmond possessed "a singular ignorance concerning our reverses around Petersburg." She admitted, "There were hunger and nakedness and death and pestilence and fire and sword everywhere," but she also contended that "we fugitives from shot and shell knew it well, but somehow we laughed and sang and . . . never believed in actual defeat and subjugation." Avary did admit, "As darkness came upon the city confusion and disorder increased. People were running around everywhere with plunder. . . . Barrels of liquor were broken open and the gutters ran with whiskey . . . There were plenty of staggering soldiers . . . who had too much whiskey, rough women had it plentifully, and many negroes were drunk."[44]

Avary also noted, "During the night detonations of exploding gunboats could be heard for miles, the noise and shock and lurid lights adding to the wretchedness of those within the city." She was more prescient than she knew when she pondered how the "advancing enemy" would "find Richmond, as Napoleon found Moscow, in ashes."[45]

British war correspondent Francis Lawley was equally appalled at what he witnessed:

Upon the edge of the roaring crackling flames, larcenous negroes, crazy Irishwomen, in a word all the dangerous classes of Richmond (many of them infuriated and made reckless by whiskey, of which hundreds of barrels had been emptied into the streets), danced and dived into cellars and into the open and undefended doors or warehouses, plying their search after plunder, with the howls of demoniacs. . . . Never might Prospero's words, "Hell is empty, and all its devils here," have been more appositely spoken. It was a scene unparalleled, I believe, even among the ghastly revelations of this war.[46]

At the Danville depot, Davis, his cabinet, and what records and baggage they could load were put on the train to Danville. At the station, Robert Lumpkin appeared, the notorious slave dealer in Richmond. His slave pens had been labelled "Hell's Half Acre." Out of the "iron-riveted door" of Lumpkin's pen "came a gang of slaves—fifty or more men, women, and children, with clanking chains." It was, correspondent Charles Carleton Coffin observed, "the last coffle of the Confederacy, the last vestige of its corner-stone, of the last institution for the preservation of which the war had been inaugurated." Chagrined there was no room on the train for him and his slaves, Lumpkin was forced to let those fifty slaves loose. Coffin concluded, "Those bodies and souls owned by Mr. Lumpkin would have commanded fifty thousand dollars in the market a few days before, but with the rising of to-morrow's sun they will not be worth a cent to him."[47]

Colonel E. P. Alexander, Lee's artillery chief, watched the Confederates march out of the city and saw the fires as mobs ransacked and pillaged local and government stores. The mob grew enraged when it discovered warehouses that were full of provisions while they—and Lee's army—starved. Alexander continued, "It was after sunset of a bright morning when from the Manchester high ground we turned to take our last look at the old city for which we had fought so long & so hard. It was a sad, a terrible & a solemn sight. I don't know that any moment in the whole war impressed me more deeply with all its stern realities than this." He noted, "The whole river front seemed to be in flames . . . & the black smoke spreading & hanging over the city seemed to be full of dreadful portents." Alexander sadly concluded, "I rode on with a distinctly heavy heart."[48]

Only the Tredegar Iron Works escaped the conflagration. From the beginning of the war, owner Joseph R. Anderson had formed the Tredegar Battalion with workers for the firm. As escapees from the penitentiary and other looters swarmed toward the Tredegar after torching the Confederate Armory, the battalion surrounded the works. As soon as the mob saw the armed cordon of Tredegar defenders, they withdrew.[49]

On the run but ever defiant, Jefferson Davis issued a proclamation to the people of the Confederate States. He admitted that General Lee had had to evacuate the city. But Davis saw an advantage: "Relieved from the necessity of guarding cities and particular points, important but not vital to our defense, with an army free to move . . . and strike in detail . . . the garrisons of the enemy, operating on the interior of our own country, where supplies are more accessible . . . nothing [sic] is now needed to render our triumph certain but the exhibition of our own unquenchable resolve." Davis went on to urge "my countrymen" not to "despond," but to "meet the foe with fresh defiance."[50]

The people of Richmond did not share Davis's optimism. On April 3, Mayor Joseph Mayo and other members of the Richmond City Council rode out to the New Market Road, where they met an advance party of Union cavalry attached to the Fourth Massachusetts. The mayor gave Major A. H. Stevens a piece of paper addressed to "the General Commanding the United States Army in front of Richmond." The message read: "General, The Army of the Confederate Government having abandoned the City of Richmond, I respectfully request that you will take possession of it with an organized force, to preserve order and protect women, children and property."[51] Major Stevens accepted the letter and promised Mayor Mayo he would hand carry it to Major General Godfrey Weitzel.

Mayor Mayo and the city council members who had accompanied him returned to Richmond and awaited the arrival of General Weitzel. The Union Twenty-Fourth Corps entered the burning city first. At approximately 8:15 a.m., Major General Weitzel accepted officially the surrender from Mayor Mayo at Richmond's city hall. After meeting with General Weitzel, Mayor Mayo noted that he and his compatriots had no idea how they would be received. Mayo wrote, "Nor could [the Federal officers] have received the instrument of submission with profounder courtesy. We went not knowing what we would encounter" but were relieved by the respect they received.[52]

Richmond Unionists greeted the arrival of Federal forces with jubilation. Chief among them was Elizabeth Van Lew, who had, especially during 1864 and 1865, supplied Federal generals with information about enemy movements. She welcomed a couple of escaped Federal prisoners of war from Castle Thunder into her home on April 2 as shells burst all around the city. "Amid all this turmoil," Van Lew recalled, "quietly, noiselessly, the Federal army entered the city. There were wild bursts of welcome from the negroes and many whites as they poured in. In an incredibly short space of time, as by magic, every part of our city was under the most kind and respectful of guards." She concluded, "Oh! Army of my country, how glorious was your welcome."[53]

People in the former capital of the Confederacy were in a state of shock. Mary Tucker Magill noted, "Upon the grass of [Capitol] [S]quare sat, lay or stood hundreds upon hundreds of human beings of all ages, sexes and ranks of life in the various attitudes of despondency. They were the homeless outcasts of the fire." Magill noted that, to add insult to injury, the Stars and Stripes were hoisted above the capitol and the Southern colors struck: "Above [Richmonders] waved and flapped the United States flag, the token of their defeat and humiliation, and around them the negro soldiers and the negroes of the city exulted and shouted over the triumphs of the day." Myrta Lockett Avary was similarly disconsolate. "Was it to this end we had fought and starved and gone naked and cold?" she asked. "To this end that the wives and children and many a dear and gallant friend were husbandless and fatherless? To this end that our homes were in ruins, our state devastated?" Undoubtedly, many others in the beleaguered city had the same thoughts.[54]

At Richmond's Chimborazo Hospital, matron Phoebe Yates Pember sent away all her nurses and, wrapped in a blanket, resolved to stay with her patients. She noted that as the explosions sounded and word that the Federals were approaching, "every man who could crawl had tried to escape a Northern prison. Beds in which paralyzed, rheumatic and helpless patients had laid for months were empty. The miracles of the New Testament had been re-enacted," stated Pember dryly. "The lame, the halt, and the blind had been cured."[55]

General Weitzel recalled that before his troops began the journey into the Confederate capital, he was awakened by a subordinate, who informed him that flames could be seen in the vicinity of Richmond. Shortly thereafter, Weitzel received a prisoner who informed him the Confederates had evacuated the city. He ordered rations to be distributed among the troops and the army to begin preparations to enter the city at dawn. According to Weitzel, "A sad sight met us on reaching Capitol Square. It was covered with women and children who had fled here to escape the fire." He went on to note, "Their poor faces were perfect pictures of utter despair. It was a sight that would have melted a heart of stone."[56]

The occupying Federals' first concern was putting out the fires that raged through the business section of the city. They were significantly hampered in that task because the prisoners who had broken out of the state penitentiary had "cut the hoses of some of the fire engines." As Weitzel's men battled the flames, they also attempted to restore some order in the tumultuous former Confederate capital: the Union general immediately declared martial law. Weitzel was struck at the irony of the scene: "Thus the rebel capitol [*sic*], fired by the men placed in it to defend it, was saved from total destruction by soldiers of the United States who had taken possession."[57]

Meanwhile, President Abraham Lincoln was aboard Admiral David Dixon Porter's flagship, *Malvern,* when he received news that Richmond had fallen. "'Thank God,' said the President, fervently, 'that I have lived to see this! It seems to me that I have been dreaming a horrid dream for four years, and now the nightmare is gone. I want to see Richmond.'"[58]

Undoubtedly concerned about the president's safety, Porter had to be extremely careful entering the James River because the Confederates had sunk mines and naval vessels to block the riverine approach to the city. The president's river escort slowly advanced up the James. It could not reach Rocketts Wharf, so the official party stopped on a sandbar near Seventeenth Street, where the president and his son Tad disembarked. The heat of the day, the dust, and the lingering fires, not to mention the hordes of newly freed African Americans who greeted Lincoln, made walking difficult. Admiral Porter recalled, "What an ovation [Lincoln] had, to be sure, from those so-called ignorant beings! They all had their souls in their eyes, and I don't think I ever looked upon a scene where there were so many passionately happy faces." Charles Carleton Coffin, a war correspondent for the *Boston Journal,* had journeyed to the late Confederate capital to report to his readers the scene on April 5. Astonished, he noted, "There was no committee of reception, no guard of honor, no grand display of troops. . . . Lincoln entered the city unheralded."[59]

Lincoln walked slowly toward the White House of the Confederacy at the corner of Twelfth Street and Clay Street, where General Weitzel had established his headquarters. The former slaves, thousands of them, cheered and cheered and strained to catch a glimpse of "Father Abraham." As African American Thomas Chester, news correspondent for the *Philadelphia Press,* described the scene, "The colored population was wild with enthusiasm. Old men thanked God in a very boisterous manner, and old women shouted upon the pavement as high as they had ever done at a religious revival."[60]

Most Richmonders whose homes had survived the conflagration stayed indoors to avoid the freedmen's jubilant actions. Irish visitor Thomas Conolly wrote to a friend, "The scene was terrific[.] [T]he Yankees advancing on &

the whole city apparently in flames. It reminded me of the burning of Moscow." J. B. Jones noted, "The cheers that greeted President Lincoln were mostly from the negroes and Federals comprising the great mass of humanity. The white citizens felt annoyed that the city should be held mostly by negro troops. If this measure were not unavoidable, it was impolitic if conciliation be the purpose." One individual who was especially bitter was Mary Custis Lee, wife of General Lee. She wrote to a distant cousin, "I wish you could have witnessed Lincoln's triumphal entry into Richmond. He was surrounded by a crowd of blacks, whooping & cheering like so many demons[.] [T]here was not a single respectable person to be seen." She was especially disgusted to see a "Yankee woman" waving her "kerchief" in triumph from the Spotswood Hotel. Mary concluded by writing, "We must submit to the will of Heaven but this is a bitter pill for the South to swallow."[61]

The route Lincoln took to the capitol was a symbolic one: as the party moved up Franklin Street, they traversed through the heart of Richmond's slave pens and slave auction houses.[62] Lincoln eventually arrived at the Confederate White House and sat in a chair in Jefferson Davis's reception room. After Weitzel arrived, Lincoln was informed that Judge John A. Campbell and General Joseph R. Anderson requested a meeting with the Union's commander in chief. According to Weitzel, "Mr. Lincoln insisted that he could not treat with any rebels until they had laid down their arms and surrendered." There was a brief discussion regarding allowing the Virginia legislature to meet, but that proposal was quickly dismissed. Weitzel then took Lincoln to visit Libby Prison, where Union prisoners of war had been incarcerated but which now housed captured Confederates. Weitzel "had considerable conversation with him in regard to the treatment of the conquered people." According to Weitzel, "The pith of [the president's] answer was that he did not wish to give me any orders on that subject," but as the general noted, Lincoln advised, "If I were in your place, I'd let 'em up easy—let 'em up easy."[63]

Abraham Lincoln was not the only Northerner to visit the former rebel capital. Numerous reporters, Union officials, and others flocked to Richmond to see the city the Union had struggled to capture for four years. Secretary of War Edwin Stanton appointed Assistant Secretary of War Charles A. Dana to be a special commissioner to Grant's army. Stanton ordered Dana to report to him on the situation in Richmond. Dana arrived on April 5 and was quite surprised by what he saw. "The Confederates in retreating," Dana wrote, "had set fire, and the damage done in that way was enormous;

nearly everything between Main Street and the river, for almost three quarters of a mile, was burned." Dana met with General Weitzel, who relayed that Mayor Mayo had surrendered the city. Dana went on to observe, "There was much suffering and poverty among the population, the rich as well as the poor being destitute of food. Weitzel had decided to issue supplies to all who would take the [loyalty] oath."[64]

Another account came from the pen of J. T. Trowbridge, who traveled from Fredericksburg to Richmond and was struck by how desolate the countryside was. As the train approached the outskirts of the city, he remarked, "And is this indeed Richmond into which the train glides so smoothly? Is this the fort-encircled capital whose gates refused so long to open to our armies?" Trowbridge was surprised by how small the former Confederate capital seemed to be. He encountered a local who was disgusted at what the retreating Confederates had done to the city. Trowbridge asked the gentleman why the locals had torched the place. "The devil only knows," he replied. "It was spite, I reckon. If they couldn't hold the city, they determined nobody else should. They kept us here four years under the worst tyranny under the sun; then when they found they couldn't keep us any longer, they just meant to burn us up."[65]

Perhaps one of the richest accounts of Richmond after the evacuation was George Alfred Townsend's report of what he discovered upon arriving in the former Confederate capital. Townsend arrived by boat at Rocketts Wharf. "A few minutes' walk," he recounted, "and we tread the pavements of the capital. . . . [T]here is no sound of life, but the stillness of a catacomb, only as our footsteps fall dull on the deserted sidewalk, and a funeral troop of echoes bump their elfin heads against the dead walls and closed shutters in reply. 'And this is Richmond,' says a melancholy voice. 'And this is Richmond.'" Townsend proceeded to survey the city. "We are under the shadow of ruins," he wrote. "A white smoke-wreath rising occasionally, enwraps a shattered wall as in a shroud." Everywhere, according to Townsend, there were "huge piles of debris." He concluded, "We are among the ruins of half a city. The wreck, the loneliness, seem interminable."[66]

Amid all this devastation was the reality that the whole population was poverty-stricken. Emma Mordecai noted in her diary, "The state of destitution to which the greater part of all classes in Richmond is reduced is almost unprecedented." Samuel Mordecai wrote to his brother George, "I live for the day and by the day, leaving the future and all its events in His hands without care or conjecture." Edmund Myers reported to a friend that business was gradually returning to the capital city, but much work still needed to be done. All were not as sanguine as these locals. Thomas Chester noted that Richmond's women in particular seemed defiant, some refusing to walk under the Union flags that flew everywhere. "This is but one of the little meannesses in which these rebels indulge, by which they comfort the spirits of treason." Chester went on to observe, "One thing is evident, that it matters not how much enmity these people bear against the Government . . . [for] they do not hesitate to draw rations from the [Union] commissary."[67]

As Sallie Putnam noticed, once the Federals occupied Richmond, "all tidings from our friends in the Confederate army were as entirely cut off as though an ocean rolled between us and them." After Lee's army left the Petersburg defenses, it had headed west in the hopes of reaching Lynchburg and then linking up with General Joseph Johnston in a last-ditch effort to defeat Sherman in North Carolina and then turning to the threat that Grant's army posed in Virginia. A week after the evacuation, Putnam and others in Richmond heard the sound of heavy artillery. As Putnam, noted, "It boded no good to us." She went on, "Soon from lip to lip ran the dreadful intelligence: 'General Lee has surrendered!'"[68]

Thomas Chester and the occupying Union army responded quite differently, as was to be expected. According to Chester, early on April 10 "the loyal hearts of Richmond pulsated with fear, in consequence of the heavy firing of artillery which was thundering around the city. They supposed that Lee, in accordance with the wishes of the rebels here, was making an effort to recapture this citadel of treason." Quite the contrary was the case, as Chester noted: "It was salute after salute over the good news that *Lee had surrendered*. . . . It was the funeral service over a God-forsaken Confederacy."[69]

In many respects, the *Richmond Examiner*'s editorial, published several weeks before the city was evacuated and occupied by Federal troops, captured the essence of what the Confederate capital represented to the South: "The evacuation of Richmond would be the loss of all respect and authority towards the Confederate Government, the disintegration of the army, and the abandonment of the scheme of an independent Southern Confederation. Each contestant in the war has made Richmond the central object of all its plans and all its exertions. It has become the symbol of the Confederacy. Its loss would be material ruin to the cause, and in a moral point of view, absolutely destructive, crushing the heart and extinguishing the last hope of the country."[70]

The end of the war in Virginia presented Richmond with daunting challenges. Its business district was a charred, burned-out ruin. Its labor system had been totally destroyed. Former slaves, free people of color, refugees, and locals were cast adrift. Then the city received word that President Lincoln, who had visited Richmond just days earlier, was dead, a victim of John Wilkes Booth's derringer. The vice president, Andrew Johnson, had sworn to punish the Southern traitors who supported the Confederacy, and Union troops continued to patrol Richmond's streets. Many prominent citizens, anxious to protect what property they had salvaged or that had escaped the evacuation fires, were taking the oath of allegiance to the United States. Finally, Northern teachers and administrators of the newly formed Bureau of Freedmen and Refugees arrived in the former Confederate capital to assist the freedmen in garnering employment contracts and establishing schools.

As early as April 20, 1865, a Freedmen's Bureau teacher was writing to a colleague that she and her sister "formally opened school in the 1st African Church. . . . We had more than one thousand children . . . and seventy-five adults." She noted that the number of teachers was far too small to instruct the children and adults who flocked to the church to be schooled. Others who visited Richmond were struck by how literate and industrious the freedmen were.[71]

Many curious people descended on the former capital of the Confederacy and were struck that the burned district was still dominated by its "toppling walls, forlorn-looking chimneys, heaps of bricks, with here and there a ruined safe lying in the midst, warped . . . from the effects of the intense heat." These individuals also saw that the vast majority of people left in the city, both white and black, were destitute and that the problem was so severe "the military authorities have divided the city into districts." The occupying Union army was sending soldiers door to door to ascertain the locals' needs.[72]

This was the situation after four long years of war that had tested the people of Richmond and its refugees as never before. The city had become the very essence of the Confederacy. But when it fell on April 2, 1865, the Confederate dream of independence became a nightmare of burned-out dwellings, worthless money, and empty chairs where loved ones had once relaxed. The end also ushered in a world alien to most whites: their "servants" were now free and working assiduously to create their own new order. It remained to be seen if the once-proud city on the James would regain its lofty stature among Southern cities.

Epilogue

"The Smoking Ruins"

On April 9, 1865, General Robert E. Lee met General Ulysses S. Grant at Appomattox Court House to surrender what remained of the Army of Northern Virginia. As he returned to his men after signing the surrender document, he was approached by many of his soldiers. Lee's artillery chief, E. Porter Alexander, recorded that "he told the men in a few words that he had done his best for them & advised them to go home & become good citizens as they had been soldiers." Alexander noted that as Lee addressed his soldiers, "a wave of emotion seemed to strike the crowd & a great many men were weeping & many pressed to shake his hand & to try & express in some way the feelings which shook every heart."[1]

Shortly thereafter, Lee left General John B. Gordon to handle the details of the formal surrender on April 12, and he began the trip back to Richmond; his wife, Mary, confined to a wheelchair, had stayed in the capital as its residents burned the city around her. Accompanied by various members of his staff, including his sons, W. H. F. "Rooney" and Custis Lee, the general approached Richmond from the Manchester side. He was undoubtedly unprepared for the sight that greeted him as he crossed the James on a hastily constructed pontoon bridge. The city was still smoldering from the evacuation fires, and debris littered the streets. As Lee's eminent biographer, Douglas Southall Freeman, writes, "The streets that had shown the proudest bustle in the days of the Confederacy now were mere tracks amid debris that had been hastily pushed back to the sidewalk to afford a passageway."[2]

Lee had hoped to return to his family quietly, but, according to Sallie Brock Putnam, rumors that he was approaching traveled "quickly through the city." The crowd swelled and included both paroled Confederates and the Union occupiers. Cheers went up spontaneously. Putnam noted Lee

Richmond across the Canal Basin, capitol building in the distance, 1865.

raised his hat several times to those gathered, and "as he dismounted" outside 707 East Franklin Street, large numbers pressed around him and shook his hand warmly and sympathetically. "Disengaging himself," he bowed to the crowd "and passed into his house." As one historian has written, "For Robert E. Lee, the war was over."[3]

Sallie Putnam recorded that word of Lee's surrender spread slowly through the Old Dominion and other parts of the Confederacy. "Nor had the people of Richmond more than begun to digest the unwelcome truth," Putnam wrote, "when there came another startling piece of information to disturb the public mind." On April 16, word swept through Richmond that President Abraham Lincoln had been assassinated while attending a play at Ford's Theater in Washington. "The man," noted Putnam, "who so short a time before had trodden the streets of our subjugated capital, a conqueror, cut down by the hand of violence!"[4] Many in the city wondered what their fate would be under the new president, Andrew Johnson, for he had sworn revenge upon all traitors. For people in Richmond and elsewhere in the South, the future was very uncertain.

It was under this pall that the people of the former capital of the Confederacy struggled to rebuild their shattered city. One local noted, "Several months have elapsed since the close of the war, and Richmond is but beginning to breathe again after the long paralysis which succeeded its final scenes." This woman was struck by the reality that "sickly odors are still ascending from the ruins, and where the foundations of houses were dug deepest a sullen cloud of smoke still rises from smoldering fires, [which] continue with a strange pertinacity to live on without food to sustain them."[5] Would Richmond rise from the ashes like the proverbial phoenix? Could it return to being the former Confederacy's industrial backbone? This was surely a daunting task for city leaders to confront in the uncertain days following the assassination of the president. Like the late war, Reconstruction would challenge the former capital of the Confederate States of America.

Acknowledgments

Anyone who writes a book incurs enormous debts. I am no exception, but my concern is I may neglect or omit someone because so many individuals and institutions made this book possible.

Perhaps my greatest debt is to the University Press of Kentucky. Not only have the press staff been encouraging and enthusiastic about this project, but they have also been extraordinarily patient. Professional obligations and personal issues derailed this manuscript on more than one occasion. But the press stood behind me. Special thanks go to senior acquisitions editor Anne Dean Dotson. My copyeditor, Annie Barva, and senior editing supervisor Ila McEntire also deserve my thanks for all their assistance.

My outside peer reviewers crafted comments, suggestions, and criticisms that substantially improved the final manuscript. Two of my reviewers identified themselves to me: Emory M. Thomas and Michael D. Gorman. My thanks to them for taking the time to provide such good input. The anonymous third reviewer also offered significant suggestions. I have tried to answer all their queries.

The respective staffs at the various archives I visited proved once again that they are the researcher's key ally. The Virginia Historical Society granted me several Mellon fellowships that allowed me to conduct research there. Frances Pollard and E. Lee Shephard deserve special thanks for informing me about collections that would be critical to this book. At the Library of Virginia, Brent Tarter, John Kneebone, and Gregg Kimball alerted me to collections I should review. Gregg even gave me copies of some primary work he had done for his splendid book *American City, Southern Place.* Teresa Roane, who at that time was at the Valentine Museum, helped me find important photographic images as well as manuscript collections. Finally, close to the Valentine was the Museum of the Confederacy's Eleanor Brockenbrough Library. As always, John Coski answered my countless queries about documents, certain collections, and the like. Because of all these people and archives, I was able to gain a much better insight into the people and events that affected the Confederacy's capital city for four years.

I also conducted research in the Earl Swem Library at the College of William and Mary. While I was there, the collections had been relocated to a warehouse, so to speak, while the library was being renovated. Nonetheless, the staff there effortlessly located all the manuscripts I asked to see. At the Perkins Library at Duke University and the Henry L. Huntington Library in San Marino, California, I was accorded similar assistance and worked in beautiful settings.

No Southern or Civil War historian can conduct research without engaging the Southern Historical Collection at the University of North Carolina at Chapel Hill. The archivists there never ceased to amaze me with their efficiency and suggestions concerning other collections.

The photographs in this book are courtesy of the Virginia Museum of History and Culture, the Valentine Museum, and the Library of Congress. Special thanks go to Graham Dozier of the Virginia Historical Society and Kelly Kerney of the Valentine for their assistance. I am also indebted to Richard Gilbreath, who fashioned the maps for 1860, 1862 and 1864, and to Mark Adams of Old South Art.

At the United States Naval Academy, a semester sabbatical from teaching and service commitments allowed me to concentrate on completing my research. The Nimitz Inter-Library Loan staff there tracked down all my requests, no matter how old or obscure the work was. My colleagues in the History Department were and continue to be supportive of my scholarly work. Parts of the manuscript were presented to the department's Works-in-Progress Seminar. There, I was queried and challenged and forced to recast certain arguments. Particular colleagues at the seminar deserve special mention for their critical insights: Tom Brennan, Nancy Ellenberger, Fred Harrod, Molly Lester, Kelcy Sagstetter, and Amanda Scott. Any errors in the manuscript are mine alone.

Like any historian of the nineteenth century, I was constantly stymied by technological issues. But once again two colleagues in the History Department bailed me out: Lee Pennington and Captain Bill Fouse of the U.S. Marine Corps. They patiently helped this dinosaur realize that scanning, pdf files, and jpgs are our friends.

Fortunately, the United States Naval Academy Information Technology Division and its director, Lou Giannotti, ensured I had everything I needed technologically, both at the Academy and at the various archives I visited, to do my work. Both he and Julie O'Dell Bloom assisted me in conducting Academy business with laptops, modems, and the Google cloud.

Janet Lauder was instrumental in helping me with the copyediting process.

Without family and friends I would have given up long ago. K. J. and Nancy Shults and Libby Krakow deserve special mention for all their love and support. My parents did not live to see this work in print, but they certainly heard a great deal about Confederate Richmond. I dedicate this book to them, Joseph and Alexandra DeCredico, as well as to the memory of my favorite Richmonder, my cousin Martha Reynolds Belk.

Soli Deo Gloria.

Notes

Abbreviations

Duke   Duke University Special Collections, William R. Perkins Library, Durham, N.C.

LVA   Library of Virginia, Richmond

MOC   Museum of the Confederacy, Eleanor S. Brockenbrough Library, Richmond, Va.

OR   U.S. War Department, *The War of Rebellion: Official Records of the Union and Confederate Armies* (Washington D.C.: U.S. Government Printing Office, 1880–1901)

SHC   Southern Historical Collection, University of North Carolina at Chapel Hill

VHS   Virginia Historical Society, Richmond, Va.

W&M   College of William and Mary, Manuscripts and Rare Books Department, Earl Gregg Swem Library, Williamsburg, Va.

Prologue

1. *Richmond Whig,* evening ed., April 7, 1865. See also Edward Pollard, *The Lost Cause: The Standard Southern History of the War of the Confederates* (1867; reprint, New York: Books for Libraries, 1970), 127.

2. U.S. Bureau of the Census, *Population of the United States in 1860 Compiled from the Original Returns of the Eighth Census* (Washington, D.C.: U.S. Government Printing Office, 1864).

3. For a full discussion on the party politics in the 1850s and how the Upper South differed, see Michael F. Holt, *The Political Crisis of the 1850s* (New York: Wiley, 1978), and William J. Cooper, *We Have the War Upon Us: The Onset of the Civil War, November 1860–April 1861* (New York: Knopf, 2012).

4. *Richmond Daily Dispatch,* June 18, 1864.

1. From the City on the James to Confederate Capital

1. Alfred Paul to "Thouvenel," March 9, 1861, Alfred Paul Papers, Library of Virginia (LVA), Richmond; Sallie A. Brock Putnam, *Richmond during the War:*

Four Years of Personal Observation by a Richmond Lady (1867; reprint, Lincoln: University of Nebraska Press, 1996), 17.

2. J. B. Jones, *A Rebel War Clerk's Diary,* 2 vols. (1866; reprint, Ann Arbor: Michigan Historical Reprint Series, n.d.), 1:15.

3. Jones, *A Rebel War Clerk's Diary,* 1:19–20.

4. *Richmond Enquirer,* April 16, 1861; see also Charles B. Dew, *Ironmaker to the Confederacy: Joseph Reid Anderson and the Tredegar Iron Works* (New Haven, Conn.: Yale University Press, 1966), 83–84.

5. Unidentified Richmond woman's diary, April 15, 1861, Valentine Museum, Richmond, Va.

6. Sara (Mrs. Roger A.) Pryor, *Reminiscences of Peace and War* (New York: McMillan, 1940), April 16–17, 1861, 122–23; William A. Link, *Roots of Secession: Slavery and Politics in Antebellum Virginia* (Chapel Hill: University of North Carolina Press, 2003), 240–41.

7. Putnam, *Richmond during the War,* 21, 22; Robert A. Graniss Diary, April 18, 1861, Virginia Historical Society (VHS), Richmond; Tucker Randolph Journal, April 19, 1861, Southern Women History Collection, Museum of the Confederacy (MOC), Eleanor S. Brockenbrough Library, Richmond, Va.; Jones, *A Rebel War Clerk's Diary,* 1:24. See also Samuella Hurt Curd Diary, April 16, 1861, VHS; Richard Eppes Diary, April 18, 1861, VHS; unidentified Richmond woman's diary, April 18, 1861, Valentine Museum.

8. Botts quoted in Link, *Roots of Secession,* 221; Van Lew quoted in Elizabeth R. Varon, *Southern Lady, Yankee Spy: The True Story of Elizabeth Van Lew, a Union Agent in the Heart of the Confederacy* (New York: Oxford University Press, 2003), 51.

9. Gregg D. Kimball, *American City, Southern Place: A Cultural History of Antebellum Richmond* (Athens: University of Georgia Press, 2000), 4.

10. *Richmond Daily Dispatch,* July 28, 1853, quoted in David R. Goldfield, *Urban Growth in an Age of Sectionalism: Virginia, 1847–1861* (Baton Rouge: Louisiana State University Press, 1977), 2–6, 26–27.

11. Wise quoted in *Richmond Daily Dispatch,* July 7, 1858.

12. Goldfield, *Urban Growth,* 224.

13. Michael B. Chesson, *Richmond after the War, 1865–1890* (Richmond: Virginia State Library, 1981), 5; Henry T. Shanks, *The Secession Movement in Virginia, 1847–1861* (1934; reprint, Richmond, Va.: Garrett and Massie, 1971), 1–3.

14. Samuel Mordecai, *Richmond in By-Gone Days* (1856; reprint, New York: Arno Press, 1975), 297–301.

15. Goldfield, *Urban Growth,* 192–93; U.S. Bureau of the Census, *The Eighth Census of the United States, 1860* (Washington, D.C.: U.S. Government Printing Office, 1865), manufacturing schedule, clxxx; Chesson, *Richmond after the War,* 8–9.

16. Quoted in Goldfield, *Urban Growth,* 194.

17. The definitive work on Anderson and the Tredegar Iron Works is Dew, *Ironmaker to the Confederacy;* see esp. 10–17.

18. See Richmond Manufacturing Census, 1840 and 1860, LVA, cited in Midori Takagi, *"Rearing Wolves to Our Own Destruction": Slavery in Richmond, Virginia, 1782–1865* (Charlottesville: University Press of Virginia, 1999), 159; Ira Berlin and Herbert G. Gutman, "Natives and Immigrants, Free Men and Slaves: Urban Workingmen in the Antebellum American South," *American Historical Review* 88 (December 1983): 1182; Takagi, *"Rearing Wolves to Our Own Destruction,"* 71–74.

19. Takagi, *"Rearing Wolves to Our Own Destruction,"* 74.

20. Kimball, *American City, Southern Place,* 181–82; Link, *Roots of Secession,* 82–89.

21. Dew, *Ironmaker to the Confederacy,* 23–25; Takagi, *"Rearing Wolves to Our Own Destruction,"* 82–83; Claudia Dale Goldin, *Urban Slavery in the American South, 1820–1860: A Quantitative History* (Chicago: University of Chicago Press, 1976), 28–30; Kathleen Bruce, *Virginia Iron Manufacture in the Slave Era* (New York: Kelly, 1968), 237, 309. Goldin also notes that white laborers in the city were equally resistant to the employment of free blacks (*Urban Slavery in the American South,* 30–31).

22. Takagi, *"Rearing Wolves to Our Own Destruction,"* 96–103, 115, 123.

23. Robert Russell, *North America: Its Agriculture and Climate* (Edinburgh: Black, 1857), 157; Michael Tadman, *Speculators and Slaves: Masters, Traders, and Slaves in the Old South* (Madison: University of Wisconsin Press, 1989), 5.

24. *Richmond Daily Dispatch,* January 3, 1853; see also Takagi, *"Rearing Wolves to Our Own Destruction,"* 77–78.

25. Frederic Bancroft, *Slave Trading in the Old South* (Baltimore: Furst, 1931), 96; John S. Wise, *The End of an Era* (Boston: Houghton, Mifflin, 1899), 58.

26. Wise, *The End of an Era,* 80–81, 85–86.

27. Marie Tyler-McGraw, *At the Falls: Richmond, Virginia, and Its People* (Chapel Hill: University of North Carolina Press for the Valentine Museum of the Life and History of Richmond, 1994), 114; Virginius Dabney, *Richmond, the Story of a City* (Garden City, N.Y.: Doubleday, 1976), 153; Kimball, *American City, Southern Place,* 74–75; Goldfield, *Urban Growth,* 197–201.

28. David R. Goldfield, *Cotton Fields and Skyscrapers: Southern City and Region, 1607–1980* (Baton Rouge: Louisiana State University Press, 1982), 28–35. See also Eugene Genovese, *The Political Economy of Slavery: Studies in the Economy and Society of the Slave South* (New York: Vintage Books Edition, 1967), 16–25. In *New Men, New Cities, New South: Atlanta, Nashville, Charleston, Mobile, 1860–1910* (Chapel Hill: University of North Carolina Press, 1990), Don H. Doyle argues a slightly different view. He sees active entrepreneurs in the Southern interior from secession through war and the rise of the New South.

29. James M. McPherson, *Battle Cry of Freedom: The Civil War Era* (New York: Oxford University Press, 1988), 9; Gavin Wright, *The Political Economy of the Cotton South: Households, Markets, and Wealth in the Nineteenth Century* (New York: Norton, 1978), 110; Don Dodd and Wynelle Dodd, *Historical Statistics of the South, 1790–1970* (Tuscaloosa: University of Alabama Press, 1978), 58.

30. Link, *Roots of Secession,* 122–23.

31. Ibid., 163.

32. Vicki Vaughn Johnson, *The Men and the Vision of the Southern Commercial Conventions, 1845–1871* (Columbia: University of Missouri Press, 1992), 129–31.

33. Roger A. Pryor, quoted in Goldfield, *Urban Growth,* 245.

34. Goldfield, *Urban Growth,* 236–37.

35. Link, *Roots of Secession,* 180–82, 195, 209–10; Shanks, *The Secession Movement in Virginia,* 93–96.

36. Daniel W. Crofts, *Reluctant Confederates: Upper South Unionists in the Secession Crisis* (Chapel Hill: University of North Carolina Press, 1989), 75–81; Link, *Roots of Secession.*

37. The popular vote for president in the Old Dominion in 1860 was: Bell, 74, 681; Breckinridge, 74, 323; Douglas, 16,290; and Lincoln, 1,929. Lincoln was strongest in the Wheeling area. See Charles Henry Ambler, *Sectionalism in Virginia from 1776 to 1861* (1910; reprint, New York: Russell & Russell, 1964), 330.

38. Paul to Thouvenel, December 8, 1860, Paul Papers, LVA; Eppes Diary, November 11, 1860, VHS.

39. *Richmond Daily Dispatch,* November 8, 1860; *Richmond Enquirer,* November 10, 1861, quoted in Shanks, *The Secession Movement in Virginia,* 120–21, emphasis in original.

40. Graniss Diary, December 28, 1860, VHS; Eppes Diary, December 12, 1860, VHS.

41. James A. Riddick to William Gray, November 27, 1860, William Gray Papers, VHS.

42. Michael F. Holt's book *The Political Crisis of the 1850s* offers the most thorough discussion of the difference in politics between the Deep South and the border South.

43. See Eppes Diary, February 4, 1861, VHS; Paul to Thouvenel, January 18 and 26, 1861, Paul Papers, LVA; P. Pegram to Powhatan Ellis, February 25, 1861, Ellis Family Papers, VHS; Curd Diary, February 19, 1861, VHS.

44. Link, *Roots of Secession,* 222–23.

45. Emory M. Thomas has argued this most effectively in *The Confederacy as a Revolutionary Experience* (1971; reprint, Columbia: University of South Carolina Press, 1991), and *The Confederate Nation, 1861–1865* (New York: Harper Torchbooks, 1979).

46. Abraham Lincoln, Inaugural Address, March 4, 1861, in *The Collected Works of Abraham Lincoln,* 8 vols., ed. Roy P. Basler (New Brunswick, N.J.: Rutgers University Press, 1953), 4:271, emphasis in original; Graniss Diary, March 14 and April 2, 1861, VHS. See also Paul to Thouvenel, March 9, 1861, Paul Papers, LVA; Henry Pelouze to Jennie Pelouze, March 17, 1861, Henry Lafayette Pelouze Papers, Duke University Special Collections (hereafter Duke), William R. Perkins Library, Durham, N.C.; Eppes Diary, March 1, 1861, VHS.

47. Link, *Roots of Secession*, 228–29, 233, 241; Shanks, *The Secession Movement in Virginia*, 139–41, 142–43, 145, 171.

48. Randolph Journal, April 9, 1861, MOC.

49. Mary Chesnut, *Mary Chesnut's Civil War*, edited by C. Vann Woodward (New Haven, Conn.: Yale University Press, 1981), April 12, 1861, 45–47.

50. Curd Diary, April 13, 1861, VHS; Putnam, *Richmond during the War*, 17; Randolph Diary, April 13, 1861, MOC. See also Henry Pelouze to Jennie Pelouze, April 14, 1861, Duke, and unidentified Richmond woman's diary, April 13, 1861, Valentine Museum.

51. James C. Chesnut Jr. was one who boasted, "The man most averse to Southern blood might safely drink every drop shed in establishing a Southern Confederacy" (quoted in W. A. Swanburg, *First Blood: The Story of Fort Sumter* [New York: Scribner's, 1957], 16).

52. Chesnut, *Mary Chesnut's Civil War*, June 21, 1861, 83.

53. Unidentified Richmond woman's diary, April 22, 1861, Valentine Museum; Randolph Journal, April 21, 1861, MOC. See also Putnam, *Richmond during the War*, 25–26, and T. C. DeLeon, *Four Years in Rebel Capitals: An Inside View of Life in the Southern Confederacy, from Birth to Death; from Original Notes, Collected in the Years 1861 to 1865* (Mobile, Ala.: Gossip Printing, 1892), 103–4.

54. Clifford Dowdey and Louis H. Manarin, introduction to chapter 1 in Robert E. Lee, *The Wartime Papers of Robert E. Lee*, ed. Clifford Dowdey and Louis H. Manarin (Boston: Little, Brown, 1961), 3–8 (Lee's resignation was sent to Secretary of War Simon Cameron on April 20, 1861; see page 9 for that letter); Douglas Southall Freeman, *R. E. Lee*, 4 vols. (New York: Scribner's, 1934), 1:461.

55. Louis H. Manarin, ed., *Richmond at War: The Minutes of the City Council, 1861–1865* (Chapel Hill: University of North Carolina Press, 1966), May 9, 1861, 35.

56. Robert E. Lee to Colonel Andrew Talcott, April 29, 1861, in *The Wartime Papers of Robert E. Lee*, 14; Freeman, *R. E. Lee*, 1:474–90.

57. Dowdey and Manarin, introduction to Lee, *The Wartime Papers of Robert E. Lee*, 5–6.

58. Robert E. Lee to Governor John Letcher, June 14, 1861, in *The Wartime Papers of Robert E. Lee*, 50.

59. Manarin, ed., *Richmond at War*, July 8, 1861, 58–59.

60. Henry Cleveland, *Alexander H. Stephens, in Public and Private: With Letters and Speeches before, during, and since the War* (Philadelphia: National Publishing, 1866), quoted in Thomas, *The Confederate Nation*, 13; *Richmond Enquirer*, May 3, 1861; Manarin, ed., *Richmond at War*, 40; *Richmond Daily Dispatch*, "Arrival of President Davis," May 30, 1861. William C. Davis presents a detailed discussion of the jockeying to relocate the capital in *"A Government of Our Own": The Making of the Confederacy* (New York: Free Press, 1994), 388–91.

61. DeLeon, *Four Years in Rebel Capitals*, 104; Edmund Ruffin, *The Diary of Edmund Ruffin*, 3 vols., ed. William Kauffman Scarborough (Baton Rouge: Louisiana State University Press, 1972), May 2, 1861, 2:16.

62. Varina Davis, *Jefferson Davis: A Memoir by His Wife,* 2 vols. (1890; reprint, Baltimore: Nautical & Aviation, 1990), 2:86; Edward Porter Alexander, *Fighting for the Confederacy: The Personal Recollections of General Edward Porter Alexander,* ed. Gary W. Gallagher (Chapel Hill: University of North Carolina Press, 1989), 37; Judith W. McGuire, *Diary of a Southern Refugee during the War by a Lady of Virginia* (1867; reprint, Lincoln: University of Nebraska Press, 1996), June 6, 1861, 26.

63. Putnam, *Richmond during the War,* 27; John Gottfried Lange Memoirs, VHS.

64. DeLeon, *Four Years in Rebel Capitals,* 86, 87; T. C. DeLeon, *Belles, Beaux, and Brains of the '60s* (New York: Dillingham, 1907), 99, 59–60, italics in the original.

65. V. Davis, *Jefferson Davis,* 2:202–3. See also Mrs. Burton Harrison (Constance Cary), *Recollections Grave and Gay* (New York: Scribner's, 1911), 127; Varina Davis, "Our New Home," in *Heroines of Dixie: Confederate Women Tell Their Story of the War,* ed. Katherine M. Jones (Indianapolis, Ind.: Bobbs-Merrill, 1955), 68; DeLeon, *Belles, Beaux, and Brains of the '60s,* 66–67; unidentified Richmond woman's diary, May 31, 1861, Valentine Museum. Some of the best accounts of entertaining at the Confederate White House can be found in Chesnut, *Mary Chesnut's Civil War.*

66. DeLeon, *Belles, Beaux, and Brains of the '60s,* 136–39.

67. Putnam, *Richmond during the War,* 34.

68. *Richmond Daily Dispatch,* June 26, 1861.

69. Putnam, *Richmond during the War,* 78–79, 81; Kate Pleasants Minor Memoir, Kate Pleasants Minor Papers, Southern Women History Collection, MOC; DeLeon, *Four Years in Rebel Capitals,* 269–70. See also Eppes Diary, May 13, 1861, VHS.

70. *Richmond Examiner,* November 11, 1861.

71. Bell Irvin Wiley, *The Life of Johnny Reb: The Common Soldier of the Confederacy* (1943; reprint, Baton Rouge: Louisiana State University Press, 1994), 53–54; *Richmond Daily Dispatch,* May 6, 1862, quoted in Wiley, *The Life of Johnny Reb,* 53–54. Wiley notes that little is known about prostitution in the camps, towns, and cities largely because the subject was considered taboo. Private letters and medical records corroborate that it was a problem. See also *Richmond Daily Dispatch,* June 20, 1861, and the website Civil War Richmond at https://www.civil warrichmond.com.

72. *Richmond Whig,* July 9, 1861.

73. See Douglas Southall Freeman, *Lee's Lieutenants: A Study in Command,* 3 vols. (New York: Scribner's, 1942–1944), 1:17–19; also unidentified Richmond woman's diary, June 10, 1861, Valentine Museum.

74. A good, succinct account of the battle can be found in McPherson, *Battle Cry of Freedom,* 335–48. For a full-length account, see William C. Davis, *Battle at Bull Run: A History of the First Major Campaign of the Civil War* (Baton Rouge: Louisiana State University Press, 1981).

75. McGuire, *Diary of a Southern Refugee,* July 30, 1861, 46.

76. William C. Davis, *Jefferson Davis: The Man and His Hour, a Biography* (New York: HarperCollins, 1991), 351; General Joseph E. Johnston, "Responsibilities of the First Bull Run," in *Battles & Leaders of the Civil War,* 4 vols., ed. Robert Underwood Johnson and Clarence Clough Buel (New York: Century, 1884–1888), 1:252.

77. DeLeon, *Four Years in Rebel Capitals,* 143; Putnam, *Richmond during the War,* 63. See also Jones, *A Rebel War Clerk's Diary,* 1:64–65.

78. Putnam, *Richmond during the War,* 63; DeLeon, *Four Years in Rebel Capitals,* 147.

79. DeLeon, *Four Years in Rebel Capitals,* 149–50; Putnam, *Richmond during the War,* 65; McPherson, *Battle Cry of Freedom,* 347. McPherson correctly notes that exact Civil War casualties remain in doubt because of incomplete records and reports.

80. Putnam, *Richmond during the War,* 65, 68; unidentified Richmond woman's diary, July 26, 1861, Valentine Museum; Thomas, *The Confederate State of Richmond,* 54–56.

81. Jones, *A Rebel War Clerk's Diary,* 1:66; *Richmond Whig,* quoted in Allan Nevins, *The War for the Union,* vol. 1: *The Improvised War* (New York: Scribner's, 1959–1971), 221.

82. Chesnut, *Mary Chesnut's Civil War,* July 24, 1861, 111; DeLeon, *Four Years in Rebel Capitals,* 159.

83. Manarin, ed., *Richmond at War,* September 9, November 4, and December 9, 1861, also June 5 and April 26, 1861, 70, 78–79, 91–92, 44, 33.

84. St. Paul's Episcopal Church Vestry Book, Fall 1861, VHS.

85. Putnam, *Richmond during the War,* 89.

86. DeLeon, *Four Years in Rebel Capitals,* 172–73.

2. The Campaigns of 1862

1. Maria Clopton to "My Dear Child," February 18, 1862, Maria G. Clopton Papers, MOC; unidentified Richmond woman's diary, February 22, 1862, Valentine Museum; Thomas Rutherfoord Diary, February 22, 1862, Rutherfoord Family Papers, VHS; *Richmond Daily Dispatch,* February 24, 1862; Pollard, *The Lost Cause,* 215.

2. Harrison, *Recollections Grave and Gay,* 68–69; DeLeon, *Four Years in Rebel Capitals,* 188–89; Ruffin, *The Diary of Edmund Ruffin,* 2:241; Jefferson Davis, Inaugural Address, February 22, 1861, in *Jefferson Davis, Constitutionalist: His Letters, Papers, and Speeches,* 10 vols., ed. Dunbar Rowland (1923; reprint, New York: AMS Press for the Mississippi Department of Archives and History, 1973), 5:200.

3. George W. Bagby Diary, March 12, 1862, George William Bagby Papers, 1828–1917, VHS; Maria Clopton to Mamie, March 7, 1862, Clopton Papers,

MOC; Catherine Cochran Diary, VHS; Chesnut, *Mary Chesnut's Civil War,* April 27, 1862, 330.

4. *Richmond Daily Dispatch,* February 25, 1862.

5. Emory M. Thomas, *The Confederate Nation, 1861–1865* (New York: Harper Torchbooks, 1979), 148. See also Jones, *A Rebel War Clerk's Diary,* 1:116.

6. Samuel Mordecai to George, March 1, 1862, George W. Mordecai Papers, Southern Historical Collection (SHC), University of North Carolina at Chapel Hill; Ruffin, *The Diary of Edmund Ruffin,* 2:246.

7. W. Asbury Christian, *Richmond: Her Past and Present* (Richmond, Va.: Jenkins, 1912), 238–39; Adelaide Clopton to Joyce, March 5, 1862, Clopton Family Papers, Duke; unidentified Richmond woman's diary, March 7, 1862, Valentine Museum; Ruffin, *The Diary of Edmund Ruffin,* March 3, 1862, 2:246; John Gottfried Lange Memoirs, VHS.

8. *Richmond Daily Dispatch,* May 13, 1862.

9. Thomas, *The Confederate Nation,* 154–55; unidentified Richmond woman's diary, March 7, 1862, Valentine Museum.

10. V. Davis, *Jefferson Davis,* 2:454.

11. Ibid., 2:454–55 (including the reference to Johnston).

12. Putnam, *Richmond during the War,* 100.

13. Ruffin, *The Diary of Edmund Ruffin,* 2:288; DeLeon, *Four Years in Rebel Capitals,* 197; Constance Cary Harrison, "Richmond Scenes in '62," in *Battles & Leaders of the Civil War,* ed. Underwood and Buel, 2:442; Putnam, *Richmond during the War,* 125.

14. M. H. Ellis to Powhatan Ellis, April 14, 1862, Ellis Family Papers, VHS; Phillip Whitlock Recollections, VHS; Jones, *A Rebel War Clerk's Diary,* May 23, 1862, 1:104; Putnam, *Richmond during the War,* 113; *Richmond Enquirer,* April 25, 1862; *Richmond Daily Dispatch,* March 24, 1862.

15. Stephen W. Sears, *To the Gates of Richmond: The Peninsula Campaign* (New York: Ticknor & Fields, 1992), 5–6.

16. Ruffin, *The Diary of Edmund Ruffin,* 2:252.

17. Sears, *To the Gates of Richmond,* 24, including quotation from McClellan.

18. Ibid., 46–48; Thomas, *The Confederate Nation,* 158–59; Joseph E. Johnston, *Narrative of Military Operations Directed during the Late War between the States,* Civil War Centennial series (1874; reprint, Bloomington: Indiana University Press, 1959), 119.

19. Caroline Kean Hill Davis Diary, April 5, 1862, VHS; unidentified Richmond woman's diary, April 9, 1862, Valentine Museum; letter by soldier quoted in Sears, *To the Gates of Richmond,*; Mary Taylor Diary, May 23, 1862, VHS.

20. Sears, *To the Gates of Richmond,* 14; Johnston, *Narrative of Military Operations,* 98–99, 102.

21. Maria Clopton to "Son," April 18, 1862, Clopton Family Papers, Duke. See also Sears, *To the Gates of Richmond,* 44, and Putnam, *Richmond during the War,* 39–40.

22. Manarin, ed., *Richmond at War*, April 30, 1862, 167; Bruce Levine, *Confederate Emancipation: Southern Plans to Free and Arm Slaves during the Civil War* (New York: Oxford University Press, 2006), 62; George Alfred Townsend, *Campaigns of a Non-combatant* (1866; reprint, New York: Arno Press, 1970), 70.

23. Sears, *To the Gates of Richmond*, 90–92; Henry W. Smart to "Sister," May 26, 1862, Civil War Collection, Earl Gregg Swem Library, Manuscripts and Rare Books Department, College of William & Mary (W&M).

24. Robert Ritchie to Belle Harrison, May 17, 1862, Ritchie-Harrison Papers, W&M; Samuel Mordecai to George Mordecai, George W. Mordecai Papers, SHC; Kate Rowland Diary, May 14, 1862, Kate Mason Rowland Collection, Southern Women History Collection, MOC.

25. Putnam, *Richmond during the War*, 129.

26. Thomas, *The Confederate State of Richmond*, 92; Rowland Diary, May 14, 1862, Rowland Collection, MOC.

27. DeLeon, *Four Years in Rebel Capitals*, 221–22.

28. DeLeon, *Four Years in Rebel Capitals*, 218–19, 224–25; Jones, *A Rebel War Clerk's Diary*, May 19, 1862, 1:126; Putnam, *Richmond during the War*, 130–31; V. Davis, *Jefferson Davis*, 2:271; Jefferson Davis to Varina Davis, May 16, 1862, in *Jefferson Davis, Constitutionalist*, 5:246.

29. U.S. War Department, *The War of Rebellion: Official Records of the Union and Confederate Armies*, series 1, 53 vols.; series 2, 8 vols.; series 3, 5 vols.; series 4, 4 vols. (Washington D.C.: U.S. Government Printing Office, 1880–1901), Series 1, 4:674 (hereafter, series are referred to as *OR*-1, *OR*-2, and so on); Dew, *Ironmaker to the Confederacy*, 179–83.

30. *Richmond Daily Dispatch*, May 15, 1862.

31. Sears, *To the Gates of Richmond*, 92–94.

32. Jones, *A Rebel War Clerk's Diary*, May 23, 1862, 1:126; J. H. Reagan, *Memoirs: With Special References to Secession and Civil War*, ed. Walter Flavius McCaleb, with an introduction by George P. Garrison (1906; reprint, New York: AMS Press, 1973), 139, quoted in Freeman, *R. E. Lee*, 2:48.

33. Samuel Mordecai to George, May 18, 1862, George W. Mordecai Papers, SHC; George M. Waddy to "Dear Aunt," May 23, 1862, Civil War Collection, W&M; Manarin, ed., *Richmond at War*, May 27, 1862, 184; Maria Clopton to "My Children," May 29, 1862, Clopton Family Papers, Duke; Henry W. Smart to "sister," May 26, 1862, Civil War Collection, W&M.

34. Putnam, *Richmond during the War*, 130; Jones, *A Rebel War Clerk's Diary*, 1:129–30; McGuire, *Diary of a Southern Refugee*, May 31, 1862, 118; Henry W. Smart to "Sister," May 26, 1862, Civil War Collection, W&M. See also Ruffin, *The Diary of Edmund Ruffin*, 2:324–27.

35. Sears, *To the Gates of Richmond*, 120, 129–30, 138.

36. Lee first named the army in Special Orders No. 22. See *OR*-1, vol. 11, pt. 3, p. 569. Douglas Southall Freeman notes in *R. E. Lee* that "the more famous

name that Lee bestowed upon the army rested thereafter on usage, not on formal, authorized adoption" (2:78 n. 6).

37. DeLeon, *Four Years in Rebel Capitals*, 228; Pryor, *Reminiscences of Peace and War*, 170–71.

38. DeLeon, *Four Years in Rebel Capitals*, 228; Harrison, "Richmond Scenes in '62," *Battles & Leaders* 2:443.

39. Putnam, *Richmond during the War*, 135.

40. Pryor, *Reminiscences of Peace and War*, 181–83.

41. Harrison, *Recollections Grave and Gay*, 82–83, and "Richmond Scenes in '62," *Battles & Leaders* 2:443–44. See also Christian, *Richmond*, 233.

42. Robert E. Lee to Jefferson Davis, June 5, 1862, in *The Wartime Papers of Robert E. Lee*, 184; Davis to Varina, June 11, 1862, in V. Davis, *Jefferson Davis*, 2:316; *Richmond Examiner* quoted in Edward A. Pollard, *The First Year of the War* (New York: Richardson, 1863), 168; Chesnut, *Mary Chesnut's Civil War*, June 16, 1862, 387.

43. Sears, *To the Gates of Richmond*, 189.

44. Clifford Dowdey, *The Seven Days: The Emergence of Robert E. Lee* (Boston: Little Brown, 1966), 192–96.

45. Sears, *To the Gates of Richmond*, 209; George B. McClellan to Edwin Stanton, June 27, 1862, in *OR-1*, vol. 11, pt. 3, 266.

46. McClellan to Stanton, June 28, 1862, in *OR-1*, vol. 11, pt. 1, 61. See also Sears, *To the Gates of Richmond*, 251.

47. Pryor, *Reminiscences of Peace and War*, 178; Jones, *A Rebel War Clerk's Diary*, May 23, 1862, 1:104.

48. Chesnut, *Mary Chesnut's Civil War*, June 27, 1862, 397, 370.

49. Maria Clopton to Joyce, July 3, 1862, Clopton Family Papers, Duke; Maggie Munford to Jennie Munford, July 2, 1862, Munford-Ellis Family Correspondence, W&M.

50. DeLeon, *Four Years in Rebel Capitals*, 234; Jones, *A Rebel War Clerk's Diary*, 1:141; George Cary Eggleston, *A Rebel's Recollections*, Civil War Centennial series (Bloomington: Indiana University Press, 1959), 88, 90.

51. Putnam, *Richmond during the War*, 149.

52. Jones, *A Rebel War Clerk's Diary*, June 28, 1862, 1:139, quoting Reynolds. The numbers of Federal prisoners forced Richmond officials to establish another prison camp for enlisted soldiers on Belle Isle in the James River.

53. Putnam, *Richmond during the War*, 151; V. Davis, *Jefferson Davis*, 2:324; Bagby quoted in Ernest B. Furgurson, *Ashes of Glory: Richmond at War* (New York: Knopf, 1996), 153.

54. Manarin, ed., *Richmond at War*, July 11, 1862, 192–93.

55. Putnam, *Richmond during the War*, 151–52.

56. *OR-1*, vol. 11, pt. 2, pp. 97, 84.

57. Josiah Gorgas, *The Journals of Josiah Gorgas, 1857–1878*, ed. Sarah Woolfolk Wiggins (Tuscaloosa: University of Alabama Press, 1995), July 8, 1862, 48;

Putnam, *Richmond during the War,* 166–67; Chesnut, *Mary Chesnut's Civil War,* June 29, 1862, 400–401.

58. *OR-1,* vol. 11, pt. 2, p. 973, for casualty statistics; Chesnut, *Mary Chesnut's Civil War,* June 29, 1862, 401.

59. DeLeon, *Four Years in Rebel Capitals,* 263; Jones, *A Rebel War Clerk's Diary,* May 23, 1862, 1:128; Ruffin, *The Diary of Edmund Ruffin,* October 12, 1862, 2:461.

60. Branch & Company to Secretary of War George Randolph, August 18, 1862, Branch & Company Records, VHS.

61. DeLeon, *Four Years in Rebel Capitals,* 236–37; Putnam, *Richmond during the War,* 113–14, 105.

62. Putnam, *Richmond during the War,* 78; McGuire, *Diary of a Southern Refugee,* February 6, 1862, 88; Chesnut, *Mary Chesnut's Civil War,* 1862–1863, 429–30.

63. Varon, *Southern Lady, Yankee Spy,* 80–81, 82.

64. Robert E. Lee to General Gustavus W. Smith, August 14, 1862, and to Jeremy Gilmer, August 25, 1862, in *The Wartime Papers of Robert E. Lee,* 254–55, 265.

65. McPherson, *Battle Cry of Freedom,* 524–26. For a complete account of Cedar Mountain and Second Manassas, see Freeman, *Lee's Lieutenants,* 2:16–51, 120–43.

66. Jones, *A Rebel War Clerk's Diary,* September 1, 1862, 1:151, emphasis in original.

67. Robert E. Lee to Jefferson Davis, September 3, 1862, in *The Wartime Papers of Robert E. Lee,* 292–93; McPherson, *Battle Cry of Freedom,* 534.

68. Mary Bedinger Mitchell, "A Woman's Recollections of Antietam," in *Battles & Leaders of the Civil War,* ed. Johnson and Buel, 2:687–88.

69. DeLeon, *Four Years in Rebel Capitals,* 276, 278.

70. McGuire, *Diary of a Southern Refugee,* September 22, 1862, 156; Jones, *A Rebel War Clerk's Diary,* September 21, 1862, 1:154.

71. Jefferson Davis to Joint Session of Confederate Congress, response to Emancipation Proclamation, in *Jefferson Davis, Constitutionalist,* 5:409; Jones, *A Rebel War Clerk's Diary,* September 27, 1862, 1:157; McGuire, *Diary of a Southern Refugee,* September 30, 1862, 159; Ruffin, *The Diary of Edmund Ruffin,* September 28, 1862, 2:453.

72. Harrison, *Recollections Grave and Gay,* 94; Jones, *A Rebel War Clerk's Diary,* October 1, 1862, 1:161; Chesnut, *Mary Chesnut's Civil War,* 434.

73. Jones, *A Rebel War Clerk's Diary,* November 4, 5, 1862, 1:182–83.

74. Ibid., 1:186, emphasis in the original.

75. *Richmond Daily Dispatch,* November 15, 1862.

76. Manarin, ed., *Richmond at War,* June 14, July 28, September 8, November 10, 1862, 189–91, 198, 218, 236.

77. Ibid., May 29, 1862, 186; see also April 30 and March 24, 1862, 168, 135–37.

78. Ibid., December 8, 1862, 247–28.

79. McGuire, *Diary of a Southern Refugee*, November 29, 1862, 173; Jones, *A Rebel War Clerk's Diary*, December 1, 1862, 1:200.

80. Manarin, ed., *Richmond at War*, December 12, 1862, 252–56; Rowland Diary, December 15, 1862, Rowland Collection, MOC.

81. Thomas Goree, *Longstreet's Aide: The Civil War Letters of Major Thomas Goree*, ed. Thomas W. Cutrer (Charlottesville: University Press of Virginia, 1995), 72.

82. McGuire, *Diary of a Southern Refugee*, November 29, 1862, 172–73; Jones, *A Rebel War Clerk's Diary*, November 23, 1862, 1:195; DeLeon, *Four Years in Rebel Capitals*, 281.

83. Quoted in Shelby Foote, *The Civil War: A Narrative*, 3 vols. (New York: Random House, 1958–1973), 2:44.

84. Rowland Diary, December 15, 1862, Rowland Collection, MOC; Putnam, *Richmond during the War*, 201.

85. Jones, *A Rebel War Clerk's Diary*, December 20 and 25, 1862, 1:219, 224–25; W. C. Corsan, *Two Months in the Confederate States: An Englishman's Travels through the South*, ed. Benjamin Trask (Baton Rouge: Louisiana State University Press, 1996), 83–84; Rowland Diary, December 26, 1862, Rowland Collection, MOC; Putnam, *Richmond during the War*, 201.

3. Hardship and Despair, 1863

1. Jones, *A Rebel War Clerk's Diary*, 1:228.

2. "Agnes" to Sara Pryor, January 7, 1863, in *Ladies in Richmond, Confederate Capital*, ed. Katharine M. Jones (Indianapolis, Ind.: Bobbs-Merrill, 1962), 202–3.

3. Jones, *A Rebel War Clerk's Diary*, January 9 and 18, 1863, 1:235, 240.

4. Robert Garlick Hill Kean, *Inside the Confederate Government: The Diary of Robert Garlick Hill Kean*, ed. Edward Younger (New York: Oxford University Press, 1957), March 4, 1863, 40, 43; Gorgas, *The Journals of Josiah Gorgas*, March 23, 1863, 27. See also Betty Herndon Maury, "We Are to Be Turned out of Doors," January 30, 1863, in *Heroines of Dixie*, ed. Jones, 208.

5. Samuel to George Mordecai, February 18, 1863, George W. Mordecai Papers, SHC; Chesnut, *Mary Chestnut's Civil War*, "Memoirs" portion, 432, 434; "Chronicles of the Life of Lucy Parke Chamberlayne," 136–37, VHS. In her diary, Chestnut notes, above her entry for September 23, 1863, "I destroyed all my notes and journals—from the time I arrived at Flat Rock [N.C.]—during a raid upon Richmond in 1863. Afterward—I tried to fill up the gap from memory." She resumed regular entries on October 27, 1863; by "a raid," she is referring to Union general George Stoneman's raid on May 3 and May 4, 1863 (*Mary Chesnut's Civil War*, 425).

6. Jones, *A Rebel War Clerk's Diary*, February 18, 1863, 1:261; Virginia Clopton Clay, *A Belle of the Fifties: Memoirs of Mrs. Clay of Alabama Covering Social and*

Political Life in Washington and the South, 1853–1866 (New York: Doubleday, Page, 1905), 194; Robert E. Lee to James Seddon, March 27, 1863, in *The Wartime Papers of Robert E. Lee,* 418. See also Samuel French to Lucius Northrup, August 3, 1863, in *OR*-1, vol. 29, part 2, p. 656. Richard D. Goff's superb work *Confederate Supply* (Durham, N.C.: Duke University Press, 1969) notes that weather throughout 1863 dogged efforts to feed both the army and the civilian population of Richmond. In fact, "incessant rains in Virginia ruined the wheat crop. This destroyed any hope of building up substantial flour reserves . . . and of lessening dependence on railroad transportation" (153).

7. Christopher Tompkins Diary, March 3 and March 31, 1863, Tompkins Family Papers, VHS.

8. Jones, *A Rebel War Clerk's Diary,* February 10 and 18, 1863, 1:257, 260–61.

9. *Richmond Daily Dispatch,* February 27, 1863; Kean, *Inside the Confederate Government,* March 21, 1863, 45, 46; Jones, *A Rebel War Clerk's Diary,* January 18 and March 22, 1863, 1:240, 278.

10. Angus Johnston II, *Virginia Railroads in the Civil War* (Chapel Hill: University of North Carolina Press, 1961), 126; *Richmond Daily Dispatch,* February 27, 1863; Tompkins Diary, February 24, 1863, Tompkins Family Papers, VHS; Jones, *A Rebel War Clerk's Diary,* January 18, 1863, 1:240–41.

11. Jones, *A Rebel War Clerk's Diary,* November 5, 1863, 2:89. See also Gorgas, *The Journals of Josiah Gorgas,* November 8, 1863, 85.

12. *Richmond Whig,* February 16, 1863; *Richmond Daily Dispatch,* January 29, 1863.

13. Jones, *A Rebel War Clerk's Diary,* March 11, 1863, 1:272; *Richmond Daily Dispatch,* February 27, 1863; David Schenk Diary, March 20, 1863, SHC.

14. The chapter "Duty, Honor, and Frustration: The Dilemmas of Female Patriotism" in George C. Rable's book *Civil Wars: Women and the Crisis of Southern Nationalism* (Urbana: University of Illinois Press, 1989) does an excellent job of presenting the tensions here. See also Bertram Wyatt-Brown, *Southern Honor: Ethics and Behavior in the Old South* (New York: Oxford University Press, 1982), 234–35.

15. Rable, *Civil Wars,* 50, 51; Drew Gilpin Faust, *Mothers of Invention: Women of the Slaveholding South in the Civil War* (Chapel Hill: University of North Carolina Press, 1996), 32, 134. See also Donna Krug, "The Folks Back Home: The Confederate Home Front during the Civil War," Ph.D. diss., University of California at Irvine, 1990, 24, 28.

16. Lucy Breckinridge quoted in Anya Jabour, *Scarlett's Sisters: Young Women in the Old South* (Chapel Hill: University of North Carolina Press, 2007), 260–63; Chesnut, *Mary Chesnut's Civil War,* August 29 and October 15, 1861, 172, 217, emphasis in original; Faust, *Mothers of Invention,* 220–21, 231–33.

17. DeLeon, *Belles, Beaux, and Brains of the '60s,* 62, italics in original; *Richmond Daily Dispatch,* May 31, 1862; V. Davis, *Jefferson Davis,* 2:208.

18. Myrta Lockett Avary, *A Virginia Girl in the Civil War: Being a Record of the Actual Experiences of the Wife of a Confederate Officer* (1903; reprint, Santa Barbara, Calif.: Narrative Press, 2004), xcix; Chesnut, *Mary Chesnut's Civil War,* 459; Rable, *Civil Wars,* 94–95.

19. Maria Clopton to "Son," April 18, 1862, Clopton Family Papers, Duke; Ladies Aid & Defence Association, Correspondence, Southern Women History Collection, MOC; Maria G. Clopton to the *Richmond Dispatch,* 1862–1863, and Association Minutes, 1862–1863, Ladies Defence & Aid Association Minute Book, 1862–1863, Southern Women History Collection, MOC; DeLeon, *Four Years in Rebel Capitals,* 220; Rable, *Civil Wars,* 138–40.

20. David McKenzie to "Madam," March 31, 1863, Maria Clopton Papers, Southern Women History Collection, MOC.

21. Faust, *Mothers of Invention,* 24.

22. Jabour, *Scarlett's Sisters,* 278–29.

23. See Faust, *Mothers of Invention,* 82–85; "The Education of Southern Women," *De Bow's Review* 31 (October–November 1861): 382–83, quoted in Faust, *Mothers of Invention,* 84. The comments regarding a woman's abilities are strikingly current.

24. Rable, *Civil Wars,* 131; Faust, *Mothers of Invention,* 82–88; Moses Hoge to Bessie Hoge, July 30, 1862, Hoge Family Papers, VHS.

25. Putnam, *Richmond during the War,* 173–75; Emma Read to C. G. Memminger, August 19, 1862, Read Family Papers, 1862–1914, VHS. See also Stanard Ledger, Stanard Family Papers, VHS; *Richmond Daily Dispatch,* October 23, 1863.

26. Rowland Diary, February 5, March 19, 1863, Rowland Collection, MOC; "Chronicles of the Life of Lucy Parke Chamberlayne," VHS.

27. Putnam, *Richmond during the War,* 173–75; McGuire, *Diary of a Southern Refugee,* 238, 244; Faust, *Mothers of Invention,* 88.

28. James H. Brewer, *The Confederate Negro: Virginia's Craftsmen and Military Laborers, 1861–1865* (1969; reprint, Tuscaloosa: University of Alabama Press, 2007), chap. 4.

29. Faust, *Mothers of Invention,* 92; Chesnut, *Mary Chesnut's Civil War,* June 29, 1861, 85.

30. Faust, *Mothers of Invention,* 96–98.

31. Brewer, *The Confederate Negro,* 95 (quote from McCaw), 96, 106–10.

32. Phoebe Yates Pember, *A Southern Women's Story: Life in Confederate Richmond,* ed. Bell I. Wiley (1959; reprint, St. Simons Island, Ga.: Mockingbird Books, 1988), 16. See also Faust, *Mothers of Invention,* 108–9.

33. Phoebe Pember to Eugenia Pember Phillips, November 29, 1862, in Pember, *A Southern Woman's Story,* 109–110, emphasis in original.

34. Pember, *A Southern Woman's Story,* 17, emphasis in original.

35. Ibid., 32–36.

36. Faust, *Mothers of Invention,* 113.

37. Pember, *A Southern Woman's Story,* 46–47.

38. Pember, *A Southern Woman's Story,* 22–25, 105, emphasis in original.

39. Catherine Clinton, *Tara Revisited: Women, War, and the Plantation Legend* (New York: Abbeville Press, 1995), 85, 86; Furgurson, *Ashes of Glory,* 82–83; E. Merton Coulter, *A History of the South,* vol. 7: *The Confederate States of America, 1861–1865* (Baton Rouge: Louisiana State University Press, 1950), 432–34.

40. Chesnut, *Mary Chesnut's Civil War,* August 5 and 23, 1861, 133, 158.

41. Faust, *Mothers of Invention,* 112–13; Rable, *Civil Wars,* 129; *Richmond Daily Dispatch,* June 2, 1862; Brewer, *The Confederate Negro,* 5. Sallie Putnam writes at length about the exertions of women in the hospitals specifically as nurses, as does Constance Cary Harrison. See Putnam, *Richmond during the War,* 136, and Harrison, *Recollections Grave and Gay,* 82–83.

42. *Richmond Daily Dispatch,* January 5, 1863.

43. Tompkins Diary, March 13, 1863, Tompkins Family Papers, VHS.

44. Gorgas, *The Journals of Josiah Gorgas,* March 21, 1863, 57.

45. *Richmond Daily Dispatch,* March 14 and 16, 1863. McGuire, *Diary of a Southern Refugee,* March 15, 1863, 198; Jones, *A Rebel War Clerk's Diary,* March 13, 1863, 1:273. See also *Richmond Examiner,* March 14, 1863.

46. J. T. Trowbridge, *The Desolate South, 1865–1866, a Picture of the Battlefields and of the Devastated Confederacy* (1866; New York: Duell, Sloane and Pearce, 1956), 92; *Richmond Examiner,* April 4, 1863.

47. Jones, *A Rebel War Clerk's Diary,* March 15, 16, 19–23, 28, 1863, 1:274–82; *Richmond Daily Dispatch,* February 27, 1863. See also Kean, *Inside the Confederate Government,* March 19–20, 1863, 45. Southerners in general religiously noted the weather in their personal correspondence, diaries, memoirs, and the like. J. B. Jones and Robert Garlick Kean were typical.

48. Samuel Mordecai to George Mordecai, March 29, 1863, George W. Mordecai Papers, SHC. See also Jane S. Dupuy to Mary Windrow, March 4, 1863, Dorsey-Coupland Papers, 1840–1876, W&M; *Richmond Daily Dispatch,* January 23, 1863; Putnam, *Richmond during the War,* 207–8; Rowland Diary, January 15, 1863, Rowland Collection, MOC.

49. The most thorough account of the Richmond Bread Riot is Michael B. Chesson, "Harlots or Heroines? A New Look at the Richmond Bread Riot," *Virginia Magazine of History and Biography* 92 (April 1984): 131–75. See also Emory M. Thomas, "The Richmond Bread Riot of 1863," *Virginia Cavalcade* 18 (Summer 1968): 41–47.

50. John R. Coupland to Sue Coupland, June 3, 1863, Dorsey-Coupland Papers, W&M.

51. Chesson, "Harlots or Heroines?" 144.

52. Jones, *A Rebel War Clerk's Diary,* April 2, 1863, 1:284–85.

53. Gorgas, *The Journals of Josiah Gorgas,* April 3, 1863, 28–29; Putnam, *Richmond during the War,* 208–9, emphasis in original; V. Davis, *Jefferson Davis,* 2:373–74.

54. Pryor, *Reminiscences of Peace and War,* 238.

55. Chesson, "Harlots of Heroines?" 145–46; Manarin, ed., *Richmond at War,* December 23, 1861, 103.

56. Hal Tutwiler to Nettie, April 3, 1863, published in Stephen E. Ambrose, "Notes," *Virginia Magazine of History and Biography* 71 (1963): 203; the original letter is located in the Southern Historical Association Archive at the University of North Carolina.

57. "Mother" to "Son," April 3, 1863, Civil War Collections, National Civil War Museum, Harrisburg, Pa., emphasis in original.

58. Tompkins Diary, April 2, 1863, Tompkins Family Papers, VHS, emphasis in original; Rowland Diary, April 4, 1863, Rowland Collection, MOC.

59. George M. Waddy to "Aunty," April 9, 1863, George M. Waddy Papers, W&M; Chesson, "Harlots or Heroines?" 138, 145–50; "Chronicles of the Life of Lucy Parke Chamberlayne," April 1863, VHS.

60. Chesson, "Harlots or Heroines?" 172–73; General Arnold Elzey to General James Longstreet, April 6, 1863, in *OR-1,* vol. 17, 965–66; McGuire, *Diary of a Southern Refugee,* 203–4.

61. Gorgas, *The Journals of Josiah Gorgas,* April 3, 1863, 59; Samuel Mordecai to George Mordecai, April 3, 1863, George W. Mordecai Papers, SHC; Putnam, *Richmond during the War,* 210. See also Jones, *A Rebel War Clerk's Diary,* April 2, 1863, 1:284–86; McGuire, *Diary of a Southern Refugee,* April 2, 1863, 202–3; and Chesson, "Harlots or Heroines?" 172.

62. Chesson, *Richmond after the War,* 40–42; Hustings Court Records, 1863, 395, LVA.

63. Margaret Brown Wight Diary, April 2, 1863, Wight Family Papers, VHS.

64. Thomas, *The Confederate Nation,* 204; *New York Times,* April 8, 1863. For examples of letters petitioning the press not to publish stories about the riot, see Jonathan Withers, assistant adjutant general, "to the Richmond Press," April 2, 1863, in *OR-1,* vol. 18, p. 958. The *Richmond Examiner,* April 3, 1863, characterized the mob as "a handful of prostitutes, professional thieves, Irish and Yankee hags."

65. Thomas, *The Confederate Nation,* 204–5; Chesson, *Richmond after the War,* 44; Manarin, ed., *Richmond at War,* April 3 and 4, 1863, 314–15.

66. Chesson, "Harlots or Heroines?" 163–66; Catherine Clinton, "Public Women and Sexual Politics during the American Civil War," in *Battle Scars: Gender and Sexuality in the American Civil War,* ed. Catherine Clinton and Nina Silber (New York: Oxford University Press, 2006), 62, 69.

67. Manarin, ed., *Richmond at War,* April 13, 1863, 320–21.

68. Ibid., June 5, 1861, 44.

69. "Annual Report of the State Board of Charities," Virginia, in *The Almshouse Experience: Collected Reports,* ed. David J. Rothman (New York: Arno Press and New York Times, 1970), 1101–7; Goldfield, *Urban Growth,* 161–65. See also Mordecai, *Richmond in By-Gone Days,* 181–85.

70. *Richmond Examiner,* April 11, 1863.

71. Paul D. Escott, *After Secession: Jefferson Davis and the Failure of Confederate Nationalism* (Baton Rouge: Louisiana State University Press, 1978), x, 146, 269–70. See also Paul D. Escott, "'The Cry of the Sufferers': The Problem of Welfare in the Confederacy," *Civil War History* 23 (1977): 228–40.

72. Confederate States of America, *The Statutes at Large of the Confederate States of America . . . Third Session. . . First Congress,* ed. James M. Mathews (Richmond, Va.: R. M. Smith Printer to Congress, 1862–1864), 102–4, 127–28; Thomas, *The Confederate Nation,* 196–97; Chesson, *Richmond after the War,* 44–45. For a full analysis of the impressment policy and the tax-in-kind, see Goff, *Confederate Supply.*

73. Thomas, *The Confederate Nation,* 198; Confederate States of America, *Statutes at Large . . . Third Session . . . First Congress,* 115–26. The best accounts of Confederate fiscal policy can be found in Richard C. Todd, *Confederate Finance* (Athens: University of Georgia Press, 1954), and Douglas B. Ball, *Financial Failure and Confederate Defeat* (Urbana: University of Illinois Press, 1991).

74. Thomas, *The Confederate Nation,* 198; Robert E. Lee to James Seddon, March 27, 1863, in *The Wartime Papers of Robert E. Lee,* 418; Freeman, *Lee's Lieutenants,* 2:477 n. 51; McPherson, *Battle Cry of Freedom,* 638–39.

75. *Richmond Daily Dispatch,* May 16, 1863.

76. *Richmond Daily Dispatch,* May 16, 1863; *Richmond Examiner,* May 16, 1863; Dew, *Ironmaker to the Confederacy,* 193–94.

77. Jones, *A Rebel War Clerk's Diary,* April 30 and May 2, 1863, 1:302, 304.

78. Gorgas, *The Journals of Josiah Gorgas,* May 3 and 4, 1863, 64.

79. Rowland Diary, May 12, 1863, Rowland Collection, MOC; Jones, *A Rebel War Clerk's Diary,* May 11, 1863, 1:319.

80. V. Davis, *Jefferson Davis,* 2:383. See also Gorgas, *The Journals of Josiah Gorgas,* May 13, 1863, 66; *Richmond Daily Dispatch,* May 12, 1863; Rowland Diary, May 12, 1863, Rowland Collection, MOC.

81. Harrison, *Recollections Grave and Gay,* 137; Ellen Mordecai to George Mordecai, May 14, 1863, George W. Mordecai Papers, SHC.

82. Gorgas, *The Journals of Josiah Gorgas,* June 13 and 24, 1863, 70, 71; Kean, *Inside the Confederate Government,* June 28, 1863, 76–77.

83. McPherson, *Battle Cry of Freedom,* 646–47; James A. Riddick to William Gray, July 3, 1863, William Gray Papers, VHS.

84. Putnam, *Richmond during the War,* 229; Tompkins Diary, July 14, 1863, Tompkins Family Papers, VHS; Pryor, *Reminiscences of Peace and War,* 250; Gorgas, *The Journals of Josiah Gorgas,* July 17 and 28, 1863, 74, 75; Kean, *Inside the Confederate Government,* July 10, 1863, 79. See also DeLeon, *Four Years in Rebel Capitals,* 288.

85. *Richmond Daily Dispatch,* August 5, 1863.

86. Manarin, ed., *Richmond at War,* August 10, October 2, 12, and 15, 1863, 357, 373, 383–84; Eugene Lerner, "Inflation and the Confederacy," in *Studies in*

the Quantity Theory of Money, ed. Milton Friedman (Chicago: University of Chicago Press, 1956), 171.

87. Harrison, *Recollections Grave and Gay,* 117; Lerner, "Inflation in the Confederacy"; Manarin, ed., *Richmond at War,* October 15, 1863, 383–84; Cochran Diary, December 25, 1863, VHS.

88. *Acts,* called session, 1863, chap. 33, cited in Thomas, *The Confederate State of Richmond,* 147–48.

89. *Richmond Daily Dispatch,* October 12, 1863, provides extensive coverage of the workers meeting.

90. *Richmond Daily Dispatch,* October 23, 1863.

91. Kean, *Inside the Confederate Government,* October 4, 1863; Jones, *A Rebel War Clerk's Diary,* September 30 and October 22, 1863, 2:56–57, 78.

92. Gorgas, *The Journals of Josiah Gorgas,* October 22, 1863, 66–67; Jones, *A Rebel War Clerk's Diary,* October 11 and November 20–21, 1863, 2:68, 100–101; *Richmond Whig,* October 30, 1863; *Richmond Daily Dispatch,* October 7 and 14, 1863, emphasis in original.

93. *Richmond Daily Dispatch,* October 14 and May 29, 1863.

94. Clinton, *Tara Revisited,* 101; Coulter, *A History of the South,* 7:236–37.

95. Jones, *A Rebel War Clerk's Diary,* December 25, 1863, 2:118–19; Gorgas, *The Journals of Josiah Gorgas,* December 28, 1863, 89; *Richmond Daily Dispatch,* December 25, 1863.

96. Chesnut, *Mary Chesnut's Civil War,* December 25, 1863, 515.

97. *Richmond Examiner,* December 31, 1863, in John M. Daniel, *The* Richmond Examiner *during the War, or the Writings of John M. Daniel* (1868; reprint, New York: Arno Press, 1970), 155–56; Thomas, *The Confederate Nation,* 199.

4. The Overcrowded and Hungry City, 1864

1. Rable, *Civil Wars,* 181.

2. See, for example, Putnam, *Richmond during the War,* 303, 314.

3. Ibid., 320; Emma Moredecai Diary, July 4, 1864, VHS; Gorgas, *The Journals of Josiah Gorgas,* April 11, 1864, 98–99.

4. Gorgas, *The Journals of Josiah Gorgas,* March 23, 1864, 96; Harrison, *Recollections Grave and Gay,* 190–91; Putnam, *Richmond during the War,* 319.

5. Elizabeth Van Lew, *A Yankee Spy in Richmond: The Civil War Diary of "Crazy Bet" Van Lew,* ed. David D. Ryan (1996; reprint, Mechanicsburg, Pa.: Stackpole Books, 2001), January 24, 1864, 54; Jones, *A Rebel War Clerk's Diary,* January 26, 1864, 2:135

6. Clara Minor Lynn Diary, 1864, Clara Minor Lynn Writings, Southern Women History Collection, MOC; Putnam, *Richmond during the War,* 303; John Godwin to wife, February 14, 1864, Godwin Family Papers, VHS.

7. Gorgas, *The Journals of Josiah Gorgas,* March 23, 1864, 96; Samuel Mordecai to George Mordecai, January 15, 1864, George W. Mordecai Papers, VHS. See also Cochran Diary, February 1864, VHS.

8. F. F. Cavada, *Libby Life: Experiences of a Prisoner of War in Richmond, Virginia, 1863–64* (New York: Lippincott, 1865), 132.

9. Jones, *A Rebel War Clerk's Diary,* January 1 and 25, 1864, 2:122–23, 185, emphasis in original; "Chronicles of the Life of Lucy Parke Chamberlayne," 151, VHS; John Godwin to wife, June 24, 1864, Godwin Family Papers, VHS; McGuire, *Diary of a Southern Refugee,* February 15, 1864, 252. See also Chestnut, *Mary Chesnut's Civil War,* January 22, 1864, 548, and Putnam, *Richmond during the War,* 319.

10. Putnam, *Richmond during the War,* 345–46; Confederate officer quoted in Dabney, *Richmond,* 188.

11. *Richmond Enquirer,* February 12, 1864.

12. Jones, *A Rebel War Clerk's Diary,* September 30, 1864, 2:290.

13. *Richmond Whig,* February 10, 1864, emphasis in original.

14. "Agnes" to Sara Pryor, January 30, 1864, in in Pryor, *Reminiscences of Peace and War,* 263–64.

15. Chesnut, *Mary Chesnut's Civil War,* January 22, 1864, 548.

16. Ibid., January 31, 1864, 551.

17. Ibid., February 26, 1864, 573–74.

18. Harrison, *Recollections Grave and Gay,* 150.

19. *Richmond Examiner,* February 11, 1864.

20. The fullest account of the Kilpatrick–Dahlgren raid can be found in Bruce M. Venter, *Kill Jeff Davis: The Union Raid on Richmond, 1864* (Norman: University of Oklahoma Press, 2016), especially chapters 10 and 11. See also *Richmond Daily Dispatch,* March 2, 3, and 5, 1864.

21. Quoted in Venter, *Kill Jeff Davis,* 267–68.

22. Chesnut, *Mary Chesnut's Civil War,* March 3, 1864, 577–78; Jones, *A Rebel War Clerk's Diary,* March 5, 1864, 2:166; Gorgas, *The Journals of Josiah Gorgas,* March 4, 1864, 94; Robert E. Lee to James Seddon, March 6, 1864, in *The Wartime Papers of Robert E. Lee,* 678.

23. *Richmond Daily Dispatch,* March 11, 1864.

24. *Richmond Daily Dispatch,* March 8 and 11, 1864.

25. Benjamin Butler to Robert Ould, March 11, 1864, OR-2, vol. 6, pp. 1034–35. For a full account of Van Lew's role, see Varon, *Southern Lady, Yankee Spy,* 135–52. Despite being at war, many soldiers and civilians attempted to continue Victorian-era practices regarding death. To enjoy a "good death," one must be surrounded by loved ones and admit they were Christians. Battlefield deaths often precluded these requirements. Van Lew attempted to give Dahlgren a "good death" to assuage Admiral Dahlgren's grief. For an analysis of "the good death," see Drew Gilpin Faust, *This Republic of Suffering: Death and the American Civil War* (New York: Knopf, 2008).

26. Gorgas, *The Journals of Josiah Gorgas,* April 4, 1864, 98.

27. Manarin, ed., *Richmond at War,* March 23, 1864, 450–51; Louis H. Manarin and Clifford Dowdey, *The History of Henrico County* (Charlottesville: University Press of Virginia, 1984), 290.

28. *Richmond Enquirer,* March 24, 1864; *Richmond Daily Dispatch,* March 26, 1864.

29. Gorgas, *The Journals of Josiah Gorgas,* April 11, 1864, 98–99; Jones, *A Rebel War Clerk's Diary,* April 11, 1864, 2:185; *Richmond Daily Dispatch,* June 22, 1864.

30. *Richmond Daily Dispatch,* June 22, 1864.

31. Cochran Diary, n.d., 1864, VHS.

32. Robert E. Lee to Jefferson Davis, April 12, 1864, in *The Wartime Papers of Robert E. Lee,* 659.

33. Jones, *A Rebel War Clerk's Diary,* April 15, 1864, 2:188; Lee to Seddon, April 12, 1864, in *The Wartime Papers of Robert E. Lee,* 696–97.

34. Quoted in McPherson, *Battle Cry of Freedom,* 566.

35. Mary Tucker Magill to "mother," April 26, 1864, Mary Tucker Magill Letter, VHS.

36. *Richmond Enquirer,* May 6, 1864; John R. Coupland to Juliana Dorsey, April 3, 1864, Dorsey-Coupland Papers, W&M, emphasis in original.

37. YMCA, "An Appeal to the People of the Confederate States," *Richmond Daily Dispatch,* May 13, 1864.

38. See Brewer, *The Confederate Negro,* 53–73; Takagi, *"Rearing Wolves to Our Own Destruction,"* 137.

39. Takagi, *"Rearing Wolves to Our Own Destruction,"* 136–37.

40. *Richmond Daily Dispatch,* March 26, 1864.

41. General Ulysses S. Grant to Edwin Stanton, June 22, 1865, in *OR-1,* vol. 46, pt. 1, p. 11; George Gordon Meade, *The Life and Letters of George Gordon Meade,* 2 vols. (New York: Scribner's, 1913), 2:246.

42. For an excellent detailed account of these battles, see Noah Andre Trudeau, *Bloody Roads South: The Wilderness to Cold Harbor, May–June 1864* (New York: Fawcett Columbine, 1989).

43. General Ulysses S. Grant to General Henry Halleck, May 11, 1864, *OR-1,* vol. 36, pt. 1, p. 4.

44. Robert E. Lee to General Jubal Early, late May 1864, quoted in McPherson, *Battle Cry of Freedom,* 743, which cites Foote, *The Civil War,* 3:442.

45. Van Lew, *A Yankee Spy in Richmond,* 94; Henri Garidel, *Exile in Richmond: The Confederate Journal of Henri Garidel,* ed. Michael Bedout Chesson and Leslie Jean Roberts (Charlottesville: University Press of Virginia, 2001), May 14, 1864, 137–38; Sarah Lawton to Sister Louisa, May 16, 1864, in *The Alexander Letters, 1787–1900,* ed. Marion Alexander Boggs (Athens: University of Georgia Press, 1980), 267. See also Emma Mordecai Diary, May 23, 1864, VHS, and James Thomas Butler Diary, May 21, 1864, VHS.

46. *Richmond Daily Dispatch,* May 13, 1864.

47. Jones, *A Rebel War Clerk's Diary,* May 13, 1864, 2:209, emphasis in original.

48. Garidel, *Exile in Richmond,* June 1, 1864, 153; *Richmond Enquirer,* June 2, 1864.

49. Putnam, *Richmond during the War,* 314–15; Minor Diary, MOC; Lange Memoirs, VHS.

50. Lange Memoirs, VHS.

51. Jones, *A Rebel War Clerk's Diary,* August 24, 1864, 2:271.

52. "Agnes" to Sara Pryor, August 26, 1864, in Pryor, *Reminiscences of Peace and War,* 293; Jones, *A Rebel War Clerk's Diary,* July 3, 1864, 2:244, emphasis in original.

53. Manarin, ed., *Richmond at War,* May 31, 1864, 473, 474.

54. Manarin, ed., *Richmond at War,* June 13, 1864, 479, 478; *Richmond Daily Dispatch,* July 13, 1864; Christian, *Richmond,* June 6, 1864, 253.

55. Kean, *Inside the Confederate Government,* July 11, 1864, 164; Jones, *A Rebel War Clerk's Diary,* July 10, 1864, 2:246–47. By "raiders," Jones was referring to General Philip Sheridan's raid against Richmond.

56. *Richmond Daily Dispatch,* July 30, 1864.

57. General Ulysses S. Grant to Major General Philip Sheridan, August 26, 1864, in *OR*-1, vol. 43, pt. 2, 202.

58. Sheridan to Grant, October 7, 1864, in *OR*-1, vol. 43, pt. 1, 30.

59. Sallie C. Bird to Sarah Hamilton Yancey, January 8, 1865, Benjamin C. Yancey Papers, SHC, quoted in Rable, *Civil Wars,* 200–221.

60. Warren Akin, *Letters of Warren Akin, Confederate Congressman,* ed. Bell I. Wiley (Athens: University of Georgia Press, 1959), December 27, 1864, 56.

61. Garidel, *Exile in Richmond,* November 17, 1864, 234, 235.

62. *Richmond Sentinel,* July 1, 1864; Thomas P. Lowry, M.D., *The Story the Soldiers Wouldn't Tell: Sex in the Civil War* (Mechanicsburg, Pa.: Stackpole Books, 1994), 70.

63. *Richmond Enquirer,* August 22, 1864; *Southern Punch,* April 2, 1864. *Southern Punch* was designed "to be the legitimate son of the *London Punch*" (Thomas, *The Confederate State of Richmond,* 151).

64. Putnam, *Richmond during the War,* 341–42; Manarin, ed., *Richmond at War,* January 18, 1864, 420.

65. Jones, *A Rebel War Clerk's Diary,* March 18 and April 3, 1864, 2:173, 180–81, emphasis in original.

66. Ulysses S. Grant, *Personal Memoirs* (1885; reprint, New York: Penguin Classics, 1999), 484.

67. Jones, *A Rebel War Clerk's Diary,* April 19, 1864, 2:190; Freeman, *R. E. Lee,* 3:495–96; Robert E. Lee to Jefferson Davis, September 2, 1864, in *The Wartime Papers of Robert E. Lee,* 848.

68. Jones, *A Rebel War Clerk's Diary,* July 30, 1864, 2:257; Kean, *Inside the Confederate Government,* November 2, 1863, 116, emphasis in original.

69. Grant to Halleck, August 1, 1864, in Ulysses S. Grant, *The Papers of Ulysses S. Grant,* vol. 11, ed. John Y. Simon (Carbondale: Southern Illinois University Press, 1984), 361.

70. Putnam, *Richmond during the War,* 310; Abraham Lincoln to cabinet, sealed memorandum, August 23, 1864, in *The Collected Works of Abraham Lincoln,* 7:514.

71. Putnam, *Richmond during the War,* 310, 321.

72. *Richmond Examiner,* September 5, 1864.

73. *Richmond Whig,* December 2, 1864.

74. *Richmond Daily Dispatch,* December 22 and 23, 1864; *Richmond Whig,* December 28, 1864; Freeman, *Lee's Lieutenants,* 3:621.

75. Jones, *A Rebel War Clerk's Diary,* December 25, 1864, 2:384, emphasis in original.

76. Putnam, *Richmond during the War,* 340–41.

77. McGuire, *Diary of a Southern Refugee,* December 26 and 28, 1864, 323–24, 326.

5. The Fall of Richmond, 1865

1. Putnam, *Richmond during the War,* 340, 342. See also Gorgas, *The Journals of Josiah Gorgas,* December 26, 1864, 145.

2. Jefferson Davis relieved Joseph Johnston of command on July 17, 1864, and named John Bell Hood as his successor. Having complained to the president about the constant retreating, Hood was forced to go on the offensive. The result was a series of defeats that led Hood to evacuate from the inner defenses of Atlanta, which allowed that city to fall to Sherman. Hood then embarked on an ill-fated invasion of Tennessee that resulted in the slaughter at Franklin, Tennessee, on November 30, 1864. Hood then proceeded to Nashville, where his army was almost destroyed on December 15–16, 1864. Lee gave Johnston the unenviable task of trying to cobble together what was left of the Army of Tennessee. See McPherson, *Battle Cry of Freedom,* 811–16.

3. Putnam, *Richmond during the War,* 341; Jones, *A Rebel War Clerk's Diary,* January 9, 1865, 2:381; Akin, *Letters of Warren Akin,* January 30, 1865, 105.

4. Garidel, *Exile in Richmond,* January 29, 1865, 298; Thomas Conolly, *An Irishman in Dixie: Thomas Conolly's Diary of the Fall of the Confederacy,* ed. Nelson Lankford (Columbia: University of South Carolina Press, 1988), March 8, 1864, 37; Akin, *Letters of Warren Akin,* January 14, 1865, 79.

5. Gorgas, *Journals of Josiah Gorgas,* February 27, 1865, 153; Akin, *Letters of Warren Akin,* January 10, 1865, 75, emphasis in original.

6. Jones, *A Rebel War Clerk's Diary,* February 3, 1865, 2:408; Thomas Morris Chester, *Thomas Morris Chester, Black Civil War Correspondent: His Dispatches from the Virginia Front,* ed. R. J. M. Blackett (Baton Rouge: Louisiana State University Press, 1989), January 1, 1865, 245–46.

7. Gorgas, *Journals of Josiah Gorgas,* February 27, 1865, 153, emphasis in original; Garidel, *Exile in Richmond,* February 18 and 28, 1865, 332; McGuire, *Diary of a Southern Refugee,* March 11, 1865, 340.

8. Major General Patrick Cleburne to Commanding General, the Corps, Division, Brigade and Regimental Commanders of the Army of Tennessee, January 2, 1864, in *OR*-1, vol. 52, pt. 2, pp. 586–92. Cleburne's proposal ended his chances of promotion. He was killed at the Battle of Franklin in Tennessee on November 15, 1864.

9. Howell Cobb to James Seddon, quoted in Robert F. Durden, *The Gray and the Black: The Confederate Debate on Emancipation* (Baton Rouge: Louisiana State University Press, 1972), 184; Robert E. Lee to Jefferson Davis, March 10, 1865, in *The Wartime Papers of Robert E. Lee,* 914. See also Robert E. Lee to John C. Breckinridge, March 27, 1865, and Jefferson Davis to Virginia governor William Smith, March 30, 1865, in *OR*-1, vol. 46, pt. 3, pp. 1339, 1336–67.

10. *Richmond Daily Dispatch,* February 20, 1865; *Richmond Enquirer,* February 14, 1865.

11. Rowland Diary, January 23, 1865, Rowland Collection, MOC.

12. Durden, *The Gray and the Black,* 147–49.

13. George Patterson to George Mordecai, February 2, 1865, George W. Mordecai Papers, SHC; Jones, *A Rebel War Clerk's Diary,* February 24 and March 17, 1865, 2:431, 451, emphasis in original.

14. Putnam, *Richmond during the War,* 351; Jones, *A Rebel War Clerk's Diary,* March 22, 1865, 2:457.

15. Kean, *Inside the Confederate Government,* February 5, 1865, 198, emphasis in original; Gorgas, *The Journals of Josiah Gorgas,* February 8 and 10, 1865, 151; Caroline Kean Hill Davis Diary, February 8, 1865, VHS, emphasis in original; Putnam, *Richmond during the War,* 350.

16. Chesnut, *Mary Chesnut's Civil War,* March 5, 1865, 747; Kean, *Inside the Confederate Government,* March 23, 1865, 120; Mrs. William Simmons Diary, March 23, 1865, Southern Women History Collection, MOC, emphasis in original.

17. Harrison, *Recollections Grave and Gay,* 134; Garidel, *Exile in Richmond,* January 24, 1865, 292; Jones, *A Rebel War Clerk's Diary,* January 27, 1865, 2:400.

18. V. Davis, *Jefferson Davis,* 2:571.

19. *Richmond Daily Dispatch,* March 29, 1865.

20. William Smith, *Memoirs of Governor William Smith of Virginia: His Political, Military, and Personal History,* ed. John W. Bell (New York: Moss Engraving, 1891), 57.

21. Ibid., 57–58.

22. McGuire, *Diary of a Southern Refugee,* January 8, 1865, 328–29.

23. Pember, *A Southern Woman's Story,* 91.

24. DeLeon, *Four Years in Rebel Capitals,* 388–89; Malvina Gist Diary, March 5 and 1, 1865, in *Heroines of Dixie,* ed. Jones, 378, 377.

25. Rowland Diary, January 23, 1865, Rowland Collection, MOC.

26. DeLeon, *Four Years in Rebel Capitals,* 391.

27. Robert E. Lee to Mary Custis Lee, February 21, 1865, in *The Wartime Papers of Robert E. Lee,* 907.

28. Lee wrote to Jefferson Davis in June 1864 that "[Ewell's] health & nervous system has been shaken by his great injury [amputated leg after Second Manassas] & though active & attentive he cannot without breaking himself down undergo the arduous duties of a Corps Commandr [*sic*]." As a consequence, Ewell was appointed to command the Department of Richmond. See Robert E. Lee to Jefferson Davis, June 1864, in Robert E. Lee, *Lee's Dispatches: Unpublished Letters of General Robert E. Lee, C.S.A. to Jefferson Davis and the War Department of the Confederate States of America, 1862–1865,* ed. Douglas Southall Freeman and Grady McWhiney (New York: Putnam's, 1957), 255–56.

29. Manarin, ed., *Richmond at War,* February 24, 1865, 571.

30. William M. Brown to "Mother Ann," March 27, 1865, Alexander Gustavus Brown Papers, VHS; Putnam, *Richmond during the War,* 303; Kean, *Inside the Confederate Government,* February 10, 1865, 200; George T. Lee, "Reminiscences of General Robert E. Lee, 1865–1868," typescript, special collections, Washington and Lee University, cited in Elizabeth Brown Pryor, *Reading the Man: A Portrait of Robert E. Lee through His Private Letters* (New York: Viking, 2007), 393.

31. Robert E. Lee to John C. Breckinridge, April 2, 1865, in *OR*-1, vol. 46, pt. 1, p. 1264.

32. Simmons Diary, April 2, 1865, MOC; Pryor, *Reminiscences of Peace and War,* April 5, 1865, 354; Fannie Taylor Dickinson Diary, April 4, 1865, VHS.

33. Lee to Breckinridge, April 2, 1865; Jefferson Davis to Robert E. Lee, April 2, 1865, and Lee to Davis, April 2, 1865, in *OR*-1, vol. 46, pt. 3, p. 1378.

34. Captain Clement Sulivane, "The Fall of Richmond," in *Battles & Leaders of the Civil War,* ed. Johnson and Buel, 4:725.

35. V. Davis, *Jefferson Davis,* 2:574–77.

36. Manarin, ed., *Richmond at War,* April 2, 1865, 591–92.

37. Putnam, *Richmond during the War,* 363; Pollard, *The Lost Cause,* 695–96; Gorgas, *The Journals of Josiah Gorgas,* April 30, 1865, 159.

38. "Chronicles of the Life of Lucy Parke Chamberlayne," VHS; Lange Memoir, VHS.

39. Conolly, *An Irishman in Dixie,* April 2, 1865, 83–84; Emmeline Crump Lightfoot Memoir, VHS.

40. James W. Llewellen to John P. Parker, Llewellen Family Papers, April 5, 1865, VHS.

41. Harrison, *Recollections Grave and Gay,* 212.

42. Raphael Semmes, *Memoirs of Service Afloat during the War between the States* (1869; reprint, Whitefish, Mont.: Kessinger, 2007), 809–10, 811–12. The fullest and most comprehensive account of the Confederate evacuation of Richmond is Nelson Lankford, *Richmond Burning: The Last Days of the Confederate Capital* (New York: Viking Press, 2002).

43. Emma Mordecai to Edward Cohen, April 5, 1865, typescript, Vertical File, Valentine Museum, emphasis in original.

44. Avary, *A Virginia Girl during the Civil War*, 357, 360–61.

45. Myrta Lockett Avary, *Dixie after the War: An Exposition of Social Conditions Existing in the South in the Twelve Years Succeeding the Fall of Richmond* (1906; reprint, Freeport, N.Y.: Books for Libraries Press, 1970), 11.

46. Francis Lawley, *Lawley Covers the Confederacy*, ed. William Stanley Hoole (Tuscaloosa, Ala.: Confederate Publishing, 1964), 118.

47. Charles Carleton Coffin, *Freedom Triumphant: The Fourth Period of the War of Rebellion, from September 1864, to Its Close* (New York: Harper, 1891), 422.

48. Alexander, *Fighting for the Confederacy*, 518, 519.

49. Dew, *Ironmaker for the Confederacy*, 286.

50. Jefferson Davis, proclamation, "To the People of the Confederate States of America," April 4, 1865, in *OR*-1, vol. 46, pt. 3, pp. 1382–83.

51. Manarin, ed., *Richmond at War*, April 3, 1865, 595.

52. Ibid.

53. Elizabeth Van Lew, "Oh, Army of My Country!" in *Ladies of Richmond*, ed. Jones, 279–80.

54. Mary Tucker Magill, "Chronicles," in *From Civility to Survival: Richmond Ladies during the Civil War*, ed. Neal E. Wixon (Bloomington: Indiana University Press, 2012), 111; Avary, *A Virginia Girl in the Civil War*, 364.

55. Pember, *A Southern Woman's Story*, 98.

56. Godfrey Weitzel, *Richmond Occupied: Entry of the United States Forces into Richmond, Virginia, April 3, 1865; Calling Together of the Virginia Legislature and Revocation of the Same*, ed. Louis H. Manarin (Richmond, Va.: Civil War Centennial Committee, 1965), 10, 51–53.

57. Ibid., 53.

58. Quoted in David Dixon Porter, *Incidents and Anecdotes of the Civil War* (New York: Appleton, 1885), 294.

59. Porter, *Incidents and Anecdotes of the Civil War*, 297; Coffin, *Freedom Triumphant*, 753, cited in Michael D. Gorman, "Peacemaker or Conqueror? Abraham Lincoln in Richmond," *Virginia Magazine of History and Biography* 123, no. 1 (2015): 23.

60. Chester, *Thomas Morris Chester*, April 6, 1865, 295.

61. Thomas Conolly to Nanny Thomas, April 27, 1865, in *An Irishman in Dixie*, 116; Jones, *A Rebel War Clerk's Diary*, April 5, 1865, 2:471; Mary Custis Lee to "My Dear Louisa," April 16, 1865, quoted in Pryor, *Reading the Man*, 427.

62. Gorman, "Peacemaker or Conqueror?" 30.

63. Weitzel, *Richmond Occupied*, 56.

64. Charles A. Dana, *Recollections of the Civil War: With the Leaders at Washington and in the Field in the Sixties* (New York: Appleton, 1902), 264–66.

65. J. T. Trowbridge, *The South: A Tour of Its Battlefields and Ruined Cities* (1866; reprint, New York: Arno Press, 1969), 83–85.

66. Townsend, *Campaigns of a Non-combatant,* 336–37.

67. Emma Mordecai Diary, May 4, 1865, SHC; Samuel Mordecai to George Mordecai, April 21, 1865, George W. Mordecai Papers, SHC; Edmund Myers to George Mordecai, May 20, 1865, George W. Mordecai Papers, SHC; Chester, *Thomas Morris Chester,* April 24, 1865, 320.

68. Putnam, *Richmond during the War,* 374.

69. Chester, *Thomas Morris Chester,* April 10, 1865, 300, emphasis in original.

70. *Richmond Examiner,* n.d., quoted in Putnam, *Richmond during the War,* 375; Putnam gave the date as "several weeks before the fall of the city."

71. Lucy Chase to "Miss Lowell," April 20, 1865, in *Dear Ones at Home: Letters from Contraband Camps,* ed. Henry L. Swint (Nashville: Vanderbilt University Press, 1966), 157–58; John Thomas O'Brien Jr., *From Bondage to Citizenship: The Richmond Black Community, 1865–1867* (New York: Garland, 1990), 80–81.

72. John Richard Dennett, *The South as It Is, 1865–1866* (1865–1866; reprint, London: Sidgwick & Jackson, 1965), 53.

Epilogue

1. Alexander, *Fighting for the Confederacy,* 539–40.

2. Freeman, *R. E. Lee,* 4:162.

3. Putnam, *Richmond during the War,* 379; Joseph T. Glatthaar, *General Lee's Army: From Victory to Collapse* (New York: Free Press, 2008), 471.

4. Putnam, *Richmond during the War,* 380–81.

5. Mary Tucker Magill, "Chronicles," in *From Civility to Survival,* ed. Wixon, 145.

Selected Bibliography

Primary Sources

Manuscript Collections

College of William and Mary (W&M), Manuscripts and Rare Books Department, Earl Gregg Swem Library, Williamsburg, Va.

Civil War Collection
Dorsey-Coupland Papers, 1840–1876
Hope, James Barron, Papers
Myers, Gustavus A., Papers
Ritchie-Harrison Papers
T. C. William & Company Journal
Tompkins, Christopher, Papers
Van Lew, Elizabeth, Papers
Waddy, George M., Papers

Duke University Special Collections (Duke), William R. Perkins Library, Durham, N.C.

Clopton Family Papers
Danforth, John B., Papers
Munford-Ellis Family Correspondence, 1859–1862
Pelouze, Henry Lafayette, Papers

Henry E. Huntington Library and Art Gallery, San Marino, Calif.

BROCK, ROBERT A., COLLECTION

Anderson, Joseph Reid, Correspondence and Documents, 1846–1896
Department of Virginia Collection, Military Correspondence and Documents, 1865–1866
Lyons Family Correspondence and Documents, 1863–1866
Minor Family Correspondence and Documents, 1787–1903
Miscellaneous File, Midlothian Coal Mining Company
Richmond & Petersburg Railroad Correspondence and Documents, 1860–1865

Ripley, Edward Hastings. "The Burning of Richmond." Unpublished manuscript.
Virginia Central Railroad Correspondence, 1859–1867
Virginia General Assembly, Senate Documents, 1861–1864; February 1865, March 1865
Wynne, Thomas Hicks, Papers, 1848–1901

Library of Virginia (LVA), Richmond

Anderson, Joseph R., Papers, 1861–1867
Fay, William, Papers
First African Baptist Church Minute Book 1, 1841–1859
Hammond, Isaac, Papers
Hustings Court Records
Irby, William H., Civil War Diary and Account Book, 1860–1865
Jones, E. V., letter, Richmond Arsenal, December 12, 1863
Jones, George Watson, Notebook, n.d.
McNiven, Thomas, Papers
Paul, Alfred, Papers
Puckett, William T., Personal Papers
Tredegar Company Business Records, letters from Francis T. Glasgow to J. R. Anderson & Company
Tredegar Company Business Records, November 1862–February 1863; February 1863–July 1864; August 1864–December 1864; August 1864–November 1865
Tredegar Company Day Books, 1836–1924
Tredegar Company Journals, 1840–1881
Tredegar Company Records, 1857–1868
Van Lew, Elizabeth, Papers
Virginia Census Schedules
Virginia Governor's Office, John Letcher Executive Papers

Museum of the Confederacy (MOC), Eleanor S. Brockenbrough Library, Richmond, Va.

SOUTHERN WOMEN HISTORY COLLECTION

Clopton, Maria G., Papers
Cook, Leila M., Diary
Fontaine, Mary Burrows, letter, April 30, 1865
Ladies Aid & Defence Association Correspondence, 1862–1863
Ladies Defence & Aid Association Minute Book, 1862–1863
Lightfoot, Emmie Crump, Papers
Loughborough, Margaret, Reminiscences
Lynn, Clara Minor, Writings

Minor, Kate Pleasants, Papers
Rowland, Kate Mason, Collection
Simmons, Mrs. William, Diary
Sublett, Emmie, letter, April 29, 1865

AFRICAN AMERICAN COLLECTION

MISCELLANEOUS

Randolph, Tucker, Journal

National Civil War Museum, Harrisburg, Pa.

Civil War Collections

University of North Carolina at Chapel Hill, Southern Historical Collection (SHC), Wilson Library

Albinson Letters, 1861–1864
Hubard Family Papers
Lacy, Drury, Papers
Mordecai, Emma, Diary, 1864–1865
Mordecai, George W., Papers
Schenk, David, Diary
Seddon, James Alexander, Papers
Trenhom, Anna Holmes, Diary, 1865
Withers, Anita Dwyer, Diary

Valentine Museum, Richmond, Va.

Mordecai, Emma, letter, April 5, 1865
Unidentified Richmond woman's diary

Virginia Historical Society (VHS), Richmond, Va.

Anderson, Archer, Papers
Archer, Edward R., Account Book, 1861–1863
Archer, Edward R., Diary, 1864–1865
Bagby, George William, Papers, 1828–1917
Beckwith, Margaret Stanley, Papers
Branch & Company Records
Brown, Alexander Gustavus, Papers
Butler, James Thomas, Diary
Cabell Family Papers
Carlton, Cornelius Hart, Diary, 1864–1869

"Chronicles of the Life of Lucy Parke Chamberlayne"
Claiborne, Mary Anna, Account Book
Claiborne Family Papers
Cochran, Catherine, Diary
Confederate Imprints
Confederate States of America, Army Department of Henrico
Cook, Lelian M., Diary
Curd, Samuella Hurt, Diary
Davis, Caroline Kean Hill, Diary
Dickinson, Fannie Taylor, Diary
Ellis Family Papers
Eppes, Richard, Diary
Godwin Family Papers
Graniss, Robert A., Diary
Gray, William, Papers
Green, Thomas, Collection
Hoge Family Papers
Hubard, Maria Mason Tabb, Diary
Lange, John Gottfried, Memoirs
Lightfoot, Emmeline Crump, Memoir
Llewellen Family Papers
Magill, Mary Tucker, Letter, 1864
Phillips, William B., Papers
Read Family Papers, 1862–1914
Rutherfoord Family Papers
Stanard Family Papers
St. Paul's Episcopal Church Vestry Book
Talbott & Brother Papers
Taylor, Mary, Diary
Tompkins Family Papers
Van Lew, Elizabeth, Papers
Whitlock, Philip, Recollections
Wight Family Papers

Newspapers

New York Times
Richmond Daily Dispatch
Richmond Enquirer
Richmond Examiner
Richmond Sentinel
Richmond Whig
Southern Punch

Official Publications

Confederate States of America. *The Statutes at Large of the Confederate States of America . . . Third Session. . . First Congress.* Edited by James M. Mathews. Richmond, Va.: R. M. Smith, Printer to Congress, 1862–1864.

U.S. Bureau of the Census. *The Eighth Census of the United States, 1860.* Washington, D.C.: U.S. Government Printing Office, 1865.

———. *Population of the United States in 1860 Compiled from the Original Returns of the Eighth Census.* Washington, D.C.: U.S. Government Printing Office, 1864.

U.S. War Department. *The War of Rebellion: Official Records of the Union and Confederate Armies.* Series 1, 53 vols.; series 2, 8 vols.; series 3, 5 vols.; series 4, 4 vols. Washington D.C.: U.S. Government Printing Office, 1880–1901.

Published Diaries, Letters, Memoirs, and Other Primary Writings

Akin, Warren. *Letters of Warren Akin, Confederate Congressman.* Edited by Bell I. Wiley. Athens: University of Georgia Press, 1959.

Alexander, Edward Porter. *Fighting for the Confederacy: The Personal Recollections of General Edward Porter Alexander.* Edited by Gary W. Gallagher. Chapel Hill: University of North Carolina Press, 1989.

Avary, Myrta Lockett. *Dixie after the War: An Exposition of Social Conditions Existing in the South in the Twelve Years Succeeding the Fall of Richmond.* 1906. Reprint. Freeport, N.Y.: Books for Libraries Press, 1970.

———. *A Virginia Girl in the Civil War: Being a Record of the Actual Experiences of the Wife of a Confederate Officer.* 1903. Reprint. Santa Barbara, Calif.: Narrative Press, 2004.

Bancroft, Frederic. *Slave Trading in the Old South.* Baltimore: Furst, 1931.

Beers, Mrs. Fannie A. *Memories: A Record of Personal Experiences and Adventure during Four Years of War.* Philadelphia: Lippincott, 1888.

Boggs, Marion Alexander, ed. *The Alexander Letters, 1787–1900.* Athens: University of Georgia Press, 1980.

Borcke, Heros von. *Memoirs of the Confederate War for Independence.* 2 vols. New York: Peter Smith, 1938.

Botts, John Minor. *The Great Rebellion: Its Secret History, Rise, Progress, and Disastrous Failure.* New York: Harper, 1866.

Cavada, F. F. *Libby Life: Experiences of a Prisoner of War in Richmond, Virginia, 1863–64.* New York: Lippincott, 1865.

Chesnut, Mary. *Mary Chesnut's Civil War.* Edited by C. Vann Woodward. New Haven, Conn.: Yale University Press, 1981.

Chester, Thomas Morris. *Thomas Morris Chester, Black Civil War Correspondent: His Dispatches from the Virginia Front.* Edited by R. J. M. Blackett. Baton Rouge: Louisiana State University Press, 1989.

Clay, Virginia Clopton. *A Belle of the Fifties: Memoirs of Mrs. Clay of Alabama Covering Social and Political Life in Washington and the South, 1853–1866*. New York: Doubleday, Page, 1905.

Coffin, Charles Carleton. *Freedom Triumphant: The Fourth Period of the War of Rebellion, from September, 1864 to Its Close*. New York: Harper, 1891.

Conolly, Thomas. *An Irishman in Dixie: Thomas Conolly's Diary of the Fall of the Confederacy*. Edited by Nelson D. Lankford. Columbia: University of South Carolina Press, 1988.

Corsan, W. C. *Two Months in the Confederate States: An Englishman's Travels through the South*. Edited by Benjamin Trask. Baton Rouge: Louisiana State University Press, 1996.

Dana, Charles A. *Recollections of the Civil War: With the Leaders at Washington and in the Field in the Sixties*. New York: Appleton, 1902.

Daniel, John M. *The* Richmond Examiner *during the War, or the Writings of John M. Daniel*. 1868. Reprint. New York: Arno Press, 1970.

Davis, Jefferson. *Jefferson Davis, Constitutionalist: His Letters, Papers, and Speeches*. 10 vols. Edited by Dunbar Rowland. 1923. Reprint. Jackson: AMS Press for the Mississippi Department of Archives and History, 1973.

———. *The Messages and Papers of Jefferson Davis and the Confederacy, Including Diplomatic Correspondence, 1861–1865*. 2 vols. Edited by James D. Richardson. New York: Bowker, 1966.

———. *The Papers of Jefferson Davis*. Vol. 9: *January–September, 1863*. Edited by Linda Lasswell Crist, Mary Seaton Dix, and Kenneth H. Williams. Baton Rouge: Louisiana State University Press, 1997.

———. *The Papers of Jefferson Davis*. Vol. 10: *October 1863–August 1864*. Edited by Linda Lasswell Crist, Mary Seaton Dix, and Kenneth H. Williams. Baton Rouge: Louisiana State University Press, 1999.

Davis, Varina. *Jefferson Davis: A Memoir by His Wife*. 2 vols. Baltimore: Nautical & Aviation, 1990.

DeLeon, T. C. *Belles, Beaux, and Brains of the '60s*. New York: Dillingham, 1907.

———. *Four Years in Rebel Capitals: An Inside View of Life in the Southern Confederacy, from Birth to Death; from Original Notes, Collected in the Years 1861 to 1865*. Mobile, Ala.: Gossip Printing, 1892.

Dennett, John Richard. *The South as It Is, 1865–1866*. Reprint. London: Sidgwick & Jackson, 1965.

Durden, Robert F. *The Gray and the Black: The Confederate Debate on Emancipation*. Baton Rouge: Louisiana State University Press, 1972.

Eggleston, George Cary. *A Rebel's Recollections*. Civil War Centennial series. Bloomington: Indiana University Press, 1959.

Ely, Alfred. *Journals of Alfred Ely, a Prisoner of War in Richmond*. New York: Appleton, 1862.

Garidel, Henri. *Exile in Richmond: The Confederate Journal of Henri Garidel.* Edited by Michael Bedout Chesson and Leslie Jean Roberts. Charlottesville: University Press of Virginia, 2001.

Girard, Charles. *A Visit to the Confederate States of America in 1863: Memoir Addressed to His Majesty Napoleon III.* Tuscaloosa, Ala.: Confederate Publishing, 1962.

Goree, Thomas. *Longstreet's Aide: The Civil War Letters of Major Thomas Goree.* Edited by Thomas W. Cutrer. Charlottesville: University Press of Virginia, 1995.

Gorgas, Josiah. *The Journals of Josiah Gorgas, 1857–1878.* Edited by Sarah Woolfolk Wiggins. Tuscaloosa: University of Alabama Press, 1995.

Grant, Ulysses S. *The Papers of Ulysses S. Grant.* Vol. 11. Edited by John Y. Simon. Carbondale: Southern Illinois University Press, 1984.

———. *Personal Memoirs.* 1885. Reprint. New York: Penguin Classics, 1999.

Harrison, Mrs. Burton [Constance Cary] . *Recollections Grave and Gay.* New York: Scribner's, 1911.

Hoge, Peyton Harrison. *Moses Drury Hoge: Life and Letters.* Richmond, Va.: Presbyterian Committee of Publication, 1899.

Johnson, Robert Underwood, and Clarence Clough Buel, eds., *Battles & Leaders of the Civil War.* 4 vols. New York: Century, 1884–1888.

Johnston, Joseph E. *Narrative of Military Operations Directed during the Late War between the States.* Civil War Centennial series. Bloomington: Indiana University Press, 1959.

Jones, J. B. *A Rebel War Clerk's Diary.* 2 vols. 1866. Reprint. Ann Arbor: Michigan Historical Reprint Series, n.d.

Jones, Katharine M., ed. *Heroines of Dixie: Confederate Women Tell Their Story of the War.* Indianapolis, Ind.: Bobbs-Merrill, 1955.

———, ed. *Ladies of Richmond, Confederate Capital.* Indianapolis, Ind.: Bobbs-Merrill, 1962.

Kean, Robert Garlick Hill. *Inside the Confederate Government: The Diary of Robert Garlick Hill Kean.* Edited by Edward Younger. New York: Oxford University Press, 1957.

Kimball, William J., ed. *Richmond in Time of War.* Boston: Houghton-Mifflin, 1960.

Lawley, Francis. *Lawley Covers the Confederacy.* Edited by William Stanley Hoole. Tuscaloosa, Ala.: Confederate Publishing, 1964.

Lee, Robert E. *Lee's Dispatches: Unpublished Letters of General Robert E. Lee, C.S.A. to Jefferson Davis and the War Department of the Confederate States of America, 1862–1865.* Edited by Douglas Southall Freeman and Grady McWhiney. New York: Putnam's, 1957.

———. *The Wartime Papers of Robert E. Lee.* Edited by Clifford Dowdey and Louis H. Manarin. Boston: Little, Brown, 1961.

Lincoln, Abraham. *The Collected Works of Abraham Lincoln.* 8 vols. Edited by Roy P. Basler. New Brunswick, N.J.: Rutgers University Press, 1953.

Manarin, Louis H., ed. *Richmond at War: The Minutes of the City Council, 1861–1865.* Chapel Hill: University of North Carolina Press, 1966.

McGuire, Judith W. *Diary of a Southern Refugee during the War by a Lady of Virginia.* 1867. Reprint. Lincoln: University of Nebraska Press, 1995.

Meade, George Gordon. *The Life and Letters of George Gordon Meade.* 2 vols. New York: Scribner's, 1913.

Mordecai, Samuel. *Richmond in By-Gone Days.* 1856. Reprint. New York: Arno Press, 1975.

Olmsted, Frederick Law. *The Cotton Kingdom: A Traveller's Observations on Cotton and Slavery in the American Slave States, Based upon Three Former Volumes of Journeys and Investigations by the Same Author.* New York: Mason, 1861.

———. *A Journey in the Back Country.* 1860. Reprint. New York: Burt Franklin, 1970.

Pember, Phoebe Yates. *A Southern Woman's Story: Life in Confederate Richmond.* Edited by Bell I. Wiley. 1959. Reprint. St. Simons Island, Ga.: Mockingbird Books, 1988.

Pollard, Edward A. *The First Year of the War.* New York: Richardson, 1863.

———. *The Lost Cause: The Standard Southern History of the War of the Confederates.* 1867. Reprint. New York: Books for Libraries, 1970.

———. *Southern History of the War.* 1866. Reprint. New York: Fairfax Press, 1990.

Porter, David Dixon. *Incidents and Anecdotes of the Civil War.* New York: Appleton, 1885.

Pryor, Sara (Mrs. Roger A.). *Reminiscences of Peace and War.* New York: McMillan, 1940.

Putnam, Sally A. Brock. *Richmond during the War: Four Years of Personal Observation by a Richmond Lady.* 1867. Reprint. Lincoln: University of Nebraska Press, 1996.

Reagan, J. H. *Memoirs: With Special References to Secession and Civil War.* Edited by Walter Flavius McCaleb. With an introduction by George P. Garrison. 1906. Reprint. New York: AMS Press, 1973.

Reid, Whitelaw. *After the War: A Tour of the Southern States, 1865–1866.* Edited by C. Vann Woodward. New York: Harper & Row, 1956.

Rothman, David J., ed. *The Almshouse Experience: Collected Reports.* New York: Arno Press and New York Times, 1970.

Ruffin, Edmund. *The Diary of Edmund Ruffin.* 3 vols. Edited by William Kauffman Scarborough. Baton Rouge: Louisiana State University Press, 1972.

Scheibert, Justus. *Captain Justus Scheibert: Seven Months in the Rebel States during the North American War.* Edited by William Stanley Hoole. Tuscaloosa, Ala.: Confederate Publishing, 1958.

Semmes, Raphael. *Memoirs of Service Afloat during the War between the States.* 1869. Reprint. Whitefish, Mont.: Kessinger, 2007.

Sherman, General William T. *Memoirs of General William T. Sherman by Himself.* Bloomington: Indiana University Press, 1957.

Smith, William. *Memoirs of Governor William Smith of Virginia: His Political, Military, and Personal History.* Edited by John W. Bell. New York: Moss Engraving, 1891.

Swint, Henry L., ed. *Dear Ones at Home: Letters from the Contraband Camps.* Nashville: Vanderbilt University Press, 1966.

Teamoh, George. *God Made Man, Man Made the Slave: The Autobiography of George Teamoh.* Edited by F. N. Boney, Richard L. Hume, and Rafia Zafar. Macon, Ga.: Mercer University Press, 1990.

Townsend, George Alfred. *Campaigns of a Non-combatant.* 1866. Reprint. New York: Arno Press, 1970.

Trowbridge, J. T. *The Desolate South, 1865–1866, a Picture of the Battlefields and of the Devastated Confederacy.* 1866. Reprint. New York: Duell, Sloane and Pearce, 1956.

———. *The South: A Tour of Its Battlefields and Ruined Cities.* 1866. Reprint. New York: Arno Press, 1969.

Van Lew, Elizabeth. *A Yankee Spy in Richmond: The Civil War Diary of "Crazy Bet" Van Lew.* Edited by David D. Ryan. 1996. Reprint. Mechanicsburg, Pa.: Stackpole Books, 2001.

Weitzel, Godfrey. *Richmond Occupied: Entry of the United States Forces into Richmond, Virginia, April 3, 1865; Calling Together of the Virginia Legislature and Revocation of the Same.* Edited by Louis H. Manarin. Richmond, Va.: Civil War Centennial Committee, 1965.

Wise, John S. *The End of an Era.* Boston: Houghton-Mifflin, 1899.

Wixon, Neal E., ed. *From Civility to Survival: Richmond Ladies during the Civil War.* Bloomington: Indiana University Press, 2012.

Wright, Mrs. D. Girard [Louise Wigfall]. *A Southern Girl in '61: The War-Time Memories of a Confederate Senator's Daughter.* New York: Doubleday, Page, 1905.

Secondary Sources

Ambler, Charles Henry. *Sectionalism in Virginia from 1776 to 1861.* 1910. Reprint. New York: Russell & Russell, 1964.

Ambrose, Stephen E. "Notes." *Virginia Magazine of History and Biography* 71 (1963): 203.

———. "Yeomen Discontent in the Confederacy." *Civil War History* 8 (September 1962): 259–68.

Ayers, Edward A., and John C. Willis, eds. *The Edge of the South: Life in Nineteenth Century Virginia.* Charlottesville: University Press of Virginia, 1991.

Ball, Douglas B. *Financial Failure and Confederate Defeat.* Urbana: University of Illinois Press, 1991.

Barber, E. Susan. "'The Quiet Battles of the Home Front War': Civil War Bread Riots and the Development of a Confederate Welfare System." M.A. thesis, University of Maryland, 1986.

Berlin, Ira. *Slaves without Masters: The Free Negro in the Antebellum South.* New York: Pantheon Books, 1974.

Berlin, Ira, and Herbert G. Gutman. "Natives and Immigrants, Free Men and Slaves: Urban Workingmen in the Antebellum American South." *American Historical Review* 88 (December 2983): 1175–200.

Bill, Alfred Hoyt. *The Beleaguered City: Richmond, 1861—1865.* New York: Knopf, 1946.

Blair, William. *Virginia's Private War: Feeding Body and Soul in the Confederacy.* New York: Oxford University Press, 1998.

Boney, F. N. *John Letcher of Virginia: The Story of Virginia's Civil War Governor.* Tuscaloosa: University of Alabama Press, 1966.

Brewer, James H. *The Confederate Negro: Virginia's Craftsmen and Military Laborers, 1861–1865.* 1969. Reprint. Tuscaloosa: University of Alabama Press, 2007.

Bruce, Kathleen. *Virginia Iron Manufacture in the Slave Era.* New York: Kelly, 1968.

Chesson, Michael B. "Harlots or Heroines? A New Look at the Richmond Bread Riot." *Virginia Magazine of History and Biography* 92 (April 1984): 131–75.

———. *Richmond after the War, 1865–1890.* Richmond: Virginia State Library, 1981.

Christian, W. Asbury. *Richmond: Her Past and Present.* Richmond, Va.: Jenkins, 1912.

Clinton, Catherine. *Tara Revisited: Women, War, and the Plantation Legend.* New York: Abbeville Press, 1995.

Clinton, Catherine, and Nina Silber, eds. *Battle Scars: Gender and Sexuality in the American Civil War.* New York: Oxford University Press, 2006.

Cooper, William J. *We Have the War Upon Us: The Onset of the Civil War, November 1860–April 1861.* New York: Knopf, 2012.

Coulter, E. Merton. *A History of the South.* Vol. 7: *The Confederate States of America, 1861–1865.* Baton Rouge: Louisiana State University Press, 1950.

Crofts, Daniel W. *Reluctant Confederates: Upper South Unionists in the Secession Crisis.* Chapel Hill: University of North Carolina Press, 1989.

Dabney, Virginius. *Richmond: The Story of a City.* Garden City, N.Y.: Doubleday, 1976.

Davis, William C. *Battle at Bull Run: A History of the First Major Campaign of the Civil War.* Baton Rouge: Louisiana State University Press, 1981.

———. *"A Government of Our Own": The Making of the Confederacy.* New York: Free Press, 1994.

———. *Jefferson Davis: The Man and His Hour, a Biography.* New York: Harper-Collins, 1991.

————. *Look Away! A History of the Confederate States of America.* New York: Free Press, 2002.

Delfino, Susanna, and Michelle Gillespie, eds. *Neither Lady nor Slave: Working Women of the Old South.* Chapel Hill: University of North Carolina Press, 2002.

Dew, Charles B. *Bond of Iron: Master and Slave at Buffalo Forge.* New York: Norton, 1994.

————. *Ironmaker to the Confederacy: Joseph Reid Anderson and the Tredegar Iron Works.* New Haven, Conn.: Yale University Press, 1966.

Dodd, Don, and Wynelle Dodd. *Historical Statistics of the South, 1790–1970.* Tuscaloosa: University of Alabama Press, 1978.

Dowdey, Clifford. *Experiment in Rebellion.* Garden City, N.Y.: Doubleday, 1946.

————. *The Seven Days: The Emergence of Robert E. Lee.* Boston: Little Brown, 1966.

Dowdey, Clifford, and Louis H. Manarin. Introduction to chapter 1 in Robert E. Lee, *The Wartime Papers of Robert E. Lee,* edited by Clifford Dowdey and Louis H. Manarin, 3–8. Boston: Little, Brown, 1961.

Doyle, Don H. *New Men, New Cities, New South: Atlanta, Nashville, Charleston, Mobile, 1860–1910.* Chapel Hill: University of North Carolina Press, 1990.

Ernst, William Joel, III. "Urban Leaders and Social Change: The Urbanization Process in Richmond, Virginia, 1840–1880." Ph.D. diss., University of Virginia, 1978.

Escott, Paul D. *After Secession: Jefferson Davis and the Failure of Confederate Nationalism.* Baton Rouge: Louisiana State University Press, 1978.

————. "'The Cry of the Sufferers': The Problem of Welfare in the Confederacy." *Civil War History* 23 (1977): 228–40.

————. "Southern Yeomen and the Confederacy." *South Atlantic Quarterly* 77 (Spring 1978): 146–58.

Etheridge, Harrison. "The Jordan Hatcher Affair of 1852: Cold Justice and Warm Compassion." *Virginia Magazine of History and Biography* 84 (October 1976): 446–63.

Fahrner, Alvin Arthur. "The Public Career of William 'Extra Billy' Smith." Ph.D. diss., University of North Carolina, 1953.

Faust, Drew Gilpin. *Mothers of Invention: Women of the Slaveholding South in the American Civil War.* Chapel Hill: University of North Carolina Press, 1996.

————. *This Republic of Suffering: Death and the American Civil War.* New York: Knopf, 2008.

Foote, Shelby. *The Civil War: A Narrative.* 3 vols. New York: Random House, 1958–1973.

Freeman, Douglas Southall. *Lee's Lieutenants: A Study in Command.* 3 vols. New York: Scribner's, 1942–1944.

————. *R. E. Lee.* 4 vols. New York: Scribner's, 1935.

Furgurson, Ernest B. *Ashes of Glory: Richmond at War.* New York: Knopf, 1996.

Gates, Paul W. *Agriculture in the Civil War*. New York: Knopf, 1965.

Genovese, Eugene. *The Political Economy of Slavery: Studies in the Economy and Society of the Slave South*. New York: Vintage Books Edition, 1967

Glatthaar, Joseph T. *General Lee's Army: From Victory to Defeat*. New York: Free Press, 2008.

Goff, Richard D. *Confederate Supply*. Durham, N.C.: Duke University Press, 1969.

Goldfield, David R. *Cotton Fields and Skyscrapers: Southern City and Region, 1607–1980*. Baton Rouge: Louisiana State University Press, 1982.

———. *Urban Growth in the Age of Sectionalism: Virginia, 1847–1861*. Baton Rouge: Louisiana State University Press, 1977.

Goldin, Claudia Dale. *Urban Slavery in the American South, 1820–1860: A Quantitative History*. Chicago: University of Chicago Press, 1976.

Gorman, Michael. "Peacemaker or Conqueror? Abraham Lincoln in Richmond." *Virginia Magazine of History and Biography* 123, no. 1 (2015): 2–88.

Green, Carol C. *Chimborazo: The Confederacy's Largest Hospital*. Knoxville: University of Tennessee Press, 2004.

Green, Rodney D. "Urban Industry, Black Resistance, and Racial Restriction in the Antebellum South: A General Model and a Case Study in Urban Virginia." Ph.D. diss., American University, 1980.

Grimsley, Mark, and Brooks D. Simpson, eds. *The Collapse of the Confederacy*. Lincoln: University of Nebraska Press, 2001.

Gudmestad, Robert H. "The Richmond Slave Market, 1840–1860." M.A. thesis, University of Richmond, 1993.

Holt, Michael F. *The Political Crisis of the 1850s*. New York: Wiley, 1978.

Jabour, Anya. *Scarlett's Sisters: Young Women in the Old South*. Chapel Hill: University of North Carolina Press, 2007.

Jackson, Luther Porter. *Free Negro Labor and Property Holding in Virginia, 1830–1860*. New York: Atheneum, 1969.

Johnson, Vicki Vaughn. *The Men and the Vision of the Southern Commercial Conventions, 1845–1871*. Columbia: University of Missouri Press, 1992.

Johnston, Angus James, II. *Virginia Railroads in the Civil War*. Chapel Hill: University of North Carolina Press, 1961.

Jordan, Ervin L., Jr. *Black Confederates and Afro-Yankees in Civil War Virginia*. Charlottesville: University Press of Virginia, 1995.

Kimball, Gregg D. *American City, Southern Place: A Cultural History of Antebellum Richmond*. Athens: University of Georgia Press, 2000.

Krick, Robert K. *Civil War Weather in Virginia*. Tuscaloosa: University of Alabama Press, 2007.

Krug, Donna Rebecca. "The Folks Back Home: The Confederate Home Front during the Civil War." Ph.D. diss., University of California at Irvine, 1990.

Lankford, Nelson D. *Cry Havoc! The Crooked Road to Civil War, 1861*. New York: Viking, 2007.

———. *Richmond Burning: The Last Days of the Confederate Capital.* New York: Viking, 2002.

Lerner, Eugene. "Inflation and the Confederacy." In *Studies in the Quantity Theory of Money,* edited by Milton Friedman, 163–75. Chicago: University of Chicago Press, 1956.

Levine, Bruce. *Confederate Emancipation: Southern Plans to Free and Arm Slaves during the Civil War.* New York: Oxford University Press, 2006.

Lewis, Ronald L. *Coal, Iron, and Slaves: Industrial Slavery in Maryland and Virginia, 1715–1865.* Westport, Conn.: Greenwood Press, 1979.

Link, William A. *Roots of Secession: Slavery and Politics in Antebellum Virginia.* Chapel Hill: University of North Carolina Press, 2003.

Lowry, Thomas P., M.D. *The Story the Soldiers Wouldn't Tell: Sex in the Civil War.* Mechanicsburg, Pa.: Stackpole Books, 1994.

Majewski, John. *A House Dividing: Economic Development in Pennsylvania and Virginia before the Civil War.* New York: Cambridge University Press, 2000.

Manarin, Louis H., and Clifford Dowdey. *The History of Henrico County.* Charlottesville: University Press of Virginia, 1984.

Massey, Mary Elizabeth. *Bonnet Brigades.* New York: Knopf, 1966.

———. *Ersatz in the Confederacy.* Columbia: University of South Carolina Press, 1952.

———. *Refugee Life in the Confederacy.* Baton Rouge: Louisiana State University Press, 1964.

McGregor, James C. *The Disruption of Virginia.* New York: MacMillan, 1922.

McInnis, Maurie D. *Slaves Waiting for Sale: Abolitionist Art and the American Slave Trade.* Chicago: University of Chicago Press, 2011.

McLeod, Norman C. "Free Labor in a Slave Society: Richmond, Virginia, 1820–1860." Ph.D. diss., Howard University, 1991.

McPherson, James M. *Battle Cry of Freedom: The Civil War Era.* New York: Oxford University Press, 1988.

———. *The Negro's Civil War: How American Negroes Felt and Acted during the War for the Union.* New York: Pantheon Books, 1965.

Nevins, Allan. *The War for the Union.* Vol. 1: *The Improvised War.* New York: Scribner's, 1959–1971.

O'Brien, John Thomas, Jr. *From Bondage to Citizenship: The Richmond Black Community, 1865–1867.* New York: Garland, 1990.

Pryor, Elizabeth Brown. *Reading the Man: A Portrait of Robert E. Lee through His Private Letters.* New York: Viking, 2007.

Rable, George C. *Civil Wars: Women and the Crisis of Southern Nationalism.* Urbana: University of Illinois Press, 1989.

Rachleff, Peter J. *Black Labor in the South.* Philadelphia: Temple University Press, 1984.

Richardson, Selden. *Built by Blacks: African American Architecture and Neighborhoods in Richmond.* Charleston, S.C.: History Press, 2008.

Russell, Robert. *North America: Its Agriculture and Climate.* Edinburgh: Black, 1857.

Scott, Mary Wingfield. *Old Richmond Neighborhoods.* Richmond, Va.: Whillet & Shepperson, 1950.

Sears, Stephen W. *To the Gates of Richmond: The Peninsula Campaign.* New York: Ticknor & Fields, 1992.

Shackelford, George Green. *George Wythe Randolph and the Confederate Elite.* Athens: University of Georgia Press, 1988.

Shade, William G. *Democratizing the Old Dominion: Virginia and the Second Party System, 1824–1861.* Charlottesville: University Press of Virginia, 1996.

Shanks, Henry T. *The Secession Movement in Virginia, 1847–1861.* 1934. Reprint. Richmond, Va.: Garrett and Massie, 1971.

Simpson, Craig M. *A Good Southerner: The Life of Henry A. Wise of Virginia.* Chapel Hill: University of North Carolina Press, 1985.

Starobin, Robert S. *Industrial Slavery in the Old South.* New York: Oxford University Press, 1970.

Steger, Werner H. "United to Support but Not Combined to Injure: Free Workers and Immigrants in Richmond, Virginia, during the Era of Sectionalism." Ph.D. diss., George Washington University, 1999.

Swanburg, W. A. *First Blood: The Story of Fort Sumter.* New York: Scribner's, 1958.

Tadman, Michael. *Speculators and Slaves: Masters, Traders, and Slaves in the Old South.* Madison: University of Wisconsin Press, 1989.

Takagi, Midori. *"Rearing Wolves to Our Own Destruction": Slavery in Richmond, Virginia, 1782–1865.* Charlottesville: University Press of Virginia, 1999.

Tarter, Brent. *The Grandees of Government: The Origins and Persistence of Undemocratic Politics in Virginia.* Charlottesville: University Press of Virginia, 2013.

Thomas, Emory M. *The Confederacy as a Revolutionary Experience.* 1971. Reprint. Columbia: University of South Carolina Press, 1991.

———. *The Confederate Nation, 1861–1865.* New York: Harper Torchbooks, 1979.

———. *The Confederate State of Richmond: A Biography of a Capital.* Baton Rouge: Louisiana State University Press, 1998.

———. "The Richmond Bread Riot of 1863." *Virginia Cavalcade* 18 (Summer 1968): 41–47.

———. "To Feed the Citizens: Welfare in Wartime Richmond, 1861–1865." *Virginia Cavalcade* 22 (1972): 22–29.

Todd, Richard C. *Confederate Finance.* Athens: University of Georgia Press, 1954.

Trudeau, Noah Andre. *Bloody Roads South: The Wilderness to Cold Harbor, May–June 1864.* New York: Fawcett Columbine, 1989.

Tyler-McGraw, Marie. *At the Falls: Richmond, Virginia, and Its People.* Chapel Hill: University of North Carolina Press for the Valentine Museum of the Life and History of Richmond, 1994.

Tyler-McGraw, Marie, and Gregg D. Kimball. *In Bondage and in Freedom: Antebellum Black Life in Richmond, Virginia.* Richmond, Va.: Valentine Museum, 1988.

Vandiver, Frank E. *Ploughshares into Swords: Josiah Gorgas and Confederate Ordnance.* Austin: University of Texas Press, 1952.

Varon, Elizabeth R. *Southern Lady, Yankee Spy: The True Story of Elizabeth Van Lew, a Union Agent in the Heart of the Confederacy.* New York: Oxford University Press, 2003.

———. *We Mean to Be Counted: White Women & Politics in Antebellum Virginia.* Chapel Hill: University of North Carolina Press, 1998.

Venter, Bruce M. *Kill Jeff Davis: The Union Raid on Richmond, 1864.* Norman: University of Oklahoma Press, 2016.

Wade, Richard C. *Slavery in the Cities: The South, 1820–1860.* New York: Oxford University Press, 1964.

Walthall, Ernest Taylor. *Hidden Things Brought to Life.* Richmond, Va.: Dietz, 1933.

Wiley, Bell Irvin. *The Life of Johnny Reb: The Common Soldier in the Confederacy.* 1943. Reprint. Baton Rouge: Louisiana State University Press, 1994.

———. *Southern Negroes, 1861–1865.* New Haven, Conn.: Yale University Press, 1938.

Wright, Gavin. *The Political Economy of the Cotton South: Households, Markets, and Wealth in the Nineteenth Century.* New York: Norton, 1978.

Wyatt-Brown, Bertram. *Southern Honor: Ethics and Behavior in the Old South.* New York: Oxford University Press, 1982.

Zaborney, John J. *Slaves for Hire: Renting Enslaved Laborers in Antebellum Virginia.* Baton Rouge: Louisiana State University Press, 2012.

Index

Italic page numbers refer to illustrations.

New Directions in Southern History

Series Editors

Michele Gillespie, Wake Forest University
William A. Link, University of Florida

The Lost State of Franklin: America's First Secession
Kevin T. Barksdale

The Civil War Guerrilla: Unfolding the Black Flag in History, Memory, and Myth
edited by Joseph M. Beilein Jr. and Matthew C. Hulbert

Bluecoats and Tar Heels: Soldiers and Civilians in Reconstruction North Carolina
Mark L. Bradley

Becoming Bourgeois: Merchant Culture in the South, 1820–1865
Frank J. Byrne

Willis Duke Weatherford: Race, Religion, and Reform in the American South
Andrew McNeill Canady

Cowboy Conservatism: Texas and the Rise of the Modern Right
Sean P. Cunningham

Confederate Citadel: Richmond and Its People at War
Mary A. DeCredico

A Tour of Reconstruction: Travel Letters of 1875
Anna Dickinson (J. Matthew Gallman, ed.)

Raising Racists: The Socialization of White Children in the Jim Crow South
Kristina DuRocher

Rethinking the Civil War Era: Directions for Research
Paul D. Escott

Marriage on the Border: Love, Mutuality, and Divorce in the Upper South during the Civil War
Allison Dorothy Fredette

Lum and Abner: Rural America and the Golden Age of Radio
Randal L. Hall

Mountains on the Market: Industry, the Environment, and the South
Randal L. Hall

The New Southern University: Academic Freedom and Liberalism at UNC
Charles J. Holden

Entangled by White Supremacy: Reform in World War I–era South Carolina
Janet G. Hudson

Bloody Breathitt: Politics and Violence in the Appalachian South
T. R. C. Hutton

Cultivating Race: The Expansion of Slavery in Georgia, 1750–1860
Watson W. Jennison

De Bow's Review: *The Antebellum Vision of a New South*
John F. Kvach

Remembering The Battle of the Crater: War as Murder
Kevin M. Levin

My Brother Slaves: Friendship, Masculinity, and Resistance in the Antebellum South
Sergio A. Lussana

The Political Career of W. Kerr Scott: The Squire from Haw River
Julian Pleasants

The View from the Ground: Experiences of Civil War Soldiers
edited by Aaron Sheehan-Dean

Reconstructing Appalachia: The Civil War's Aftermath
edited by Andrew L. Slap